Brazilian Agricultural Technology and Trade

Peter T. Knight

The Praeger Special Studies program—utilizing the most modern and efficient book production techniques and a selective worldwide distribution network—makes available to the academic, government, and business communities significant, timely research in U.S. and international economic, social, and political development.

Brazilian Agricultural Technology and Trade

A Study of Five Commodities

PRAEGER SPECIAL STUDIES IN INTERNATIONAL ECONOMICS AND DEVELOPMENT

Praeger Publishers   New York   Washington   London

PRAEGER PUBLISHERS
111 Fourth Avenue, New York, N.Y. 10003, U.S.A.
5, Cromwell Place, London S.W.7, England

Published in the United States of America in 1971
by Praeger Publishers, Inc.

Library of Congress Catalog Card Number: 76-145953

Printed in the United States of America

ACKNOWLEDGMENTS

The major portion of the field research for this study was done in Brazil in the first eight months of 1968, during which time I held a Foreign Area Fellowship granted by the American Council of Learned Societies and the Social Science Research Council. I wish to acknowledge the financial support of the Foreign Area Fellowship Program and also the assistance of the Centro de Treinamento e Pesquisa Para o Desenvolvimento Econômico of the Instituto de Pesquisa Econômico-Social Aplicada (IPEA) in Rio de Janeiro, where office space and a stimulating intellectual environment were made available to me. Some additional information was obtained in December, 1968, during a brief trip to Brazil.

    The Brazilian economists, agricultural research workers, extension agents, bankers, librarians, and public officials who facilitated this research and gave abundantly of their time educating me are too numerous to mention here, but I wish to express special gratitude to Antônio Carlos Silveira Abbott and Nelson Marchezan of the Banco do Brasil in Pôrto Alegre, Soly Souza Machado and Ary Hertzog of the Instituto Rio Grandense do Arroz, and Engenheiro Agrônomo Aureo Elias of the Federação de Coperativas Tritícolas do Sul for facilitating access to large amounts of useful data and introducing me to both the agricultural realities of Rio Grande do Sul and the warmth of that state's people. My greatest intellectual debts are to Ronald McKinnon and Donald Keesing, both of whom contributed generously of their time and special competence. I also owe much to the suggestions and assistance of Alan Manne of Stanford University, Albert Fishlow of the University of California at Berkeley and IPEA, and Marvin Beatty of the University of Wisconsin and the Federal University of Rio Grande do Sul.

    The writing of the study was done at the Research Center in Economic Growth at Stanford University and at the Brookings Institution. I am grateful to Joseph Grunwald of the Brookings Institution for the material and moral support which made it possible to complete the second and final drafts. Marsha Dyer typed the final draft in record time. Of course none of the

persons or institutions mentioned above are directly responsible for the views expressed in this work, but it would be
arrogant to say they had no influence on the author.

Finally, I thank my wife Zaida for her assistance with
calculations and computer work and for the many nights and
weekends of social life foregone.

CONTENTS

LIST OF TABLES

Table   Page

LIST OF FIGURES

LIST OF ABBREVIATIONS

AID   (U.S.) Agency for International Development
                    (also known as USAID)

CACEX   Carteira de Comércio Exterior (Foreign-
                    Exchange Department of the Bank of Brazil)

CCLEF   Comissão Central de Levantamento e
                    Fiscalização das Safras Tritícolas (Central
                    Commission for the Survey and Inspection
                    of Wheat Crops)

CENTRISUL   Centro de Treinamento e Informação do Sul
                    (Southern Center for Training and Informa-
                    tion)

c.i.f.   Cost, insurance, and freight. Refers to
                    import price and value data which include
                    these charges. To be contrasted with f.o.b.
                    which does not include insurance and freight
                    and refers to cost in the port of origin,
                    loaded

COFAP   Comissão Federal de Abastecimento e
                    Preços (Federal Supply and Price
                    Commission)

CRA   Companhia Riograndense de Adubos
                    (Riograndense Fertilizer Company)

CTRIN   Comissão de Compra de Trigo Nacional
                    (Domestic Wheat Purchase Commission of
                    the Bank of Brazil)

DW   Durbin-Watson Statistic, a measure of
                    autocorrelation of residuals used in
                    regression analysis

ECLA	Economic Commission for Latin America (United Nations)
EPEA	Escritório de Pesquisa Econômica Aplicada (Office of Applied Economic Research of the Ministry of Planning), old name for IPEA
FAO	Food and Agriculture Organization (United Nations)
FAV/UFRGS	Faculdade de Agronomia e Veterinária/ Universidade Federal de Rio Grande do Sul (Faculty of Agronomy and Veterinary Science of the Federal University of Rio Grande do Sul)
FECOTRIGO	Federação de Cooperativas Tritícolas do Sul (Federation of Southern Wheat Cooperatives)
f.o.b.	Free on board. Refers to price and value data in international trade, specifically the price or value of goods loaded into a ship, plane, or other vehicle in the port of origin but exclusive of transport and insurance charges to deliver it to the port of destination
FUNFERTIL	Fundo de Estímulo Financeiro ao Uso de Fertilizantes e Suplementos Minerais (Fund for Financial Stimulus to the Use of Fertilizers and Mineral Supplements)
GDP	Gross domestic product
GNP	Gross national product
IBGE	Instituto Brasileiro de Geografia e Estatística (Brazilian Institute of Geography and Statistics)
ICM	Imposto de Circulação de Mercadorias (value-added tax)

IMF	International Monetary Fund
INSTICARNE	Instituto Sul-Riograndense de Carnes (Rio Grande do Sul Meat Institute)
IPEA	Instituto de Pesquisa Econômico-Social Aplicada (Institute of Applied Economic and Social Research, formerly known as IPEA)
IPEAS	Instituto de Pesquisa e Experimentação Agropecuárias do Sul (Southern Institute for Agricultural Research and Experimentation)
IRGA	Instituto Rio Grandense do Arroz (Rio Grande do Sul Rice Institute)
IVC	Imposto de Vendas e Consignações (sales tax)
NBM	Nomenclatura Brasileira de Mercadorias (Brazilian Goods Classification)
SEEF	Serviço de Estatística Econômica e Financeira (Economic and Financial Statistics Service of the Ministry of Finance)
SEP	Serviço de Estatística da Produção (Production Statistics Service of the Ministry of Agriculture)
SET	Serviço de Expansão do Trigo (Wheat Expansion Service of the Ministry of Agriculture)
SUMOC	Superintêndencia de Mocda e Credito (Superintendency of Money and Credit)
SUNAB	Superintêndencia Nacional de Abastecimento (National Supply Agency)

INTRODUCTION

This book is a study of technological change, public policy, and economic behavior in Brazil's agricultural sector, with emphasis on their implications for international trade. It was undertaken to shed some empirical and analytical light on a number of questions which have concerned development planners in Brazil and, on a more general level, throughout the developing world.

Most authorities agree that increased imports of producer goods and the growth of foreign-exchange earning (or saving) activities are critical to Brazil's over-all economic development. Rapid expansion of exports of minor agricultural commodities would appear necessary, in addition to stimulation of manufactured and mineral exports, to reach officially declared growth goals. What has been the response of exporters to price incentives and direct export controls in the past? Why have land and herd productivity stagnated in many regions of Brazil? What are the economic prospects for productivity increases through the application of modern agricultural technology? Wheat, the principal agricultural import, has long been the object of special import-substitution policies by Brazilian authorities. What were the effects of these policies on the production and marketing systems for wheat? What has been their cost? What is the potential for reducing production costs in the future?

These are broad questions, and it would be presumptuous to suggest that complete answers can be given within the necessarily limited scope of a single volume. The student of development has, however, an obligation to orient his research toward problems of real concern to policy makers and to supply what insights he can within the constraints imposed by his own skill and resources. To this end, five agricultural products which are important in international trade have been chosen for study. Four of them--rice, soybeans, corn, and beef--fall within the strategic class of so-called minor agricultural exports and attracted considerable attention in the late 1960's because of favorable demand conditions in the international market. The fifth, wheat, is an import-substitution good. Wheat has consistently been the largest agricultural import and accounted for from 7 to 16 percent of the total dollar value of imports during 1947-67, with an average of 11.7 percent in the years 1965-67.

In order to restrict the geographical scope of the study in a fashion permitting field research by a single investigator in a relatively brief period of time, attention is focused on a single Brazilian state, Rio Grande do Sul, which is an important producer of all five products and the dominant exporter of three--beef, rice, and soybeans.

The first chapter is introductory in character and is intended to provide a macroeconomic context within which the more specific studies of the following chapters take on added significance. Evidence is presented to support the hypothesis that Brazil has been plagued with a severe balance-of-payments problem for most of the period since World War II and that the situation as the 1960's drew to a close was not greatly improved. The important roles which modernization of the agricultural sector can play in easing the import constraint and contributing to the over-all development of Brazil during the 1970's are analyzed briefly.

In Chapter 2, a brief summary of the relevant economic history of Rio Grande do Sul, technologies utilized in the production of the commodities being studied, interrelationships between crops, and the structure of land tenure are presented to serve as background for the following chapters.

Chapter 3 examines export performance over the period 1947-67 for beef, rice, soybeans, and corn. As part of an over-all policy designed to maintain low prices of basic foodstuffs and thus favor the development of the industrial sector by holding down wages, a combination of overvalued exchange rates and direct export controls operated to reduce exports. The functioning of the rather complicated exchange system which existed over this period is explained, and the effective exchange rates for each export product are compared with two more "realistic" exchange rates. Evidence concerning both financial incentives to export and direct controls on Brazilian exports of beef, rice, soybeans, and corn is presented and export supply functions estimated. The existence of inverse seasonal price changes in Brazil and major northern hemisphere producers of rice, soybeans, and corn is investigated. Such seasonals, where they exist, are advantageous to Brazil. The appendix investigates the factors influencing beef slaughter in Rio Grande do Sul.

The Brazilian wheat-import substitution effort is analyzed and evaluated in Chapter 4. The chapter begins with a brief history of wheat production in Brazil. Then, distortions which arose under the dual-price system, whereby the price of wheat to millers and thence consumers was kept low while domestic wheat producers received higher prices, are investigated. Subsidies to wheat production and consumption are estimated, and the static efficiency of domestic-resource use in wheat production is compared with that for each of the four export goods. Reasons for the high cost of wheat production in Rio Grande do Sul, the principal producing state, are examined, and arguments in favor of domestic-wheat production are evaluated.

Chapter 5 documents the stagnation of agricultural productivity, measured as output per hectare for field crops and per head in the herd for beef cattle, which appears to have taken place in Rio Grande do Sul in the postwar period. Some fragmentary evidence concerning the types of technological change which did take place is presented. All the improvements which occurred no more than kept pace with declining soil fertility, the extension of cultivation to more marginal lands, and, in the case of wheat, the development of new strains of rust. By the late 1960's, it is shown that the process of transferring pasture and forest land to annual crops had reached a point where there was little or no scope for additional extensive growth in output of any of the products studied without the simultaneous diminution of one or more of the others.

In other words, the supply of frontier land which in the past had provided opportunities for extensive growth of agricultural production in Rio Grande do Sul, and for that matter probably in all of southern Brazil, had been exhausted. Further growth in output thus depended greatly on accelerated technological change.

Evidence has been accumulating, both in Rio Grande do Sul and elsewhere throughout the world, that the use of modern manufactured inputs in agricultural production, particularly chemical fertilizers, together with new, higher-yielding grain varieties, can result in dramatic increases in yields within relatively short periods of time. Chapter 6 examines the economics of fertilizer use in Rio Grande do Sul--its profitability with existing varieties of rice, wheat, and corn as determined from fertilizer-response functions fitted to experimental data; the past and potential demand for major plant nutrients; and the prospects for achieving significant reductions in real fertilizer prices paid by farmers through local fertilizer production and improvements in the fertilizer marketing system.

Chapter 7 draws together and summarizes the conclusions obtained in the other chapters and relates them to the broad questions which motivated this study.

Brazilian Agricultural Technology and Trade

1

MACROECONOMIC
BACKGROUND

In this chapter, the principal focus is on the relationship between the foreign and agricultural sectors and the rest of the Brazilian economy. In the first section, evidence is presented concerning the existence of a foreign-exchange constraint on Brazilian growth, with particular emphasis on the decline in the growth rate of the gross domestic product (GDP) which took place in the first half of the 1960's and the prognosis for the early 1970's. In the second part of the chapter, the policies of import substitution and export expansion are examined, with attention given to the agricultural sector and its role in Brazilian development in the 1970's. While again there is an emphasis on the implications of agricultural output growth on the balance of payments, a number of other important effects of a reordering of priorities in favor of the agricultural sector are examined briefly. These include the supply of foodstuffs to urban areas, the reduction of regional and sectoral inequalities in income distribution, and the development of a broader market for manufactured agricultural inputs as well as consumer goods. This chapter draws heavily on secondary sources and is intended primarily as an introduction to our own research which is presented in the rest of this book.

THE FOREIGN-EXCHANGE CONSTRAINT

In the period from World War II until the early 1960's, Brazil enjoyed rapid rates of economic growth based principally on import-substituting industrialization. The dramatic

Brazilian development experience and the subsequent stagnation of GDP per capita (it averaged 0.6 percent per annum in
1962-67 and was actually negative in three years) have been
the subject of frequent analyses in recent years and will not
be dealt with in any depth here. [1] Nevertheless, it may be
helpful to review this development process from the vantage
point of the balance of payments.

In the period 1948-67, as is shown in Table 1, the average growth rate of Brazil's GDP was 6.1 percent; that of imports of goods and services (including capital services) measured in 1953 prices was 4.4 percent, which is one indication
of the extent to which import substitution took place during
this period. Indeed, imports of goods and services in current
prices fell from an average of 10.5 percent of GDP in 1948-
50 to 7.5 percent in 1965-67. These figures probably under-
state the actual decline in the import coefficient because the
exchange rate was more overvalued in 1948-50 than it was in
1965-67. (Evidence concerning overvaluation is presented in
Chapter 3.)

More interesting than these over-all figures is the distinct
tendency for low or negative growth rates of imports to be
associated with low growth rates of GDP. There were five
years during which the GDP grew at a rate of 3.2 percent or
lower--1953, 1956, and 1963-65. The average GDP growth for
these years was 2.6 percent (-0.5 percent on a per capita
basis) compared with 6.7 percent for all other years in the
period 1948-67. Imports of goods and services declined on
the average of 6.9 percent in these "recession" years and
grew at 8.1 percent on the average in the remaining years.
In absolute terms, the current account balance was in surplus
at an average annual rate of $48 million in the recession years
and ran an average deficit of $281 million for the remainder
of the period.

The data in Table 1 indicate that a decline in imports led
the downturn in the rate of growth of GDP, starting in 1961.
Domestic saving began to fall in 1962, and gross fixed capital
formation, in 1964, although the rate of increase of the latter
had slackened as early as 1962. Both the 1953 and the 1956
low growth years were preceded by years of declining imports.

There is considerable support in the literature published
both in Brazil and elsewhere for the hypothesis that the bind-
ing constraint on the Brazilian growth process has, at least
at critical junctures, been the capacity to import. [2] The existence of a foreign-exchange constraint is asserted explicitly,
for example, by Celso Furtado and Nathaniel Leff and implicitly by others such as the Institute of Applied Economic and

Social Research of the Ministry of Planning and General Co-
ordination (IPEA) and the Economic Commission for Latin
America (ECLA). [3]

    None of this evidence is really conclusive, however, be-
cause a thorough testing of the hypothesis that an import constraint was responsible for the slowdown of economic growth
experienced by Brazil in the mid 1960's would require the
estimation of lags between imports and their utilization as
well as the development of a much more rigorous and complete
model than any of the authors cited have utilized. In any case,
it may be more fruitful to look at the foreign-exchange constraint in a much broader context than that implied in the above
discussion.

    It can be argued that discussion of a so-called balance-
of-payments problem is not an adequate way to consider an
import or foreign-exchange constraint in development. After
all, the balance of payments is in many ways a reflection of
all the other constraints in development--the savings-invest-
ment balance, the public budget, the skilled-manpower situation, natural-resource shortages, a lack of know-how and of
technological efficiency and capacity in specific sectors, insufficient scale economies, a lack of fit between the structure
of demand and production capacity, inexperience in exporting,
and so on. The fact remains that insufficient capacity to import seems to have appeared as a constraint to policymakers
including Presidents Jânio Quadros and João Goulart, who,
in the early 1960's, faced an exchange crisis which was at
least in part the product of their predecessor's ambitious
Target Plan and its shaky financial base. Some support for
this statement is provided in the following paragraphs.

    Toward the end of his term in office, President Juscelino
Kubitschek had relied to an increasing extent on short-term
suppliers' credits and even adopted certain emergency ex-
pedients such as the currency "swaps" described below to
finance imports crucial to the fundamental aims of his Target
Plan. These were made necessary by the accumulation of
heavy external commitments, the unfavorable trend of exports
(which were further discouraged by the low level of exchange
rates) and the expansionist trend of subsidized imports.

    The currency "swaps" worked as follows: The Bank of
Brazil would hand over cruzeiros in exchange for a deposit in
dollars, which would then be used to finance imports. In itself, this measure would have a deflationary effect if not offset by further emissions of cruzeiros, since it took cruzeiros
out of circulation and increased the supply of real goods to the

TABLE 1

Selected Macroeconomic Variables, 1948-67

Macroeconomic Variables	1948	1949	1950	1951	1952	1953	1954	1955	1956	1957	1958	1959
1. Growth rate of real GDP	7.4	6.6	6.5	6.0	8.7	2.5	10.1	6.9	3.2	8.1	7.7	5.6
2. Growth rate of real GDP per capita	4.9	4.2	4.0	2.9	5.7	-0.4	6.9	3.8	0.2	5.0	4.6	2.5
3. Growth rate of real gross capital formation	1.8	7.8	8.1	22.5	7.5	-15.6	8.8	-5.8	7.8	13.4	5.9	13.0
4. Growth rate of real domestic saving	6.8	-0.8	23.0	-1.5	8.7	0.0	10.9	6.3	-3.8	22.7	-2.3	20.9
5. Growth rate of real imports of goods and services	-12.0	2.1	18.2	49.7	-12.3	-27.0	30.9	-19.4	6.8	13.7	-5.1	19.8
6. Goods and Services imports as percent of GDP	12.3	10.3	8.9	13.2	10.2	6.9	8.6	7.9	7.0	7.3	7.3	8.4
7. Net service payments as percent of exports	26.6	24.6	23.5	30.3	29.7	25.5	24.3	24.2	28.3	28.2	26.3	31.8
8. Capital service payments as percent of exports	8.9	9.2	8.9	7.1	10.7	8.8	9.5	9.2	8.6	11.7	14.2	13.1
9. Balance on current account; $ million	-44	-121	104	-470	-709	17	-235	-34	7	-299	-266	-345

TABLE 1 - Continued

Macroeconomic Variables	1960	1961	1962	1963	1964	1965	1966	1967	1948-67	Averages Recession Year*	Averages All Other Years
1. Growth rate of real GDP	9.7	10.3	5.3	1.5	2.9	2.7	5.1	4.8	6.1	2.6	6.7
2. Growth rate of real GDP per capita	6.5	6.7	2.1	-1.5	-0.2	-0.4	1.8	1.5	3.0	-0.5	4.2
3. Growth rate of real gross capital formation	4.1	5.1	3.1	3.1	-2.8	2.5	20.1	1.9	5.6	-1.7	7.8
4. Growth rate of real domestic saving	-6.4	16.6	-3.8	-1.7	17.5	14.2	-12.0	-0.6	5.7	5.2	6.3
5. Growth rate of real imports of goods and services	14.3	-7.3	-2.3	-6.9	-8.7	1.4	19.9	11.6	4.4	-6.9	8.1
6. Goods and services imports as percent of GDP	8.1	8.0	7.7	10.7	7.0	7.3	7.7	7.4	8.6	7.8	8.9
7. Net service payments as percent of exports	40.2	29.6	33.5	21.2	21.3	28.6	31.6	34.3	28.2	25.0	29.2
8. Capital service payments as percent of exports	14.2	13.1	16.4	10.2	13.2	16.2	16.3	17.8	11.3	12.0	11.1
9. Balance on current account, $ million	-548	-288	-458	-147	102	263	-33	-277	-189	48	-281

*Column includes 1953, 1956, and 1963-65.

Sources: Variables 1 and 2, Conjuntura Econômica, October, 1969, p. 55; 3, calculated from ibid., pp. 66-67; 4, calculated as sum of net private saving, government saving, and depreciation of fixed capital deflated by implicit deflator for gross fixed capital formation, all found in ibid., pp. 60, 61, 66, and 67; 5, calculated from ibid., pp. 66-67; 6, calculated from ibid., pp. 55, 60, and 61; 7, 8, and 9, calculated from data in Escritório de Pesquisa Econômica Aplicada (EPEA), Diagnóstico Preliminar, Setor de Comércio Internacional (Rio de Janeiro, 1967), Table 41 (1947-62), and Instituto Brasileira de Geografia e Estatística, Anuário Estatístico do Brasil, various issues (1963-68).

7

economy. However, the depositor in the "swap" operation obtained the right to repeat the operation in reverse at a specified future date at the same rate of exchange. If an exchange devaluation had taken place in the meantime, this meant that the Bank of Brazil had to purchase dollars to repay the depositor at a higher cruzeiro price, which would have an inflationary effect and cause further pressure on the exchange rate.

According to Thomas Skidmore, Quadros, in his inauguration speech on January 31, 1961, described the financial situation as "terrible." There was $2 billion in foreign debt due in the new presidential term and over $600 million payable within the first year. Quadros lamented, "All this money, spent with so much publicity, we must now raise, bitterly, patiently, dollar by dollar and cruzeiro by cruzeiro. We have spent, drawing on our future to a greater extent than the imagination dares to contemplate."[4] His government then launched a stabilization campaign calculated to please the International Monetary Fund (IMF) and other foreign creditors. In March, the system was drastically reformed and the cruzeiro sharply devalued. The exchange subsidies for wheat and oil imports were reduced. This in turn doubled the retail price of bread and resulted in steep increases in bus fares and other transport costs.[5]

In May-June, 1961, the Quadros government announced a consolidation and refinancing of the foreign debt in a $2 billion package which included not only rescheduling and consolidation, but also $300 million in new financing. This operation was largely responsible for a $304 million "autonomous" net inflow of capital and made possible a net outflow of $65 million in the compensatory category.[6] According to ECLA, however, "the stabilization program was a failure in the end, largely on account of the issues that the Banco do Brasil was obliged to make for the purpose of its exchange operations."[7] In order to comply with the provisions of the "swap" agreements made in the last year of the preceding administration (1960), the Bank of Brazil had to purchase the dollars owed at a higher rate of exchange. This implied monetary emissions equivalent to those required to cover the total deficit of the federal public sector.[8]

Quadros resigned unexpectedly on August 25, 1961, and precipitated a grave political crisis that led to the assumption of the presidency by Goulart. The Goulart government prepared a Three-Year Plan for Economic and Social Development of which Celso Furtado was the principal author. Leff

quotes this plan's optimistic assessment of the situation with
respect to the foreign sector:

> On reaching a phase of development where the proc-
> ess of capital formation leans mainly on our own
> production of equipment, the development of the
> Brazilian economy has come to depend on its own in-
> ternal dynamics. Thus, no matter how important
> the external factors still may be, the rate of growth
> is determined mainly by domestic market condi-
> tions. . . . A lag in the external demand does not
> anymore, necessarily, result in a general slump
> in economic activity. [9]

Only a year and a half later, Furtado as much as admitted he
had been in error, although the careful reader will note the
escape clauses in the passage quoted above.

> There exists ample evidence that the industrialization
> brought Brazil very close to that point at which devel-
> opment becomes a cumulative, circular process,
> which itself creates the means which it requires to
> proceed forward. In Brazil's case, this point would
> have been reached when the barrier of import capac-
> ity had been overcome. . . . However, this op-
> portunity to enter the restricted club of mature
> capitalist economies as an autonomous national
> system was apparently lost. [10]

In fact, the Three-Year Plan considered the capacity to
import essential for future economic growth and proposed
another refinancing of the foreign debt as well as the promotion of exports. The first step was the (temporary) elimination of subsidies on oil and wheat imports in January, 1963,
and a further devaluation. In negotiations which took place in
Washington, D.C. in March, 1963, and included lengthy con-
versations with President John F. Kennedy, Goulart's finance
minister, San Tiago Dantas, sought a large aid package. He
met a cautious response from both the United States and the
IMF. He obtained a U.S. agreement of $398.5 million, but only
$84 million was available for immediate use. "The rest re-
mained contingent upon Brazil's carrying out a reform and stabilization program spelled out in a joint communiqué between
Dantas and David Bell, director of USAID" (U.S. Agency for International Development). [11] A tight money policy was instituted

which "actually aggravated the recession because of its de-
pressive effects on manufacturing and construction. "[12] An
IMF mission arrived in May, 1963, to study the Goulart government's attack on inflation. According to Skidmore, "the
conclusions of the mission were crucial, since both the American and European creditors were awaiting the IMF's decision
before embarking on a further refinancing of Brazil's enor-
mous short-term debt. "[13] Under heavy political pressure,
Goulart agreed to a 70 percent salary increase in early June
for the military and civil service functionaries. The IMF
mission left Brazil with a poor impression, and the attempt
to renegotiate the debt failed.

In evaluating the lessons of the Dantas-Furtado phase of
the Goulart government, Skidmore notes the contradiction between domestic political imperatives and the problem of satis-
fying foreign creditors:

> Given this debtor role, no domestic economic policy
> could fail to be heavily influenced by the need to con-
> sider how any measure would affect currency re-
> serves, Brazil's trade position, and, not least im-
> portant, the attitude of her foreign creditors. This
> necessity of paying constant heed to European and
> North American financial circles, often of the most
> orthodox type, had been a political liability to many
> governments. It gave the economic nationalists (in-
> cluding some São Paulo industrialists as well as
> left-wing intellectuals) ready ammunition with which
> to attack Goulart as he faced the unavoidable neces-
> sity of pursuing an anti-inflation program. The po-
> litical stakes grew higher as Brazil's foreign debts
> mounted and her prospects for repaying them grew
> dimmer.[14]

While the foreign debt repayment problem may appear to
be a short-term difficulty, it was the result of the heavy current account deficits of the 1950's and early 1960's. It is
perfectly true, as ECLA emphasizes, that political instability
greatly aggravated the inflation as well as the problem of re-
negotiating the debt.[15] The traditional political system was
unable to reconcile the conflicting demands of various domestic pressure groups as well as the foreign creditors while
maintaining a high rate of economic growth. The "Revolution"
of April, 1964, which resulted in a strong stabilization program and substantial measures to stimulate exports (including

a domestic recession) was the end result of incompatible,
rapidly shifting economic and political policies pursued in the
early 1960's as well as the lack of attention to noncoffee exports which had been a characteristic of Brazilian economic
policy throughout most of the postwar period. The problem
was, of course, aggravated by declining terms of trade which
fell steadily from their peak of 134 percent of the 1953 value
in 1954 to 84 percent in 1962, with the exception of a brief,
partial recovery in 1957 and 1958. [16]
    There can be little doubt that a precondition for a more
autonomous domestic economic policy is a strong balance of
payments on current account. A larger degree of independence
from the dictates of international financial circles implies an
expansion of exports and/or a further reduction of imports if
rapid economic growth is to be achieved simultaneously. Samuel Morley has documented this inconsistency. After developing a series of import-demand functions and then making
projections using these functions under alternate assumptions
with regard to growth rates of GNP, changes in relative prices,
and the growth of domestic substitutes over the period 1967-
71, and finally aggregating the results, he concludes:

> If Brazil chooses a "slow growth" path of 5 percent
> per year, her domestic industry will probably be
> growing at around 6 percent; whereas at a more dy-
> namic rate of 6 percent, the industrial sector, which
> will lead the advance if the past is any indication,
> will undoubtedly have to reach an 8 percent annual
> growth. Either way, imports will be growing at a
> rate which exceeds the expected rate of growth of
> exports. [17]

In the first alternative, assuming a 1 percent decrease in the
relative prices of imports, imports would grow at 7 percent,
and, on the hypothesis of a 6 percent growth rate in GNP with
an 8 percent increase in domestic substitutes, imports would
rise by 7.7 percent.
    Other works on Brazilian import-demand functions by
Paul G. Clark and Richard Weisskoff and by Albert Fishlow
have indicated that aggregate import demand (goods) varies
about in proportion with gross fixed-capital formation (they
found approximately unitary elasticity) and shows an elasticity
to the relative price of imports compared with domestic production on the order of -0. 3 to -0. 4, using annual data. [18]
There was a downward trend of between 3 and 4 percent per

year over the period 1953-65, due to the import-substitution
drive, but whether this trend can be maintained in the future
is debatable. In any case, there has been an opposing trend
in payments for capital services. This is obviously the result of the large capital inflows of the late 1950's and early
1960's.

In September, 1967, after a major import liberalization
which had the effect of reducing the ratio of the price index of
potential imports to domestic substitutes by about one third
the level of 1964, Clark applied the Clark-Weisskoff functions
to estimate imports for 1966 to 1971. While the 1966 import
increase was slightly underestimated, his results indicated
that "about a third of the large increase in 1966 was attributable to import liberalization, the remainder being due to the
sharp recovery of gross investment."[19] The projections suggest that if GNP were to grow at a rate of 5.5 to 6 percent in
1968-71, and if there were a moderate, further import liberalization, imports would rise at about 10 percent per year.
This assumes increases of gross fixed capital formation on
the order of 13 percent per annum, which is roughly the rate
indicated for 1968-70.[20] According to Clark, most of the
projected rise in imports is attributable to the expansion of
gross investment--only about 11 percent of the total increase
is attributable to assumed further import liberalization. Clark
concludes, given the extent of the liberalization accomplished
on the import side, that the most crucial issues of Brazilian
trade policy involve exports rather than imports.

IMPORT SUBSTITUTION, EXPORT EXPANSION, AND AGRICULTURAL DEVELOPMENT

There are only two "autonomy preserving" means of reducing the tendency to current account deficit in the Brazilian
balance of payments during periods characterized by rapid
economic growth--decreasing imports or expanding exports.
The other possibility (reliance on foreign aid, foreign loans,
and direct foreign investment to finance an import surplus),
implies a forfeiture of some degree of autonomy in the economic sphere in favor of the "international community." This
alternative may indeed be a necessary condition for assuring
rapid economic growth in the 1970's. However, in view of the
strong nationalistic pressures existing in Brazil for more
rather than less economic autonomy, it would appear appropriate to examine the possibilities for export expansion and
further import substitution.

From the discussion in the previous section, it should be
clear that, throughout the postwar period, rapid rates of economic growth have been associated with substantial net inflows
of foreign capital in various forms. In brief, predominantly
agricultural exports and imports of foreign capital have financed a rapid growth of the industrial sector, and relatively
little attention has been devoted to the expansion of exports or
to the agricultural sector.[21] One exception to the latter statement should be noted--as described in some detail in Chapter
4, considerable resources were dedicated to the objective of
increasing wheat production in the 1950's, although without
notable success. On the other hand, notable achievements in
the field of industrial import substitution resulted from these
policies, as has been amply documented in a number of important studies, to which the reader is referred for detailed
analyses.[22] For the present purpose, it is sufficient to note
that industrial import substitution has been carried very far
in Brazil, as revealed by Figure 1, which shows imports as
a percentage of total supply for different branches of industry.
As can be seen from this graph, by the 1960's, the import
coefficient had fallen below 20 percent, even in the capital-
goods industry.

Agricultural Growth and Productivity Stagnation

This industrialization policy was facilitated by the large
supplies of unexploited land and abundant agricultural man-
power which made it possible to increase the area cultivated
(and thus, agricultural production), without a parallel effort
to increase productivity in the food-production sector. In
fact, it appears that per hectare productivity of major food
crops was virtually unchanged over the period 1947-68, as is
indicated in Table 2. Rapid increases in per hectare productivity were observed only for Irish potatoes among the food
crops, with lesser increases for two industrial crops, peanuts
and sugarcane. The principal food crops--rice, corn, beans,
manioc, and wheat--were essentially stagnant and fell within
a range of plus or minus 10 percent productivity change, comparing the averages for 1947-51 with those for 1964-68. This
is equivalent to a compounded annual rate of change of considerably less than 1 percent. Cocoa and coffee, two very
important export crops, experienced substantial decreases in
productivity per hectare.

Labor productivity, if the available statistics can be be-
lieved, rose almost three times as fast in transformation

FIGURE 1

Imports as a Percentage of Total Supply, 1955-66

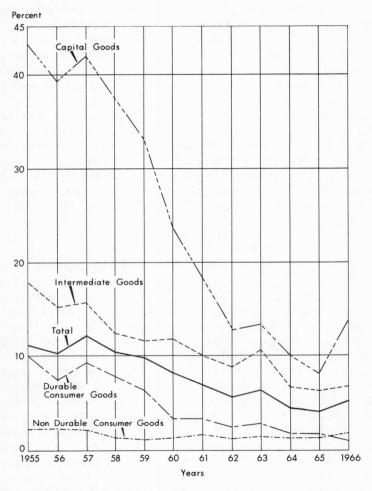

Source: Instituto de Pesquisa Econômico-Social Aplicada (IPEA), Industrialização Brasileira, Chapter 7, Figure 2.

TABLE 2

Average Yields of Major Brazilian Crops
For Selected Years (1947-51 = 100)

Crop in Kilograms per Hectare	1947-51	1956-60	1964-68	1956-60 index	1964-68 index
Rice	1583	1534	1536	97	97
Corn	1273	1254	1332	99	105
Beans	686	661	665	96	97
Manioc	13,098	12,992	14,244	99	109
Wheat	753	638	828	85	110
Irish potatoes	4790	5406	6633	113	138
Coffee	1219	1045	847	86	69
Cocoa	464	388	356	84	77
Sugarcane	38,402	41,403	45,161	107	118
Cotton	438	471	482	107	110
Peanuts	1002	1279	1082	128	123

Source: Calculated from data supplied by Serviço de Estatística da Produção (SEP) 1947-66; and Equipe de Estatística Agropecuária and Instituto Brasileiro de Café, 1967, 1968, published in various numbers of IBGE, Anuário Estatístico do Brasil. Absolute values are five-year average of annual average.

industries as in agriculture, with the result that the ratio of
industrial employment to total employment actually fell between 1950 and 1960. The relevant data are presented in Table 3.

Students of Brazil's development have stressed that productivity stagnation in the agricultural sector may present a
bottleneck to future economic growth. [23] On the other hand,
some analysts have noted that agricultural production has expanded more or less in harmony with the demands placed on
it except for livestock products, principally meats, milk, and
eggs, an approach that does not, however, take into account
potential demand, such as that of the international market,
which did not become effective in many years due to the operation of implicit export taxes and/or direct export controls.
(See Chapter 3.) In support of the latter viewpoint, it has been
shown that the level of agricultural prices as compared with
general price indexes for the economy as a whole did not increase significantly over the postwar period for most product
groups. The wholesale prices for agricultural products in
general, for example, stood at 101.3 percent of the 1951 level
in 1966 and were never higher than 111 percent in the period
1949-66; this high was reached in a year of severe agricultural
crisis, 1962. Animal products at the producer level did rise
as high as 134.6 percent of the 1949-53 average in 1962 and
were 134.3 percent in 1964 compared with 92.4 percent for
nonlivestock products. [24] However, these and other observers
note that the process of extensive agricultural growth which
made possible this relative stability in real prices of agricultural goods was reaching natural limits in the late 1960's.
These were imposed by the increasing physical distance of the
extensive agricultural frontier from the principal consuming
centers of the country, with an attendant increasing burden of
transport costs. [25] According to this analysis, which may be
called the hypothesis of the "hollow frontier," a critical point
has been reached where the exhaustion of the natural fertility
of soils in regions relatively near the major consumption centers, coupled with increasing costs of transporting goods from
a receding extensive frontier, makes imperative the adoption
of a more intensive technology in the traditional producing
areas of Brazil. The most articulate proponent of this view,
Ruy Miller Paiva, has argued that without substantial changes
in: (a) exchange-rate policy, (b) the relative prices of modern
manufactured inputs and agricultural commodities, and (c) the
quality and quantity of agricultural research, extension, and
credit, the introduction of modern technology is doomed to

TABLE 3

Relative Labor Productivity and Structure of Employment by Sectors

	Relative Labor Productivity Industry = 100		Annual Rate of Growth of Labor Productivity	Sector Employment as a Percent of Total Employment	
	1950	1960	1950-60	1950	1960
Agriculture	20.6	13.6	2.49	62.4	55.1
Transformation industries	100.0	100.0	6.83	9.8	9.1
Mining	24.8	33.5	10.05	0.7	0.5
Construction	19.0	13.8	3.48	3.6	3.6
Electricity	184.1	116.3	2.04	0.2	0.3
Commerce	123.2	75.6	1.74	5.8	6.9
Transport and communication	96.2	64.7	2.69	4.2	4.9
Services	62.2	26.6	-1.59	10.2	12.4
Government	113.3	24.1	-8.50	3.1	7.2
Total	45.0	31.0	2.92	100.0	100.0

Source: IPEA, A Industrialização Brasileira: Diagnóstico e Perspectivas, Table 5, p. 93.

failure due to the operation of a "self-controlling mechanism."
This mechanism would operate through the depression of domestic agricultural prices as output expanded faster than domestic demand and yet at costs too high to permit commercial
exports, thus eliminating the incentives for adoption of the
more intensive technology. [26]

In a somewhat similar vein, Gordon Smith's analysis of
several price-oriented agricultural policies pursued by Brazilian governments in the 1950's and 1960's led him to con-
clude: that

> If Brazil is to reduce the ever-widening gap between
> industrial and agricultural per capita incomes, the
> emphasis of policy must change from the manipula-
> tion of market incentives (although they certainly
> should not be abandoned) to direct action on the
> structural factors retarding the modernization of
> agriculture: poor rural education, ineffective re-
> search and extension, and perhaps even the land
> tenure structure. [27]

On a more positive note, it must be said that the "transforming of traditional agriculture" as it has been preached by
Theodore Schultz, John Mellor, Bruce Johnston, and others,
while not without its difficulties, is a process which in recent
years has received increasing attention by economists, sociol-
ogists, and anthropologists, and which promises high and relatively certain returns for the society in which it takes place. [28]
Today, it is considered almost trite to assert, given economic
incentives and access to modern, demonstrably superior (in
economic terms) technology, that even the most tradition-
bound, illiterate, and backward of peasants can be brought to
respond by adoption. The sticking point is really the will on
the part of policymakers to allocate the resources which make
a revolution in agricultural productivity possible. But in Brazil, little attention has been devoted to measuring the costs
and returns associated with the "transformation of traditional
agriculture." In the remaining chapters of this book, an attempt is made to provide some of the missing analysis.

Regional and Sectoral Inequalities

The heavy concentration of Brazilian industry in the Center-South region and the neglect of the agricultural sector are

also alleged to have increased existing sectoral and regional
inequalities in income distribution.[29] This is probably true,
particularly with regard to the Northeast region during the
1950's, although a comparison of per capita income by states
relative to São Paulo for the years 1947, 1957, and 1966 re-
veals that by three reasonable measures of over-all dispersion,
(mean absolute deviation, unweighted standard deviation, and
standard deviation using state populations as weights), inequality between states actually decreased very slightly between 1947 and 1966.[30] Nevertheless, the disparities in per
capita income by state are alarmingly large. Taking the Northeast region as a whole, the per capita income in 1966 was only
26 percent of the average for the state of São Paulo. The cor-
responding figures for 1947 and 1957 were 24 and 20 percent
respectively. Even within the Center-South region, moreover,
there are large differentials. In Minas Gerais, for example,
the 1966 per capita income was only 42 percent of that obtain-
ing in São Paulo. The three extreme southern states as a
region lost ground relative to São Paulo over the period studied
and moved from 61 percent in 1947, to 54 percent in 1957, and
51 percent in 1966. These states are overwhelmingly devoted
to agriculture.

Many Brazilians are coming to the conclusion that the
severe regional imbalances can be corrected only if increasing
attention is devoted to raising productivity in the agricultural
sector. The obvious advantages of such a policy, which would
help create a larger market for domestically produced agricultural inputs as well as consumer goods, should help gain
the support of the industrial sector for a major revision of
development priorities along these lines.

Import Substitution and Export Performance

In addition, several authors have expressed the view that
further import substitution in industry will be an increasingly
costly way of saving foreign exchange.[31] The case is made
that (a) the easy import substitution (in terms of technological
sophistication and low capital-output ratios) has already been
accomplished; (b) the high cost structure of many established
industries, which was facilitated by the ample protection af-
forded to import-substitution industries in the past, including
many capital goods and intermediate goods producers, places
a handicap on new industries; and (c) relatively narrow markets, which are a function of the grossly unequal sectoral and

regional distribution of income coupled with high degrees of
socioeconomic inequality within any given sector and region,
limit the realization of returns to scale in many industries
and tend to facilitate the establishment of monopolies.

In the past, a number of arguments were presented to
justify the emphasis on import substitution in the industrial
sector. Among them, the following deserve mention: (a) the
risks of depending on exports of primary products due to cyclical or random disturbances in the international economy,
such as wars and business cycles which may have led policymakers to discount by a large risk factor potential foreign-
exchange earnings from increased primary product exports;
(b) the belief that industrialization was indispensable for the
attainment of economic and technological independence in a
hostile world environment; (c) awareness that many primary
products are characterized by low income elasticities of demand; (d) the knowledge that Brazil has a large degree of
monopoly power in the world coffee market, which is characterized by relatively inelastic price and income elasticities
of demand; (e) the assumption that supply elasticities for many
exportable primary products were low; and (f) the fear that
synthetic substitutes would make increasing inroads in the
markets of some primary products.

In addition, there is strong evidence that Brazilian economic policymakers adhered to a theory of international trade
which Nathaniel Leff and Ivan Lakos have labeled the "exportable surplus theory."[32] This view holds that domestic demand
must be "satisfied" before exports are permitted. The policy
of overvaluing export-exchange rates and employing direct
export controls as well to hold down domestic prices tended
to discourage production and stimulate consumption as well as
reducing exports. Evidence to this effect for some specific
products will be presented in Chapters 3 and 4.

It is not within the scope of this study to examine all of
the arguments given above in favor of import substitution for
all products produced or producible in Brazil. Rather, this
study will focus on five agricultural commodities which are
important in international trade. The emphasis is on factors
affecting the supply of these commodities from Brazilian
sources.

To develop further the rationale for this procedure, data
on the average dollar value of selected import and export
categories in 1947-49, 1955-57, and 1965-67 are presented
in Tables 4 and 5. These years were chosen in order to reflect the situation in the immediate postwar period, at the

TABLE 4

Performance of Principal Brazilian Exports

Product[a]	1947-49 Average	Percent[b]	1955-57 Average	Percent[b]	1965-67 Average	Percent[b]	1955-57 Index[c]	1965-67 Index[c]
Coffee and preparations	511,142	44.7	906,428	63.3	731,300	44.0	177	143
Cotton	164,586	14.4	99,874	7.0	105,883	6.4	61	64
Iron ore	3,045	0.3	37,685	2.6	101,987	6.1	1238	3349
Sugar	11,960	1.6	31,461	2.2	72,564	4.4	175	404
Cocoa beans and products	57,160	5.0	93,718	6.5	66,341	4.0	164	116
Pinewood	40,570	3.6	51,650	3.6	54,018	3.3	127	133
Soybeans and products	610	0.1	3,887	0.3	27,375	1.7	637	4488
Corn	5,024	0.4	--	--	27,149	1.6	--	540
Castor oil	2,835	0.3	9,322	0.7	24,092	1.5	329	850
Beef frozen, chilled, and canned	17,875	1.6	6,485	0.5	23,367	1.4	36	131
Manganese ore	2,044	0.2	17,048	1.2	23,334	1.4	834	1141
Tobacco leaf	16,279	1.4	18,325	1.3	22,793	1.4	113	140
Sisal	5,981	0.5	13,013	0.9	21,350	1.3	218	357
Rice	25,676	2.3	3,331	0.2	20,600	1.2	13	80
Wool	4,096	0.4	12,071	0.8	19,996	1.2	295	488
Peanuts and Products	3,109	0.3	1,031	0.1	14,348	0.9	33	461
Brazil nuts	6,657	0.6	12,794	0.9	12,270	0.7	192	184
Wood other than pine	7,622	0.7	4,139	0.3	11,595	0.7	54	152

[a]Dollar values are f.o.b., in thousands of dollars.
[b]Represents percent of dollar value of total exports.
[c]Based on 1947-49 = 100.

Source: Calculated from data supplied by SEEF, Ministério da Fazenda, Rio de Janeiro.

TABLE 5

Value of Selected Categories of Brazilian
Exports and Imports, for Selected Years

Category	1947-49[a]	Percent[b]	1955-57[a]	Percent[b]	1965-67[a]	Percent[b]	1955-57[c] Index	1965-67[c] Index
1. Coffee and preparations	512,142	44.7	906,428	63.3	731,300	44.0	177	143
2. Pinewood, cotton, brazil nuts, cocoa, and cocoa products	268,973	23.5	258,512	18.1	238,512	14.3	96	89
3. Wood other than pine	7,622	0.7	4,139	0.3	11,595	0.7	54	152
4. Other minor agricultural commodities	99,445	8.7	98,926	6.9	273,634	16.5	100	275
5. Iron and manganese ore	5,089	0.5	54,733	3.8	125,311	7.5	1076	2462
6. Manufactures (SITC 5, 6, 7, 8)	52,562	4.6	13,684	1.0	116,329	7.0	26	221
7. All other exports	198,246	17.3	96,345	6.7	166,971	10.0	49	84
2 + 7	467,219	40.9	354,857	24.8	405,483	24.4	104	87
3, + 4, + 5, + 6	164,718	14.4	171,432	12.0	526,869	31.7	104	320
Total exports	1,143,079	100.0	1,432,291	100.0	1,663,652	100.0	125	146
Wheat and flour imports (c.i.f.)	130,064	11.4	128,165	9.0	164,460	9.9	99	127

[a]Average dollar value, in thousands of dollars.
[b]Represents percent of dollar value of total exports.
[c]Based on 1947-49 = 100.

Source: Calculated from Table 4 above.

height of the taxation of exports via the exchange system (see Chapter 3 for an explanation of implicit export taxes), and finally during the period of increased incentives to export which began after the military takeover of 1964. Three-year periods were chosen to smooth out fluctuations due to variations in crop yields. While the value data include the impact of changes in price as well as volume, these tables reveal certain salient features of the changing structure of Brazilian exports.

First, coffee and preparations (category 1) remained by far the most important items in 1965-67 and still accounted for over 40 percent of the value of exports. Second, four other products--pinewood, cotton, brazil nuts, and cocoa-- (category 2) which together accounted for over 23 percent of the value of exports in 1947-49, had declined in both value and relative importance and accounted for only 14 percent of the total in 1965-67. Third, exports of minor agricultural commodities (category 4), forest products (category 3), and manufactures (category 6) were stagnant or declining in value at the height of the period of discrimination against exports in 1955-57, but appeared to have responded favorably to increased incentives to export in the period 1965-67; however, by 1965-67, they added up to only 25 percent of the total value of exports. Fourth, manganese and iron ore exports (category 5) expanded very rapidly throughout the period covered. Fifth, all other exports (category 7), none of which contributed as much as an annual average of $10 million to the export bill in the period 1965-67, did even worse than category 2 and declined to 84 percent of their 1947-49 value by 1965-67. And finally, the value of wheat and flour imports was still almost 10 percent of the total value of exports in 1965-67, only slightly below their share in 1947-49 in spite of large-scale attempts to promote domestic wheat production and the much higher prices of the immediate postwar period.

What is the prognosis for the future? Export projections are notoriously inaccurate, but certain assumptions can be made with a fairly low risk of error. First, coffee exports cannot be expected to increase by more than 3 percent per year under the Indernational Coffee Agreement, or approximately in proportion with the growth in world consumption of coffee. Second, the outlook for increasing pinewood exports continues unfavorable--the southern Brazilian forest resources on which these traditional exports have been based are limited and declining. Cotton prices have shown a strong downward trend since 1955, and, given the U.S. government's announced policy of allowing world prices to seek lower levels in order

to combat increasing competition from synthetic fibers, it is
unlikely that there will be any great stimulus to cotton production in the foreseeable future. Brazil-nut production is a
primitive, extractive activity dependent on low-cost labor in
the Amazon forests. The prospects for increasing supplies of
such labor are not good. Cocoa and cocoa products have good
possibilities, but only if a major replanting program is undertaken in the principal producing region, Bahia. Because cocoa
is a tree crop, the results of even a massive program starting
in the early 1970's would only become apparent in the late
1970's. All in all, for the decade of the 1970's, the best that
can be expected is that the value of exports of category 2 commodities will be approximately constant.

     The same can probably be said for the group of unidentified
minor export products in category 7. This implies that exports of metalic ores, minor agricultural and forest products,
and manufactures will have to expand extremely rapidly if anything like a rate of growth of exports of even 5 percent is to
be obtained. Table 6 shows the initial (1969), terminal (1975),
and average annual growth rates for the aggregate value of
categories 3, 4, 5, and 6 to maintain alternative annual growth
rates for the value of total exports over the period 1969-75,
starting with the observed values for 1968 and assuming that:
(a) the value of coffee exports increases at 3 percent per annum, and (b) the aggregate value of categories 2 and 7 remains
constant. The average required rate of growth of the aggregate
of categories 3, 4, 5, and 6 (dynamic exports) ranged from
10 percent for a 5 percent growth rate of total export earnings
to 16. 4 percent for an 8 percent over-all export growth. The
rates of growth required in the early years are considerably
higher.

     In view of: (a) the relative neglect of the agricultural sec-
tor in the postwar period, (b) the importance of this sector if
anything like the planned growth rates of exports are to be
achieved, (c) the intense Brazilian interest in import-substituting wheat production, and (d) the possible benefits of a rapid
increase in agricultural production in terms of improving sectoral and regional income distribution in Brazil, we have decided to concentrate attention on the factors which influenced
production of five commodities and exports of four selected
agricultural commodities in the period 1947-67 and then to
examine the potential for technological change which might
substantially alter existing production relationships. Fertilizer use has been singled out for detailed study in view of its
strategic importance in the process of agricultural modernization. No attempt is made to analyze either domestic or foreign

TABLE 6

Required Growth Rates of Selected Export
Categories to Achieve Specified Rates of Growth
of Total Exports, 1969-75

Rate of Growth of Total Exports	5%	6%	7%	8%
Average 1969-75 growth rate of categories 3, 4, 5, and 6	10.0	12.2	14.4	16.4
1969 growth rate of categories 3, 4, 5, and 6	11.4	14.4	17.5	20.5
1975 growth rate of categories 3, 4, 5, and 6	8.9	10.6	12.1	13.4

Source: For assumptions used in these calculations, see
text. Categories are defined in Table 5 and the text.

demand in any depth--the study is fundamentally oriented toward supply.

Before ending this introductory chapter, it is worthwhile
to note that the picture of the Brazilian agricultural sector and
its relationship to the rest of the economy, sketched here and
painted in greater detail in the remainder of this volume, has
much in common with the rest of Latin America. In 1969,
ECLA described the "critical state of agricultural development
in Latin America" in the following words:

> Its principal symptoms and causes may be summed
> up under the following heads: (a) a slow rate of in-
> crease of production, especially in the livestock sec-
> tor, in relation to the rate of population growth;
> (b) little improvement in unit yields of a large number
> of products, and, as a general rule, inadequate tech-
> nological progress in most countries; (c) an unsatis-
> factory structure of production characterized by
> underdiversification; (d) overconcentration of owner-
> ship of land and agricultural income, with the result

that the income levels of living of vast numbers of the
rural population are deplorably low; (e) underutilization of available land and labor, giving rise to high
unemployment and underemployment figures in rural
areas and to substantial and increasing population
shifts from the countryside to the towns; (f) low levels
of food consumption in most countries in both rural
and urban areas, despite the steady growth of imports; (g) slow expansion of agricultural exports, and
a progressive decline in the prices of agricultural
products chiefly exported by Latin America; (h) lack
of integrated agricultural development planning, aim-
ing at the removal of the existing obstacles and the
solution of the abovementioned problems through the
adoption of continuing and consistent policies and   33
appropriate administrative and institutional reforms.

There is thus a high probability that the qualitative if not
the quantitative findings of this study may have application beyond Rio Grande do Sul and Brazil.

NOTES

1. Some basic references on the postwar Brazilian in-
dustrialization include the following: Werner Baer, Industrialization and Economic Development in Brazil (Homewood,
Illinois: Richard D. Irwin, 1965); Celso Furtado, Dialético
do Desenvolvimento (Rio de Janeiro: Editôra de Cultura,
1964), especially the second part, entitled "Diagnóstico da
Crise Brasileira"; Economic Commission for Latin America
(ECLA), "The Growth and Decline of Import Substitution in
Brazil, " and "Fifteen Years of Economic Policy in Brazil,
Economic Bulletin for Latin America (March, 1964), 1-59, "
and (November, 1964), 153-214, respectively; Instituto de
Pesquisa Econômico-Social Aplicada (IPEA), A Industrialização Brasileira: Diagnóstico e Perspectivas, Versão Prelimi-
nar, Rio de Janeiro, January, 1968; Nathaniel H. Leff, Eco-
nomic Policy-Making and Development in Brazil, 1947-1964
(New York: John H. Wiley and Sons, 1968); and Joel Bergsman,
Brazil's Industrialization and Trade Policies (New York: Oxford University Press, 1970).

2.   The concept of import-constrained growth has been
spelled out in rigorous terms by Ronald McKinnon, "Foreign

Exchange Constraints in Economic Development and Efficient Aid Allocation, " Economic Journal (June, 1964), 388-409; and Hollis Chenery and Alan Strout, "Foreign Assistance and Economic Development, " American Economic Review (September, 1968), 679-733. The rigidity of the assumptions underlying these two-gap models is discussed in Benjamin Cohen, "Comment, " and Ronald McKinnon, "Rejoinder, " Economic Journal (March, 1966), 168-171.

3. Furtado, op. cit., pp. 118-33; Nathaniel H. Leff, "Import Constraints and Development: Causes of the Recent Decline of Brazilian Economic Growth, " Review of Economics and Statistics (November, 1967), 494-501; IPEA, op. cit.; and ECLA, "Growth and Decline" and "Fifteen Years, " op. cit. Leff's analysis is criticized in Joel Bergsman and Samuel Morley, "Import Constraints and Development: Causes of the Recent Decline of Brazilian Economic Growth: A Comment," Review of Economics and Statistics (February, 1969), 101-12. See also, Nathaniel H. Leff's "Import Constraints and Development: A Reply, " Review of Economics and Statistics (February, 1969), 102-4.

4. Quoted in Thomas Skidmore, Politics in Brazil, 1930-1964: An Experiment in Democracy, (New York: Oxford University Press, 1967), p. 194.

5. Ibid., pp. 194-95.

6. Ibid., p. 195; and Escritório de Pesquisa Econômica Aplicada (EPEA), Diagnóstico Preliminar, Setor de Comércio Internacional (Rio de Janeiro, March, 1967), Table 39.

7. ECLA, "Fifteen Years of Economic Policy, " op. cit., p. 203.

8. Ibid.

9. "Plano Trienal do Desenvolvimento Econômico e Social, 1963-1965, " Rio de Janeiro, December, 1962, quoted in Leff, Economic Policy-Making, op. cit., p. 165.

10. Furtado, op. cit., pp. 120-21, my translation.

11. Skidmore, op. cit., p. 240.

12.   Leff, Economic Policy-Making, op. cit., p. 167.

13.   Skidmore, op. cit., p. 248.

14.   Ibid., p. 258.

15.   ECLA, "Fifteen Years of Economic Policy," op. cit., pp. 198-207.

16.   Conjuntura Econômica National Economic Index No. 4, June, 1968.

17.   Samuel Morley, "Import Demand and Import Substitution in Brazil," in Howard S. Ellis, ed., The Economy of Brazil (Berkeley and Los Angeles: University of California Press, 1969).

18.   Paul G. Clark and Richard Weisskoff, "Import Demand and Import Policies in Brazil," paper prepared for AID, February, 1967, mimeographed. Albert Fishlow's work is published in Ministério do Plantejamento e Coordenação Geral., Programa Estratégico de Desenvolvimento, 1968-1970, Vol. 1, Versão Preliminar (Rio de Janeiro, June, 1968), pt. I, chap. VI. The data and functions used by Fishlow are not identical with those used by Clark and Weisskoff, but the results are quite similar and therefore are lumped together in this brief review.

19.   Paul G. Clark, "Brazilian Import Liberalization," Williams College, Williamstown, Massachusetts, September, 1967, mimeographed.

20.   Ministério do Planejamento e Coordenção Geral, Programa Estratégico, op. cit., pt. I, chap. VI, p. 33.

21.   With regard to the neglect of the agricultural sector see Baer, op. cit., chap. 7; Donald L. Huddle, "Postwar Brazilian Industrialization: Growth Patterns, Inflation, and Sources of Stagnation," in Eric Baklanoff, ed., The Shaping of Modern Brazil, (Baton Rouge: Louisianna State University Press, 1969); ECLA, "Growth and Decline," and "Fifteen Years of Economic Policy," op. cit., pp. 51-54 and 185 respectively; and Agency for International Development (AID), Brazil Agriculture and Rural Development Office, "Problems and Needs of Brazilian Agriculture" (Rio de Janeiro, October 15, 1966, mimeographed.)

22. See note 1.

23. See, for example, Baer, op. cit., and his Chapter 7, "Imbalances and Bottlenecks in the Brazilian Economy, " especially pp. 150-63.

24. Statistics are from Ministério do Planejamento e Coordinação Geral, Programa Estratégico do Desenvolvimento, Áreas Estratégicas I e II, Agricultura, Abastecimento (Rio de Janeiro, January, 1968), pp. 16-25. The notable failure of production in the livestock sector to keep up with demand apparently was not a phenomenon confined to Brazil. See ECLA, "Agricultural Development in Latin America, " E/CN. 12/829, February 12, 1969, mimeographed.

25. See Ruy Miller Paiva, "Bases de uma Política para a Melhoria Técnica da Agricultura Brasileira, " Revista Brasileira de Economia (June, 1967), 5-38; Baer, op. cit., chap. 7; and ECLA, "Agricultural Development in Latin America, " op. cit., p. 36, which also notes that the cost of extensive growth is high in terms of the additional infrastructure required.

26. Paiva, op. cit.; this analysis is further developed in a more recent work by the same author, "Apreciação Geral Sôbre o Comportamento da Agricultura Brasileira, " Revista de Administração Pública (January-June, 1969), 56-117.

27. Gordon W. Smith, "Brazilian Agricultural Policy, 1950-1967, " in Howard S. Ellis, ed., The Economy of Brazil, op. cit., p. 214.

28. See Theodore W. Schultz, Transforming Traditional Agriculture (New Haven: Yale University Press, 1964); John W. Mellor, "Toward a Theory of Agricultural Development"; Bruce Johnston and Herman Southworth, "Agricultural Development Problems and Issues"; and Raj Khrishna, "Agricultural Price Policy and Economic Development, " Chapters 2, 1, and 13, respectively, in Johnston and Southworth, eds., Agricultural Development and Economic Growth (Ithaca, New York: Cornell University Press, 1967); and Lester R. Brown, The Seeds of Change: The Green Revolution and Economic Development in the 1970's (New York: Praeger Publishers, 1970). For a review of the literature on the returns to agricultural research in the United States, see Willis L. Peterson,

"The Returns to Investment in Agricultural Research in the
United States, " paper presented at the Symposium on Resource
Allocation in Agricultural Research, University of Minnesota,
Minneapolis, February 23-25, 1969. Estimates of returns to
agricultural research in Mexico by N. Ardito-Barletta are cited
in Theodore W. Schultz, Economic Growth and Agriculture
(New York: McGraw Hill Book Co., 1968), p. 85. For Japan,
see Saburo Yamada, "Changes in Output and in Conventional
and Non-Conventional Inputs in Japanese Agriculture Since
1880, " Food Research Institute Studies, II, 3, (1967), 371-
413.

29. ECLA, "Growth and Decline, " op. cit., p. 52.

30. The original data used to make these calculations was
taken from Conjuntura Econômica (October, 1969), p. 70 and
p. 80 (domestic income), and Instituto Brasileira de Geografia
e Estatística (IBGE), Anuário Estatístico do Brasil (Rio de
Janeiro, 1957 and 1969) (population).

31. ECLA, "Growth and Decline, " op. cit., pp. 66-67;
and Furtado, op. cit., pp. 115-19; Joel Bergsman and Arthur
Candal, "Industrialization: Past Success and Future Problems, " in Howard S. Ellis, ed., The Economy of Brazil, op.
cit., pp. 29-73.

32. Nathaniel H. Leff, "Export Stagnation and Autarkic
Development in Brazil, " Quarterly Journal of Economics (May,
1967), 286-301; and Ivan Andras Lakos, "The Effects of Brazil's Foreign Exchange Policy on the Value of Her Exports and
on the Flow of Private Investment with Respect to Brazil's
Economic Development: 1946-1960" (unpublished Ph. D. dissertation, Harvard University, March, 1962).

33. ECLA, "Agricultural Development in Latin America, "
op. cit., p. 1.

2

HISTORICAL BACKGROUND
AND THE STRUCTURE
OF PRODUCTION
IN RIO GRANDE DO SUL

In this chapter, a brief historical background is presented, followed by a summary of productive technologies utilized in the postwar period, interrelationships among crops, and the structure of land tenure for each of the five products discussed below--beef, rice, wheat, soybeans, and corn.

HISTORICAL BACKGROUND

Rio Grande do Sul is Brazil's southernmost state and adjoins Uruguay on the south and Argentina on the west. (See Figure 2.) The state's economy is predominantly agricultural and pastoral, although in the postwar period there has been a substantial growth of light industry in and north of Porto Alegre, the state capital.

In the past, Rio Grande do Sul's mild, temperate climate and large expanses of natural pastures made its economy largely complementary to that of the rest of tropical and semi-tropical Brazil, supplying dried beef (charque), albeit at higher prices than potential suppliers in Argentina and Uruguay, and importing some tropical products.[1] Beginning in the first decade of the twentieth century, irrigated rice became an important crop, both for sale in the rest of Brazil and for export. In addition, since the mid-nineteenth century, there has been an area of small farms settled by European colonists, mostly German and Italian, in the regions of hilly terrain unsuited to extensive grazing. The colonos, as they are called, were and still are homesteaders who produce corn, most of

FIGURE 2
Rio Grande do Sul

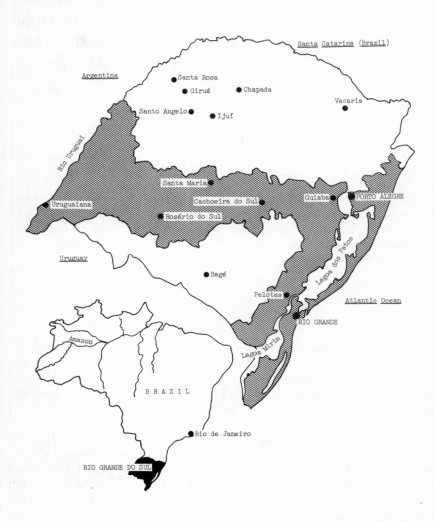

which is fed to hogs, as well as wheat, beans, and manioc. The colono economy involves a substantial percentage of essentially subsistence farming, although surplus production has been marketed within the state. The principal exception is the grape and wine industry in the area north of Pôrto Alegre which is oriented toward the national market.

In the years since World War II, there has been a rapid expansion of upland rice cultivation and a beef industry based zebu cattle (originally imported from India) in the Center-South states--principally São Paulo, Goiás, Paraná, and parts of Mato Grosso. A substantial beef industry has also developed in the south of Bahia. These surplus production areas have been putting competitive pressure on Rio Grande do Sul in the large Center-South and Northeast markets as internal transportation costs have fallen, so there has been a tendency for Rio Grandense producers to look to overseas markets as an outlet for rice and beef production. [2]

Rio Grande do Sul rice, produced in irrigated lowlands, has found an acceptance in the international market which has not yet been equaled by the upland rice produced in the rest of Brazil. As for cattle, the Gaucho (Rio Grandense) herd is composed of breeds such as the Hereford and the Shorthorn which are known to European buyers. While the quality of the Rio Grandense product is generally considered inferior to that of Argentina and Uruguay, it has found acceptance--principally in Europe for frozen and chilled beef and in the United States for canned and cooked frozen beef prepared by local subsidiaries of the large international packing companies as well as a number of locally owned cooperative packing companies.

Wheat has been cultivated in Rio Grande do Sul on a small scale by colono farmers since 1749. [3] However it was in the period following World War II that a massive effort was made to expand Brazilian wheat production in order to save foreign exchange, which was required in increasing amounts to finance wheat imports. This agricultural import-substitution campaign was concentrated overwhelmingly in Rio Grande do Sul, where large areas of natural pastureland were ploughed up and devoted to mechanized wheat culture.

Soybean production also began a rapid expansion in the 1950's. Area devoted to soybeans increased steadily through the late 1960's, and a high proportion of production has been exported in most years.

As may be seen in Table 7, in the period 1965-67 Rio Grande do Sul either produced or exported 80 percent of the Brazilian total for all the products being studied here except corn.

TABLE 7

Share by Rio Grande do Sul in Production and
Export of Five Agricultural Products, 1965-67

| Product | Rio Grande do Sul | |
	Percent of National Production	Percent of National Exports
Rice	18.6	84.7
Wheat	87.6	Brazil does not export wheat
Soybeans	81.7	85.4[a]
Corn	18.9	0.0
Beef	13.0	89.9[b]

[a]Exports include soybeans, soybean meal, soybean cake, and soybean flour.
[b]Chilled and frozen beef.

Source: Production, Anuário Estatístico do Brasil, 1969, except for wheat; CCLEF, Anuário Estatístico do Trigo, Safra 66/67; and directly from CCLEF offices in Pôrto Alegre for 1967-68 crop. Exports, SEEF, Ministério da Fazenda, Rio de Janeiro.

TECHNOLOGIES AND LAND TENURE

The remainder of this chapter is devoted to discussion of the five crops in relation to technologies utilized and land tenure.

Beef

Beef production is the most traditional agricultural activity in Rio Grande do Sul. In terms of area occupied, it is by far the most important, and there are significant interrelationships with rice, wheat, and soybean production. It is a land-extensive activity which uses relatively little labor or capital other than the cattle themselves. The data presented in Table 8, taken from

TABLE 8

Land Use in Rio Grande Do Sul

	1950	Percent[a]	1960	Percent[a]	Index
Natural pasture	14,352,549	65.03	13,178,558	60.84	91.8
Artificial pasture	263,628	1.19	301,316	1.67	137.1
Total pastures	14,616,177	66.23	13,539,874	62.51	92.6
Land under crops, other than pasture	2,502,691	11.34	3,709,781	17.13	148.2
Forests	2,270,802	10.29	2,315,149	10.67	102.0
Unproductive or unculti-vated	2,679,705	12.14	2,094,602	9.67	78.2
Total area in census	22,069,375	100.00	21,659,406	100.00	98.1
Total area of state beef herd	26,752,800 9,211,489		26,752,800 8,682,985		94.3
Sheep herd	7,916,000		10,088,000		124.4
Beef cattle [a]	.630		.641		102.0
Sheep [b]	.542		.745		137.0

[a]Figures given are percent of census areas.
[b]Figures represent animals per hectare of pasture.

Source: IBGE, Serviço Nacional de Recensamento, Censo Agrícola, 1950 and 1960; SEP estimate published in IBGE, Anuário Estatístico do Brasil, 1961, for data on sheep herd.

the two most recent agricultural censuses, are quite revealing.
The total area of Rio Grande do Sul is 26,752,800 hectares;
of these, 22,069,375 and 21,651,406 hectares respectively
were covered by the agricultural censuses of 1950 and 1960.
The remainder is accounted for by urban areas, roads, rail-
roads, and so forth.

Of the agricultural area, over 66 percent was devoted to
pastures in 1950, and that proportion had dropped to 62.5 percent by 1950, while the area devoted to crops other than
pastures increased by 48 percent, from 11.3 to 17.1 percent
of the total agricultural area. It would appear that there was
a slight increase in the intensity of use of the pasture area when
both sheep and beef cattle are taken into account. Given the
limitations of the system of extensive grazing on natural
pastures described below, this has not been sufficient to sus-
tain the growth of meat production with even the population
growth of Rio Grande do Sul, which increased at an annual rate
of 2.72 percent between 1950 and 1960 and was estimated by
the Instituto Brasileiro de Geografia e Estatística (IBGE,
Brazilian Geographic and Statistical Institute), to be growing
at 2.56 percent per annum in the 1960's. The result has been
a downtrend in beef production for export both to the rest of
Brazil and to foreign countries as greater proportions of annual
production have been consumed in the form of fresh meat
(carne verde) within Rio Grande do Sul. (See Appendix for
evidence on this point.)

In the lowland areas of the litoral, central depression, and
the valley of the Rio Uruguai, the standard practice is rotation
between rice and natural pasture. Two thirds of the rice area
is cultivated by agricultural entrepreneurs who rent the land
from ranchers (fazendeiros) for two- or three-year periods.
The fazendeiros retain the right to graze their cattle on the
rice straw after the harvest until spring ploughing for the next
year's rice crop.

The apparent inefficiency of this system, where the rice
land is usually left in natural pasture for four years out of six
with no attempt at cultivation, is self-evident. Insufficient
drainage and, in some cases, lack of irrigation capacity to handle
both rice and pasture areas are the reasons usually given for the
continuation of the practice, although the conservatism of ranchers may also be a factor.

Rice and beef production are largely complementary activities because the natural pastures have their highest carrying
capacity during the summer, when the rice land is occupied.
In the winter, when forage is in short supply and the carrying

capacity of the pastures is diminished by as much as 50 percent, the rice lands are available for grazing.

In the cooler plateau areas in the north-central part of the
state, and to a lesser extent in the south as well, mechanized
wheat production competes with beef cattle for pasture land
during the critical winter months, when the carrying capacity
of the natural pastures is at its lowest. Much of mechanized
wheat production takes place on land rented from ranchers,
although rented area accounts for a lesser percentage of the
total land under this crop than in the case of rice.

In the summer, mechanized soybean production in former
natural pasture areas, like rice in the lowlands, is not a full
competitor for land, because requirements for pasture are
diminished in this season.

The most important factor limiting productivity in the beef
sector is the winter-forage shortage. It is responsible for
live-weight losses on the order of 25 to 30 percent in the cold
winter months in the central depression and Uruguayan frontier
regions and as much as 50 percent on the colder northern
plateau near Vacaria. In effect, under the dominant technology,
the animals live off their own fat during the winter. The mortality rates are high (4 to 5 percent of the herd per year), and
fertility rates are low for the same reason. Less than half of
the cows of bearing age calve in any given year, and experiments
have shown that only 28 percent of those cows which calve bear
again in the next year under natural pasture conditions, as
opposed to over 80 percent of those maintained in artificial
pastures, which have their greatest output of green matter in
the winter months.[4]

In the beef sector, large ranches (100-1,000 hectares) and
latifundia (more than 1,000 hectares) accounted for 39.1 percent of the establishments and 92.8 percent of the total area,
and together had a mean size of 641.8 hectares in 1960.[5] The
small and medium producers are primarily those with dairy
herds. The latifundia alone were 6 percent of the establishments,
but they had 53.7 percent of the total area with an average size
of 2,434 hectares. It should be noted that large size is considered by many observers, including the World Bank, to be
necessary for efficient production of beef. From the foregoing,
it should be clear that beef production is concentrated in very
large establishments. Several studies have indicated that typi- •
cal beef production enterprises in Rio Grande do Sul would lose
money if they had to pay rents. Only the ownership of land
permits many _fazendeiros_ to earn a monetary surplus, although not, in economic terms, a profit.[6] The size of the

establishments makes this a very comfortable income. Roughly 80 percent of beef land is owned by the ranchers themselves. [7]

While the area in artificial pastures grew fairly rapidly in the 1960's, the total area as of 1965 (the last available data) was 491, 104 hectares, or about 3. 6 percent of total pasture area, an increase of 35.9 percent since the agricultural census of 1960. [8] Much of this total was for dairy herds rather than slaughter cattle. Use of artificial pastures, or perhaps even semiconfinement feeding, is necessary if the slaughter age of steers (traditionally between 4 and 5 years) is to be brought down. (Numerous studies indicate that the planting of artificial pastures can be highly profitable, and some of the evidence is presented in Chapter 6.) Thus, the slow rate of diffusion of such practices raises the question of whether fazendeiros as a class are a conservative force in economic as well as political affairs. [9]

Rice

Irrigated rice cultivation is perhaps the most advanced agricultural activity in Rio Grande do Sul in terms of complexity of agro-technical-commercial organization, the level of yields obtained, and the statistics available. As noted above, rice production is closely linked with the primitive beef sector, although in roughly 70 percent of the area devoted to the joint production of rice and beef, the two operations are conducted by separate economic units. Rancher landowners in the rice regions receive an important part of their total income from rental payments of rice farmers, which run well over the legal maximum of 25 percent of the value of production for land and water combined. [10]

Rice production is dominated by medium and large establishments (farms of 20 to 1, 000 hectares in rice), which together accounted for 87 percent of the total rice area, although only 42 percent of the production units in the 1966-67 crop year. [11] There is a strong positive association between yields obtained in irrigated rice and the size of area planted per establishment, and farms harvesting over 250 hectares of rice obtained 15 to 25 percent higher productivity per hectare than those with less than 25 hectares. [12] This would appear to indicate better management practices, including higher fertilization, on the larger farms.

There were 7, 584 tractors in the rice region in 1966. Mechanization of land preparation has proceed fairly rapidly in the postwar period. The number of hectares per tractor fell from 152.5 in 1949 to 38.6 in 1966 for the farms in the rice zone with more than 9 hectares planted to this crop. [13] Harvest mechanization has been slower due to drainage problems. In 1966, there was only one combine per 413 hectares in rice, and even this figure may overstate the extent of combine use. [14] Further mechanization of the harvest would probably have adverse social effects because this is a very labor-intensive process and the cash income it provides to agricultural laborers could not be replaced easily. Mechanization, of course, has minimal effects on yields.

Improved drainage would probably have two major effects: It would tend to increase the mechanization of the harvest and permit the rotation of rice land with artificial pastures, soybeans, and other dry land crops. Two other factors complicate the drainage situation. The first is a typical organizational problem involving economies external to the firm in that drainage normally involves substantial numbers of producing units and thus requires collective action. The second is the high proportion of rice land which is rented. Neither of these latter difficulties is insurmountable. They are primarily organizational in nature and not strictly economic.

No major breakthroughs have been made in rice breeding, although in the latter years of the 1960's varieties which appeared to yield about 10 percent above those traditionally planted were introduced and rapidly adopted. (See Chapter 5.) In particular, no rice varieties capable of efficiently using high levels of nitrogen fertilization without lodging had been developed as of 1968.

The rent burden and insecurity of tenure are important factors deterring some improvements, such as better drainage, greater use of modern land-leveling techniques, and even chemical weed control. Most tenant rice farmers with whom we talked were aware of such practices and said they would implement them if they owned the land they worked. However, they professed little interest in handing over improved land to the fazendeiros at the end of three years at most, which is about the maximum duration of a rental contract. No doubt some contractual arrangements, such as longer contracts and reduced rents for carrying out specified improvements, could be conceived which would eliminate many of these disincentive effects.

Wheat

Throughout the postwar period, wheat has been produced under two fundamentally different technologies which are distinguished by the relative size of establishments practicing them, location, and degree of mechanization.

Mechanized wheat farming, utilizing tractors and self-propelled combines, takes place on natural pasture lands, in gentle rolling areas, with increased use of terracing and contour ploughing to control soil erosion. A much less mechanized and sometimes very primitive technology has been employed on small farms owned by the descendents of European colonists in the hilly and previously forested areas of the state.

The decade of the 1950's was marked by a very rapid expansion of the mechanized wheat area, much of this by persons with little or no previous experience in wheat farming. This may have been at the same time a blessing and a disadvantage, for while the new wheat entrepreneurs were not burdened with traditional, conventional wisdom about wheat culture, and were thus eager seekers of technological advice, they also neglected some basic principles of farming and were not supported by an adequate infrastructure of marketing, research, and extension facilities.

Beginning in 1958, overexpansion without sufficient technical support, coupled with unusually bad weather, heavy attacks of stem rust, and a high incidence of other wheat diseases, resulted in four successive years of extremely low yields, even by Brazilian standards. Wheat area declined each year from 1959 through 1962.

Mention should be made at this point of the massive frauds which arose during the 1950's due to the nature of the dual-price system under which a higher price was paid for domestically produced wheat than for that which was imported at highly subsidized exchange rates. Both as a result of these frauds and the statistical collection procedures employed by the Serviço de Estatística da Produção (SEP, Production Statistics Service of the Ministry of Agriculture), wheat statistics prior to 1962 are extremely unreliable. After 1962, technological standards, marketing procedures, and statistics for wheat improved substantially. These matters are discussed in some detail in Chapter 4.

Mini (less than 5 hectares in wheat) and small (5-20 hectares) wheat farms accounted for 88.5 percent of the production units, but only 29.1 percent of the wheat area in the period 1962-66. For the purpose of description, the data on farm size

for the five years 1962-66 have been aggregated and an over-all
average calculated.   This is not the average of annual averages,
but one fifth of the average for all recorded wheat production
over the five-year period as given in the publications of the
Comissão Central de Levantamento e Fiscalização das Safras
Triticolas (CCLEF).   Medium and large producers (all others,
as no wheat farm exceeded 1,000 hectares in this period), which
were only 11.5 percent of the total establishments, occupied
70.9 percent of the area.   Of the total area, 33.2 percent was
rented.   Based on data for the only years in which data are
appropriately broken down (1964 and 1965), the rented area
was overwhelmingly concentrated in the mechanized farms.
Rents ran about 11 percent of the value of wheat production per
hectare, assuming a yield of 804 kilograms per hectare over
the three-year period, 1965-67. [15]

The mechanized technique was used in 72.4 percent of the
area, but due to the larger size of mechanized as opposed to nonmechanized farms (55.4 hectares per production unit as opposed
to 4.4 hectares for nonmechanized farms), mechanized farms
were only 17.3 percent of the total.   Yields on mechanized
farms averaged about 5 percent higher than on nonmechanized
farms, which appears to indicate that higher fertilization and
better seeds more than compensated for the poorer soils of
the natural pasture regions where the majority of mechanized
farms are located.

As in the case of rice, no wheat varieties capable of sup-
porting intensive nitrogen fertilization without lodging had been
developed for commercial use as of 1968.   Rust-resistant
varieties were created and rapidly adopted.   The most widespread, IAS 20 (Iassul), was first released to farmers in 1963
and accounted for 28.4 percent of the total wheat area in 1966.

Fertilization is a virtual necessity on the poor soils of the
mechanized wheat regions.   In the colonial areas, where the nonmechanized technique is most common, natural soil fertility is
much higher, although it has been declining over time with repeated cropping.

The growth of a strong chain of producers' cooperatives,
starting in the early 1960's and supported by the Bank of
Brazil's Domestic Wheat Purchasing Commission (CTRIN),
has made the wheat-marketing system the best for any crop in
Rio Grande do Sul.   The Bank of Brazil has been the sole buyer
of wheat since 1962.   The cooperatives market other crops,
especially soybeans, are important in certified seed production,
and together constitute one of the most important institutions
in the state for diffusing new technology.

Soybeans

Soybeans became an important crop in Rio Grande do Sul in the early 1950's. As in the case of wheat, two distinct technologies have been employed. Fully mechanized soybean culture is associated closely with wheat production in the natural pasture areas, mostly in a system of double cropping. Immediately after the wheat harvest in November and December, the same land is ploughed up, and soybeans are planted. Often, farmers do not add additional fertilizer but rely solely on the residual effects of wheat fertilization. The same tractors and combines used for wheat are also employed in soybean production and thus secure a more efficient use of capital than would otherwise be the case. Most observers feel that mechanized soybean production is of only marginal profitability unless wheat is also produced on the same land.

Nonmechanized soybean farming is practiced in the colonial areas, especially in the northwestern part of the state centered on the county (município) of Santa Rosa. There, the common Brazilian practice of interplanting with corn is usually employed. Soybeans are a cash crop, and corn is normally fed to hogs.

Data are not available on the size of soybean farms, but because soybeans are closely associated with corn, the lower limit is probably set by the size distribution of corn-producing farms described below. Probably about 30 percent of the total soybean area in 1967-68 was rented, and about half of this was mechanized. The export director of the largest soybean marketing company estimated, in 1968, that nonmechanized soybean production accounted for 70 percent of the total, mechanized production in the double cropping system with wheat, 20 percent, and mechanized production not directly associated with wheat, 10 percent. The same source estimated that only about 20 percent of the soybean area in 1967 was planted with improved varieties, which is not far from the figure cited in the Ministry of Planning's new agricultural plan, 16 percent.[16]

Corn

Even less information is available on corn in Rio Grande do Sul than in the case of soybeans. In general, production is very backward and largely confined to the colonial areas of the state. As mentioned above, in some areas, soybeans are interplanted. Black and brown beans for human consumption as well as manioc are also often associated with this product. Most

corn is an intermediate good in hog production. Corn production takes place largely on small (5-20 hectares) and
medium (21-100 hectares) farms, which together accounted
for 87 percent of the production units and 78.8 percent of the
area of farms reporting corn as their principal product for
the 1960 agricultural census. If the only available data on
area actually devoted to maize production, that of the SEP, are
accepted, about 36 percent of the area of farms producing corn
was actually used for this crop. Because other units undoubtedly produce corn as a secondary crop, an estimate of 50 percent
appears reasonable, which would imply that the area for small
producers average 5.6 hectares, and for medium producers,
17.5 hectares. About 25 percent of corn area was rented.[17]

No data on mechanization of corn production are available.
If we judge from the size distribution of farms, it is unlikely
that more than 10 percent of the area was mechanized in 1960.
As for varietal improvement, one published estimate put the
percentage of area sown to hybrid corn in Rio Grande do Sul
at 5 percent as of 1965.[18]

NOTES

1. Joseph L. Love, Jr. "Rio Grande do Sul as a Source
of Political Instability in Brazil's Old Republic, 1909-1932"
(unpublished Ph.D. dissertation, Columbia University, 1967).

2. Ibid., p. 29; in 1930, Rio Grande do Sul supplied about
80 percent of the charque produced in Brazil. By 1966, the
percentage had fallen to 26.4. The principal gainer in the production of this item was São Paulo, the largest producer in
1966, with 41.6 percent of the total; Ministério da Agricultura,
Departamento Econômico, Serviço da Estatística da Produção
(SEP), Carnes, Derivados e Subprodutos 1966 (Rio de Janeiro,
September, 1967). This figure probably overstates the increase
in São Paulo, as much of the cattle slaughtered there originates
in other states such as Goiás, Paraná, and Mato Grosso. The
weakening position of Rio Grande do Sul is discussed at length
in Banco Nacional de Desenvolvimento Economico (BNDE),
Economia da Carne no Rio Grande do Sul e Aspectos dos
Mercados Nacional e Internacional do Producto (Rio de Janeiro,
March 25, 1963), especially pp. 96-111. With regard to the
competitive position of Rio Grande do Sul rice in the national
market, a large number of published sources are available.

Among them are: Ary Hertzog, Soly Souza Machado e Manoel P. Estrella Brasil, "Comparecimento Permanente e Contínuo do Arroz Gaucho no Mercado Internacional, " Congresso Estadual da Orizicultura, Anais (Pôrto Alegre, January, 1966), 135-38; Homero Pegas Guimarães, "Perspectivas para a Lavoura Gaucha, " Anais, 161-70; Alvaro Ornellas de Souza, "Um Estudo Sôbre Exportação, " Lavoura Arrozeira (January, 1965), 17-22; and "Pronunciamento do Dr. Mario de Lima Beck, Presidente do IRGA, " Lavoura Arrozeira (January, 1965), 5-9.   The latter is a speech by the President of the Instituto Rio Grandense do Arroz, a state autarquia (autonomous, semi-governmental agency), to its Deliberative Council given on December 29, 1964.   Following is my translation of an excerpt from this speech:

> The growing production of rice in Goiás and
> other central states is impeding our placing
> of rice in the São Paulo and Rio markets.   Be-
> side the quantity, the lower price of this pro-
> duction competes with our rice principally be-
> cause the producer in those zones is exploited
> by intermediaries.   We are on the margin of
> the domestic market and in difficulties in the
> world market and everyone knows what rice
> means to the economy of our state.

3.   Govêrno do Estado de Rio Grande do Sul, Os Problemas do Trigo (Pôrto Alegre, 1961), p. 11.

4.   Instituto de Pesquisa e Experimentação Agropecuárias do Sul (IPEAS) and Centro de Treinamento e Informação do Sul (CENTRISUL), Pastagens na Zona Fronteira do Rio Grande do Sul, Circular No. 32 (Pelotas, February, 1967).

5.   Calculated from 1960 agricultural census.

6.   See, for example, PLANISUL "Estudo Econômico Sôbre a Bovinocultura No Rio Grande do Sul" (Pôrto Alegre, July 30, 1968, mimeographed), which also cites other studies.

7.   Calculated from data in 1960 agricultural census.   This figure is the highest for any of the products being studied.

8.   Secretaria de Agricultura, Área de Pastagens Cultivadas no Rio Grande do Sul (Pôrto Alegre, 1966).

9. See Love, op. cit., for an analysis of the political role of the fazendeiro class.

10. Instituto Rio Grandense do Arroz (IRGA), Subsídios para Reestruturação: Relatório Preliminar do Grupo de Trabalho Criado pela Portaria 538/66, de 3 Novembro 1966 (Pôrto Alegre, 1967).

11. Calculated from IRGA, Anuário Estatístico do Arroz, Safra 1966/67.

12. Ibid., calculated from data in various issues.

13. Ibid.

14. Ibid., Safra 1966/67.

15. Calculated from surveys made by Federação das Cooperativas Tricolas do Sul, Ltda. (FECOTRIGO) and published annually in Trigo: Estudo do Custo de Produção No Rio Grande do Sul (Pôrto Alegre, 1965, 1966, and 1967).

16. Ministério do Planejamento e Coordenação Geral, Programa Estratégico de Desenvolvimento: Areas Estratégicas I e II, Agricultura, Abastecimento (Rio de Janeiro, January, 1968), p. 110.

17. Estimate based on data in the 1960 agricultural census.

18. Ministério de Planejamento, loc. cit.

CHAPTER

3

INTERNATIONAL PRICES,
THE FOREIGN-EXCHANGE SYSTEM,
AND EXPORT PERFORMANCE

In this chapter, the factors which have influenced Brazilian exports of beef, rice, soybeans, and corn over the period 1947-67 are analyzed. The first section considers the selection of suitable international prices and examines their behavior. The functioning of the rather complex and changing exchange system which existed over the postwar period is described in the second section. Included is a comparison of effective exchange rates for each export product, with two approximations of a more realistic, or equilibrium rate of exchange. This comparison allows the calculation of the implicit export taxes involved in the foreign-exchange system. Direct export controls, which were employed with varying intensity over time and among products, are also discussed. Finally, information from the first two sections is combined with internal market price series to estimate export functions for Brazilian beef, rice, soybeans, and corn. (See the Appendix, which deals with factors influencing the rate of slaughter of beef cattle in Rio Grande do Sul.)

INTERNATIONAL PRICES

For each of the four export products, the following information is presented below: First, an explanation of the choice of an appropriate international price or price index for each commodity, and second, a brief analysis of the behavior of the chosen series over the period 1947-67. For rice, corn,

and soybeans, the existence of inverse seasonals in international
and domestic prices due to Brazil's southern hemisphere location is investigated, because such price movements operate
to Brazil's advantage in international trade.

For the analysis of annual average international prices,
the principal tool used is the fitting of time trends. It is shown
that the direction of the trend, its statistical significance, and
its magnitude are quite sensitive to the year chosen for beginning the series. Comparative data are presented for each
product over five progressively shorter time periods: 1947-67,
1950-67, 1953-67, 1955-67, and 1960-67.

Beef

The choice of an appropriate price is particularly difficult
for this product, because there is no well-defined international
price, and beef is far from being a homogeneous commodity.
Various cuts of frozen and chilled beef as well as canned corned
beef and cooked frozen beef are included in export statistics.
Furthermore, Brazilian exports, especially those of chilled
and frozen beef, have been erratic. Argentina is the world's
largest beef exporter and accounted for 28. 5 percent of total
world exports over the period 1961-65. The figure rises to
41. 6 percent of the world exports excluding European countries. [1]
Argentina is also physically located on Rio Grande do Sul's
borders. Therefore, it was decided to construct an index of
the dollar prices of Argentinian beef exports, giving equal
weights to frozen and corned beef and utilizing data published
in International Financial Statistics on dollar prices for the
years 1950-67 for frozen beef and 1952-67 for canned beef,
taking the average price of each in 1957-59 as 100. To obtain
values for earlier years, these indexes were linked to similar
indexes for the dollar unit value of Brazil's exports of the same
product categories. This technique was used because Brazil
exported relatively large quantities of both in the period 1957-59,
at prices very close to those of Argentina, and Brazilian exports of each were also large in the years for which Argentinian
data was lacking, although not for a number of other years in
the series, which was the principal reason for using the
Argentinian data in the first place.

Table 9 shows that the trend in international beef prices,
as for producer prices in Brazil (data on price trends on the
domestic market are presented in Chapter 5), has been quite
consistently upward throughout the period 1947-67, with the

TABLE 9

International Prices for Four Commodities, 1947-67

Year	International Beef Price Index[a]	International Rice Price Index[a]	Chicago Contract Soybean Prices[b]	Chicago Contract Corn Prices[b]
1947	100	116	131.77	83.78
1948	105	128	134.56	83.72
1949	115	88	93.90	53.85
1950	96	88	107.07	62.96
1951	105	94	119.57	71.91
1952	111	153	118.99	74.98
1953	119	156	109.80	64.14
1954	117	122	121.34	62.70
1955	112	101	97.31	54.61
1956	94	99	101.57	56.43
1957	90	102	89.17	51.12
1958	97	106	85.75	48.23
1959	113	92	87.21	47.32
1960	120	83	84.31	44.60
1961	118	93	145.09	44.45
1962	100	105	98.20	43.82
1963	103	103	106.14	48.86
1964	124	107	105.20	48.65
1965	144	106	111.01	50.55
1966	138	119	121.31	53.30
1967	126	150	109.63	50.26

[a]1957-59 equals 100.
[b]Prices given are in U.S. dollars per metric ton.

Source: See text.

exception of the last eight years, which have been characterized
by a sharp cyclical movement, first downward to a trough in
1961 and then up to a peak in 1964. By 1967, prices were near
the trend value for the entire period 1947-67. The same factors which were responsible for the upward trend, principally
a high-income elasticity of demand and rising per capita income levels both in the principal exporting and major importing
countries, may be expected to continue in the future according
to the United Nation's Food and Agriculture Organization
(FAO) projections. [2] The principal negative factor is a trend
toward protection of local beef industries, particularly with
the European Common Market. On the whole, beef would appear to be one of the most promising agricultural exports, assuming pressure on major industrialized countries succeeds
in keeping these markets open and that quality can be brought
up to the standards demanded by European consumers. Unless
hoof-and-mouth disease is erradicated in Brazil, which is
highly unlikely, there is no possibility of export of Brazilian
fresh, chilled, and frozen beef to the United States. Cooked,
frozen, and canned beef can and do enter the U.S. market,
however.

                              Rice

     As in the case of beef, the problem of sporadic Brazilian
exports prevented the use of data on unit value of exports.
For the years 1957-67, the FAO index of rice export prices
in private transactions was used. This price index was then
linked to the only other major price series available on an
annual basis back to 1947, the free on board (f.o.b.) export
price for fine white rice with 5 to 7 percent brokens[*] at
Bangkok, Thailand. Thailand is one of Brazil's principal competitors in the international rice trade.
     As may be seen from Table 9, international rice prices
were quite volatile over the period 1947-67. However, over
the entire period, there was no statistically significant trend.
The extremely high prices of 1967 cannot be expected to prevail, especially in the light of recent technological advances
in rice production. The future trend will probably be gradually
downward.
     Because Brazil is located in the southern hemisphere

_____

[*]Refers to broken, as opposed to whole, grains. The
larger the percentage of brokens, the lower the price.

while most of the major rice exporting countries are on the
other side of the equator, the possibility of taking advantage
of the phenomenon of inverse seasonal price movements exists
which might enhance Brazil's competitive position during
certain months.

For the years 1957-67, a series of monthly export prices
for medium grain Thai white rice with 15 percent brokens--
the counterpart, in quality, of the medium grain blue rose
especial sold on Pôrto Alegre's Commodity Exchange (Bôlsa
de Mercadorias)--was available. Using these two series,
eliminating the year 1962 in which prices were not available
for Pôrto Alegre, and converting the Brazilian price to dollars
per metric ton at the effective exchange rate prevailing in
each month, indexes of seasonality were computed by expressing each month's dollar price as a percentage of the average
of twelve months' prices for each month and then taking the
average index value for all years in the series for both Pôrto
Alegre and Bangkok prices. Mathematically, for any given
year t and month i, the seasonality index for the domestic
price, S_{it}^d, is given by

$$S_{it}^d = \frac{100\ P_{it}^d\ R_{it}}{1/12 \left(\frac{1}{12} \sum_{i=1}^{12} P_{it}^d\ R_{it} \right)}$$

where P_{it}^d is the domestic price in month i of year t and R_{it}
is the effective exchange rate in month i of year t. Then the
average seasonality index for all years is

$$S_i^d = \frac{\sum\limits_{t=\,1957}^{1967} S_{it}^d}{11}$$

The same method was used to calculate the seasonality indexes for foreign prices.

Periods of four consecutive months for each location were
then selected during which the average seasonality index over
the period 1957-67 was the most favorable for Brazilian exporters. The same process was performed on the difference
between the Bangkok and Pôrto Alegre seasonals. It was
found that the most favorable period for purchase in Rio
Grande do Sul was May-August, with an average index of 95.4,
whereas from the point of view of sales, the highest period for

Bangkok prices was July-October, with an average index of
104. 2.   As might be expected, the best period for a combined
purchase in Rio Grande do Sul and sale in the international
market was June-September, with an average differential between the two indexes of 5. 85.   A trend was also fitted to the
four-month average seasonality indexes and the differential
between them to test whether there had been any significant
changes in these measures over time.   In no case was a significant trend found.   The mean values, standard deviations,
and number of years in which the price movement was favorable are presented below.

Period and Location	Four-Month Average Index of Seasonality or Differential	Standard Deviation of Index or Differ- ential	Years Favorable for Brazil	Years Unfavor- able for Brazil
July- October, 1957-67 Bangkok	104. 2	2. 13	10	1
May- August, 1957-67, excl. 1962 Pôrto Alegre	95. 4	4. 63	9	1
Differential 1957-67, excl. 1962	5. 9	2. 16	8	2

This analysis would suggest that Brazil could have reaped
significant advantages by careful timing of its sales in the international market.   A private exporter who timed his pur-
chases to take full advantage of both seasonal movements would,
on the average, do about 6 percent better than one who distributed his transactions randomly over the year.   That

statistically significant differentials could be measured in spite
of the irregular timing and extent of exchange-rate changes
suggests that under a "crawling peg" system such as that
adopted at the end of the 1960's, the differential would have
been still more regular. This point is applicable to other
agricultural products as well.

The actual distribution of exports over the year as given
in various issues of Anuário Estatístico do Arroz, a publication
of Instituto Rio Grandense do Arroz (IRGA), for the period
1957-67 was examined, and it was found that only 43.2 percent
of the total quantity of rice exported by Rio Grande do Sul was
exported in the July-October period, 52.3 percent in the June-
October period, and only 55.9 percent in the still longer period
of May-October, which embraces the most favorable months
both for purchase and sales.

The explanation is more likely to lie in delays in granting
export licenses and imposition of direct controls than in the
failure of exporters to behave in an economically optimal
fashion. [3] The high degree of uncertainty which prevailed regarding exchange-rate changes as well as direct controls
probably dominated the attention of exporters to an extent
which made seasonal price movements of secondary importance
to them.

Soybeans

The most representative international price is that for
number 2 yellow soybeans in Chicago. The United States
dominates the international trade in soybeans and accounted
for 89.4 percent of world exports of this product over the
period 1961-65. [4] The midrange of monthly high and low prices
as reported in the official Chicago Board of Trade statistics
on Chicago Contract Cash Soybeans was calculated, and annual averages were computed and converted into dollars per
metric ton.

Soybean prices were influenced by no long-term trend of
any statistical significance, although in the years 1960-67,
the trend would certainly have been upward were it not for abnormally high prices in 1961 which increased the standard
error of trend estimate considerably, compared to what it
would have been had more "normal" prices prevailed.

The lore of the trade has it that the only thing wrong with
soybeans is that they contain soybean oil. The demand for
soybean meal and cake for high protein livestock feeds has

been the dynamic element in the world soybean industry. Exports of oil are uncommon because most countries protect the soybean processing industry. However, international trade in soybean cake and meal has been large. Demand for soybeans will probably grow still faster if techniques are perfected for producing artificial meats from soybean meal and if the trend toward greater meat production within the European Common Market continues. In the United States, one company had thirty varieties of such "meatless meats" on the market in 1969.[5]

Using the same price series and following the procedures used for rice, monthly indexes of seasonality were computed both for the entire period 1947-67 and for 1956-67. The four-month period with the highest average index of seasonality was April-July; however, that for May-August was lower by such a small amount (103.72 compared with 103.87) over the entire period 1947-67 that it was decided to use the latter period, because very little of the Rio Grande do Sul crop is marketed by April.

For neither period was the index of seasonality significantly different from 100 even at the 10 percent level. However, the average values were 104 for the full period and 103 for the period 1956-67, as shown below. Nor was a trend shown.

Period (May-August)	Mean Season-ality Index	Standard Deviation of Season-ality Index	Years Favorable to Brazil	Years Unfavor-able to Brazil
1947-67	104.0	6.63	15	6
1956-67	103.9	3.78	10	2

Brazilian prices generally reflect the international price corrected for transportation-cost differentials and converted at the effective exchange rate. There is no reliable wholesale market price for soybeans, and that of Pôrto Alegre's Bolsa de Mercadorias is considered unrepresentative. Soybean exporters are very conscious of the seasonal price movement as well as their own storage costs, and exports are concentrated in the May-August period.

Corn

The United States is also the leader in the international corn trade and accounted for 55.2 percent of the total over the period 1961-65. [6] Because Brazilian exports were sporadic and dollar values of Argentinian exports were not readily available for the earlier years, the Chicago Board of Trade Contract Cash Prices were used. As in the case of soybeans, the annual average of monthly midranges was taken as the annual international price, expressed in dollars per metric ton. The trend of corn prices over the period 1947-67 was generally downward, with a slight upturn in recent years.

In the future, the downtrend will probably continue at a very gradual rate if nitrogen prices stay at the low levels of 1967 and 1968 and progress continues in the development of hybrid and synthetic corn seeds. The European and Japanese markets are very promising if the expansion of livestock production which took place there in recent years continues. The principal qualification to this statement applies to Europe, where surplus supplies of denatured wheat from the Common Market (particularly France) are competing with corn in the feed-grain market.

The hypothesis that Brazil could profit from concentrating its corn exports in the June-September period, when the Chicago prices are normally at their highest, was tested by computing indexes of seasonality by the same methods as were used for rice and soybeans. The monthly midrange of the Chicago price was used for the period 1947-67 and also for the subperiod, 1956-67.

Period	Trend	Mean Season-ality Index	Standard Deviation of Season-ality Index	Years Favor-able to Brazil	Years Unfavor-able to Brazil
1947-1967 June-Sept.	None	104.0	4.10	18	3
1956-1967 June-Sept.	Down -.457[a]	103.9	2.75	11	1
1956-1967	Down -.499[b]	104.3	2.30	12	0

[a]Significant at the 5 percent level.
[b]Significant at the 1 percent level.

The June-September period had the highest four-month average index of seasonality, but this was not significantly different from 100 even at the 10 percent level. During the subperiod 1956-67, the June-September seasonality index was smaller but also had a smaller standard deviation. However, during reduced periods, May-August had a higher mean index than did June-September, and also a smaller standard deviation. Relevant statistics are given in the table above. The significant downtrend in the corn seasonal over the period 1956-67 may reflect improvement in intertemporal corn marketing in the United States.

A time series of monthly Brazilian wholesale prices was not available to us, but a relevant price would be that of the Bôlsa de Cereais (Cereal Exchange) in São Paulo. We have some monthly data for semihard corn on this exchange for the year 1966. In 1966, the index of seasonality for May-August was 83.39, converting the prices at the official exchange rate which was fixed throughout that year.

It may be concluded that Brazil can derive significant advantages by concentrating corn exports in the period immediately following the harvest in that country, May-August. This would both save on storage costs and take advantage of the significant, if diminishing, seasonal in international prices. If the 1966 Brazilian seasonal were typical of those prevailing in earlier years, Brazilian exporters could have gained an average of roughly 20 percent by following the policy of purchasing and exporting only in May-August as opposed to spreading their transactions evenly over the year. Comparisons of annual average prices to compute the supposed unprofitability of corn exports may therefore be quite misleading. At least one prominent Brazilian economist appears to have been guilty of this oversight. [7] On the other hand, it is possible that problems of port congestion would have prevented taking full advantage of inverse seasonals for corn, rice, and soybeans in areas where the three crops are harvested at roughly the same time of the year, such as Rio Grande do Sul. In fact, in the two years 1966 and 1967 for which monthly corn export data were obtained, 58.5 percent and 69.4 percent of exports, respectively, were so timed.

EXCHANGE RATES AND DIRECT CONTROLS

Exchange-rate policy played an important role in determining cruzeiro export and import prices for all five commodities

studied throughout 1947-67, but it was critical between 1953
and 1961, when a complex system of multiple exchange rates
flourished.

During the period 1947-52, the export rate was fixed at
18.38 cruzeiros per dollar and the import rate at 18.72.
However, beginning in 1949 and continuing into the early part
of 1952, a period in which inflation was rapidly eroding the
real value of an export dollar converted at the official rate,
the export rate was implicitly devalued for some products
which were priced out of the international market by the fixed
official rate policy. The mechanism by which this was done
was as follows: Carteria de Comércio Exterior (CACEX, the
Foreign-Exchange Department of the Bank of Brazil) paid the
exporter of a product determined by that department to be
gravoso (i.e., unable to be sold at a profit in the international
market at the official rate and threatening to depress internal
prices unduly), a sum in cruzeiros sufficient to assure him a
profit. The same exporter was then denominated as an agent
of the Bank of Brazil to sell the product in the world market.
Among the products affected by the "compensation agreements,"
or, as they were more commonly called, linked operations
(operações vinculadas), were rice, corn, and some beef derivatives. Unfortunately, the exact amount of such transactions
was unavailable to us, although it was possible to obtain a
rough idea of their magnitude from several published sources
which are cited in the next section of this chapter.[8]

In the period 1953-60, a changing system of multiple-
exchange rates prevailed. From 1961 through 1967, the exchange rate for all four export products was identical except
for an episode in 1965 and 1966 when beef exports were controlled indirectly through an exchange tax. This tax varied
between the two principal producing regions during part of the
period it was in effect. The data presented below use the rate
applicable to Rio Grande do Sul.[9]

For each export product, and also for wheat (to facilitate
comparisons), the average effective exchange rate was calculated on an annual basis. In the case of wheat and flour, the
observed average exchange rate computed from dollar and
cruzeiro values of exports during the period 1953-67 was used.
During the period of multiple rates, wheat was usually imported at the lowest import rate, called the custo de câmbio
because it was calculated from a weighted average of export
rates. Prior to 1953, the wheat rate was the same as that
for all other imports. For the four export products, the effective rate was calculated as a weighted average of the

effective rates prevailing during each year, the weight for each
rate being the fraction of the year during which it was in effect.

The effective rates for beef, rice, and soybeans were computed by taking effective rates for a number of products (which
did not include any of those being studied except corn), supplied
by the international trade division Escritório de Pesquisa
Econômica (EPEA), and using a list of directives from the
Superintendency of Money and Credit (SUMOC), published by
CACEX to determine the movements of products between exchange categories. [10] When the category was established for
soybeans, rice, and beef, a product in the group studied by
EPEA falling in the same category was used to establish the
effective rate. The effective rates included export bonuses
and, in the period following SUMOC Directive 204 (the exchange reform of March 13, 1961), corrections for compul-
sory investments of varying fractions of export proceeds in
Bank of Brazil obligations at interest rates well below the rate
of inflation. Average annual effective rates for the four export products and also for wheat are given in Table 10.

For the products being studied, the effective exchange
rates were almost always overvalued (i.e., exports were being
taxed and wheat imports subsidized via the exchange system).
It was therefore necessary to make some estimate of what an
"equilibrium" or "realistic" exchange rate would have been.
With this information, implicit rates of taxation or subsidization could be estimated for each product.

The first measure of a more realistic exchange rate is a
purchasing power parity rate, hereinafter referred to as the
parity rate. It was calculated for each year of the period
1947-67, on the assumption that the rate of 17.62 cruzeiros
per dollar prevailing in 1938 was an "equilibrium" rate, by
inflating the 1938 rate by the ratio of the general wholesale
price index, excluding coffee (<u>Conjuntura Econômica</u>, National
Index No. 45), to the U.S. wholesale-price index for all commodities prepared by the Bureau of Labor Statistics, setting
1938 equal to 100 for both indexes. [11]

This is, of course, only a very rough indicator of what
an equilibrium rate of exchange would have been. [12] In fact,
the Brazilian wholesale-price index, excluding coffee, was
not entirely independent of the U.S. wholesale-price index.
This was especially true during 1946-53, when large amounts
of U.S. goods were imported at the overvalued rate and thus
held down the rate of increase in the Brazilian price level,
which, in fact, was the object the Brazilian government had
in mind when it set the postwar exchange rates.

For the period 1954-67, another estimate of an equilibrium rate is available. This is the "quasi-free trade rate" developed by Joel Bergsman. [13] Bergsman defined this rate as that which would "compensate for the removal of all tariffs, export taxes, and subsidies except those on coffee," thus maintaining equilibrium in the balance of payments. The calculation of the quasi-free trade rate involved a large number of assumptions about demand and supply elasticities for both exports and imports. These assumptions appear reasonable, however, and this is no doubt the most sophisticated attempt to estimate an equilibrium rate which has been made to date. The parity and quasi-free trade rates are given, together with the effective rates for the five products being studied, in Table 10. The higher values of the Bergsman rate as compared with the parity rate after 1957 appear in large part to reflect the institution of an ad valorem tariff at very high rates in that year. [14] Before 1957, Brazilian tariffs were fixed in cruzeiro terms and had been rapidly reduced in real incidence by the inflation. The substantial tariff reductions by the military government of Castello Branco are also reflected in Bergsman's quasi-free trade rate to a greater extent than in the parity rate. In part, this may be an indication that many of the tariffs were redundant; prices in the domestic market seldom reached the full ceiling price implied by the tariff structure.

In order to give a graphic impression of the complexity of the exchange system prevailing in the 1950's, the rate structure is shown in Figure 3 and expresses all relevant rates as a percentage of the parity rate. The average annual exchange rate for fertilizer imports to Rio Grande do Sul over the period 1955-67 is also shown. After 1960, the fact that it was lower than the rate for exports is probably accounted for by the timing of fertilizer imports, the bulk of which normally enter in the first half of the calendar year. Table 11 gives the implicit export taxes for beef, rice, soybeans, and corn according to parity and quasi-free trade rate criteria. The tax is given by unity minus the ratio of the effective rate to the parity or quasi-free trade rate, times 100.

In addition to exchange policy, direct controls were always available to the federal government when it desired to prevent exports of products deemed vital to the national economy. CACEX was empowered to deny export licenses under certain circumstances, among them, that the domestic market had not been supplied with 107 percent of its previous year's consumption. Another ground for denying export licenses was that domestic prices for the commodity in question, although

TABLE 10

Effective Exchange Rates for Five Commodities and Two
Estimates of the Equilibrium Exchange Rate, 1947-67

Year	Effective Beef Rate	Effective Rice Rate	Effective Soybean Rate	Effective Corn Rate	Average Wheat Rate	Parity Rate	Quasi-Free Trade Rate
1947	18.38	18.38	18.38	18.38	18.72	26.34	--
1948	18.38	18.38	18.38	18.38	18.72	26.11	--
1949	18.38	18.38	18.38	18.38	18.72	28.88	--
1950	18.38	18.38	18.38	18.38	18.72	28.67	--
1951	18.38	18.38	18.38	18.38	18.72	30.96	--
1952	18.38	18.38	18.38	18.38	18.72	36.00	--
1953	20.63	20.63	20.63	20.63	20.94	41.95	--
1954	29.92	29.92	29.92	29.92	24.84	52.74	38.00
1955	40.40	40.40	37.37	40.40	25.50	62.20	57.00
1956	56.88	56.88	48.43	47.96	30.76	73.58	71.00
1957	67.00	67.00	55.00	55.00	51.74	81.74	81.00
1958	80.56	91.84	75.56	89.45	64.27	93.43	95.00
1959	99.80	157.70	99.78	145.20	99.73	131.40	160.00
1960	178.50	178.50	178.50	178.50	99.99	172.70	210.00
1961	236.40	236.40	236.40	236.40	222.20	234.20	350.00
1962	336.70	336.70	336.70	336.70	357.60	363.90	550.00
1963	556.70	556.70	556.70	556.70	560.60	643.70	830.00
1964	1080.00	1080.00	1080.00	1080.00	1110.00	1165.00	1700.00
1965	1514.00	1874.00	1874.00	1874.00	1867.00	1754.00	2500.00
1966	2145.00	2200.00	2200.00	2200.00	2220.00	2389.00	2800.00
1967	2658.00	2658.00	2658.00	2658.00	2576.00	3018.00	3100.00

Source: See text.

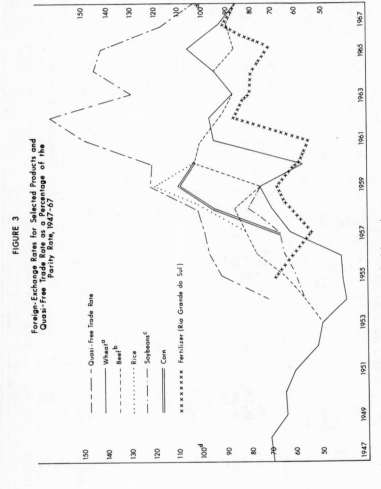

FIGURE 3

Foreign-Exchange Rates for Selected Products and
Quasi-Free Trade Rate as a Percentage of the
Parity Rate, 1947-67

– – – – Quasi-Free Trade Rate

———— Wheat[a]

– – – – Beef[b]

· · · · · · · Rice

– · – · – Soybeans[c]

═══════ Corn

x x x x x x x Fertilizer (Rio Grande do Sul)

[a]Includes all other rates if they are the same, except pseudofree trade rate.
[b]Includes rice, soybeans, and corn if they are the same.
[c]Includes corn if rate is the same.
[d]100 represents parity rate.

60

TABLE 11

Implicit Export Tax Rates Measured by Parity
and Quasi-Free Trade Criteria, 1947-67

Year	Beef		Rice		Soybeans		Corn	
	Parity	Quasi-Free Trade	Parity	Quasi-Free Trade	Parity	Quasi-Free Trade	Parity	Quasi-Free Trade
1947	30.2	--	30.2	--	30.2	--	30.2	--
1948	29.6	--	29.6	--	29.6	--	29.6	--
1949	36.4	--	36.4	--	36.4	--	36.4	--
1950	35.9	--	35.9	--	35.9	--	35.9	--
1951	40.6	--	40.6	--	40.6	--	40.6	--
1952	48.9	--	48.9	--	48.9	--	48.9	--
1953	50.8	--	50.8	--	50.8	--	50.8	--
1954	43.3	21.3	43.3	21.3	43.3	21.3	43.3	21.3
1955	35.1	29.1	35.1	29.1	39.9	34.4	35.1	29.1
1956	22.7	19.9	22.7	19.9	34.2	31.8	34.8	32.5
1957	18.0	17.3	18.0	17.3	32.7	32.1	32.7	32.1
1958	13.8	15.2	1.7	3.3	19.1	20.5	4.3	5.8
1959	24.1	37.6	-20.0	1.4	24.1	37.6	-10.5	9.3
1960	- 3.4	15.0	- 3.4	15.0	- 3.4	15.0	- 3.4	15.0
1961	- 0.9	32.5	- 0.9	32.5	- 0.9	32.5	- 0.9	32.5
1962	7.5	38.8	7.5	38.8	7.5	38.8	7.5	38.8
1963	13.5	32.9	13.5	32.9	13.5	32.9	13.5	32.9
1964	7.3	36.5	7.3	36.5	7.3	36.5	7.3	36.5
1965	13.7	39.4	- 6.8	25.0	- 6.8	25.0	- 6.8	25.0
1966	10.2	23.4	7.9	21.4	7.9	21.4	7.9	21.4
1967	11.9	14.3	11.9	14.3	11.9	14.3	11.9	14.3

Source: See Table 10 and text. Data are calculated as unity minus the ratio of the effective rate to the parity or quasi-free trade rate times 100.

61

below international prices at the effective exchange rate, were
rising. On the other hand, export licenses could be granted
if the domestic price were stable or falling. [15] More important
than specific criteria (which were not always adhered to strictly), was the philosophy behind it which Ivan Lakos and Nathaniel
Leff have termed the "exportable surplus" theory of trade.
As Nathaniel Leff describes it:

> According to this approach, a country exports only
> the "surplus" which is "left over" after the domestic
> market has been "adequately" supplied. Hence, ex-
> ports are determined by its total production and by
> domestic consumption of the commodity in question.
> Domestic demand must be served first, however,
> indeed, even if internal prices are lower than world
> market levels. [16]

The exportable-surplus theory, which was explicitly stated
by the former director of CACEX, Ignácio Tosta Filho, in a
publication of CACEX which is cited by both Lakos and Leff,
implicitly assumes that both short- and long-term price
elasticities of supply of exportable products in Brazil were
very low. [17] Only in this case would the policy fail to depress
production while at the same time encouraging consumption of
products for which Brazil is a price taker in international
markets and for which domestic demand is even moderately
price elastic. The export products being considered here
would seem to fall in this category.
    In spite of a number of efforts to determine exactly when
such direct export controls were in force for each product
studied, it was not possible to establish an exhaustive list of
dates. Since 1963, another regulatory agency, Superintendência
Nacional de Abastecimento (SUNAB), has had the power to
prohibit or curtail exports. We are indebted to SUNAB officials for preparing for us a complete list of SUNAB decrees
relevant to soybeans, corn, beef, and rice, covering the
period 1963-67, as well as a partial list of decrees of a predecessor agency. During these years, outright prohibition of
exports by SUNAB was in effect for rice, soybeans, and corn
in 1964. Exports of beef were curtailed in the same year.
In 1960, direct controls were in effect for all of the four
products. [18]
    Beef exports in Rio Grande do Sul have also been dependent
on prior provisions for the supply of the Pôrto Alegre market
during the entresafra period (between crops), from July to

February. An important role was played by the Instituto Sul-
Riograndense de Carnes (INSTICARNE, Rio Grandense Meat
Institute), and the provisions appear to have been designed to
subsidize local meat consumption. They generally had the effect of reducing but not eliminating beef exports.

EXPORT PERFORMANCE

Brazilian exports of beef, rice, soybeans, and corn were
extremely unstable over the years 1947-67, as can be seen
from the quantity data presented in Tables 12 through 15. An
explanation of these series involves a careful analysis of the
incentives facing potential Brazilian exporters, product by
product, and year by year. Such an analysis is provided in
this section.

To begin with, the international prices presented in the
first section of this chapter must be converted into cruzeiros
at the effective exchange rates prevailing for each commodity
in each year. In the case of rice and beef, the price indexes
must also be converted, which presents no real problem at
this stage. The resulting cruzeiro figures will, of course,
be in current prices, and if the existence of a relationship of
the form:

$$X_t = a_o + bP_t^{(I)} + u_t$$

were to be examined, the international prices would have to
be deflated by some domestic price index.

Before proceeding further, however, the question of what
determines the supply of exportable commodities in any given
year must be answered. In no case, except beef, was there
any reason to believe that the current year's price would determine supply, because in the absence of preannounced minimum
prices or effective futures markets, the farmers could not
know what price they would actually receive at harvest time
and presumably based their estimates on prices previously
received. The supply of exportable commodities in year t,
at least in the case of field crops, is independent of the export
price or the price in the domestic market in the year t. It is
effectively predetermined by planting decisions taken in year
t-1 and the accidents of weather, diseases, pests, and so forth.
In the case of beef, where slaughtering might be expected to
be greater in years of high prices, no evidence was found that

this in fact was the case, at least for Rio Grande do Sul. (The question of price response is discussed in some detail in the Appendix.) The relevant question is how the available supply is allocated between the domestic and world markets. While presumably the price prevailing in year t may cause farmers to use more or less fertilizer, to harvest more or less intensively, and so forth, and thus affect the supply of exportable commodities, there is no evidence that this kind of production response takes place in Rio Grande do Sul. (See Chapters 5 and 6.)

It is insufficient to know only the price available to exporters, because imports of these products were seldom permitted in any significant quantity, and it was therefore possible for the domestic price to rise above the level prevailing in the international market in some years. Furthermore, due to the system of direct controls and export licensing referred to (in the previous section of the chapter), it was also possible for the export price to remain above the domestic price for extended periods, especially if exports were prohibited outright. Of course, if exports were completely free, one would expect that the international price could not long remain above the price in the domestic market, since in that case, exports would take place until domestic prices were equal to export prices and the incentive for exports thus removed. Data on relative prices in the domestic and international markets presented for the four export products in Tables 12 through 15 indicate clearly that there were indeed very substantial fluctuations in the ratio of international to domestic prices for the commodities in question. The coefficient of variation (standard deviation divided by the mean) for the price ratios was 13. 8 for beef, 20. 3 for soybeans, 27. 3 for corn, and 27. 7 for rice, expressed in percentage terms.

Consider, then, a model which says that exports in years when the international price exceeds the domestic price are a function of the relative of these two prices and a variable indicating the presence and duration of direct controls.

$$X_t = a_o + a_1 \frac{P_t^{(I)}}{P_t^{(D)}} + a_2 C_t + u_t$$

The price relative measures the incentive to export, but its coefficient will be biased downward for the following reasons:
    1.   To the extent that the market mechanism works

TABLE 12

Brazilian Exports of Beef and Values of the
International/Domestic Beef Price Ratio Index,
1947-67

Year	Beef Exports[a]	Beef Price Ratio Index[b]
1947	31,566	119.5
1948	41,337	112.9
1949	30,540	122.5
1950	17,632	98.0
1951	7,638	82.2
1952	3,499	86.0
1953	2,397	81.9
1954	74	84.1
1955	4,457	83.2
1956	11,080	85.6
1957	29,148	91.9
1958	41,905	112.0
1959	51,310	107.1
1960	14,135	102.5
1961	28,109	100.0
1962	21,890	100.3
1963	18,371	89.6
1964	26,404	119.3
1965	52,637	114.5
1966	31,301	106.7
1967	21,117	120.0

[a]Includes frozen beef (41001), chilled beef (4105), frozen and chilled veal (41008), and preserved and canned beef (41224); numbers refer to the Nomenclatura Brasileira de Mercadorias. Figures represent thousands of metric tons.
[b]1961 equals 100.

Source: Exports, SEEF, Ministério da Fazenda, Rio de Janeiro; prices, see text.

TABLE 13

Brazilian Exports of Rice and Values of the
International/Domestic Rice Price Ratio Index,
1947-67

	Rice Exports[a]	Rice Price Ratio Index[b]
1947	218,423	97.37
1948	212,643	83.79
1949	688	46.06
1950	95,741	56.93
1951	118,121	59.28
1952	162,268	78.90
1953	2,787	52.29
1954	--	57.18
1955	2,483	63.63
1956	101,444	70.77
1957	329	60.38
1958	51,552	89.92
1959	9,816	88.88
1960	104	79.79
1961	120,833	100.00
1962	46,666	--
1963	--	58.19
1964	12,425	81.88
1965	236,788	132.38
1966	289,252	108.17
1967	31,884	100.28

[a]Includes Nomenclatura Brasileira de Mercadorias
numbers 44003-40. Figures are given in thousands of metric
tons.
[b]1961 equals 100.

Source: Exports, SEEF, Ministério da Fazenda, Rio de
Janeiro; prices, see text.

TABLE 14

Brazilian Exports of Soybeans and Soybean Products
and Values of the International/Domestic Price
Ratio Index, 1949-67

	Soybeans and Soybean Product Exports[a]	Soybean Price Ratio[b]
1949	18,704	54.81
1950	21,236	64.05
1951	39,675	53.31
1952	28,941	53.81
1953	26,117	42.69
1954	25,344	60.15
1955	51,390	58.92
1956	41,483	73.31
1957	17,399	43.01
1958	45,847	58.66
1959	57,950	58.39
1960	28,537	56.74
1961	108,310	100.00
1962	145,833	76.75
1963	95,493	68.25
1964	43,841	60.69
1965	180,363	74.04
1966	306,278	69.46
1967	429,931	71.91

[a]Includes soybeans (22075), soybean flour (22096), soybean meal (48176), and soybean cake (48276); numbers refer to the Nomenclatura Brasileira de Mercadorias. Figures are given in thousands of metric tons.
[b]1961 equals 100.

Source: Exports, SEEF, Ministério da Fazenda, Rio de Janeiro; prices, see text.

TABLE 15

Brazilian Exports of Corn and Values of the
International/Domestic Corn Price Ratio Index,
1947-67

	Corn Exports[a]	Corn Price Ratio Index[b]
1947	166, 046	150. 9
1948	110, 981	122. 3
1949	21	65. 3
1950	11, 698	93. 6
1951	295, 249	108. 2
1952	28, 416	72. 5
1953	--	54. 1
1954	11, 652	81. 5
1955	80, 094	66. 3
1956	--	70. 1
1957	--	67. 0
1958	--	90. 5
1959	--	103. 5
1960	9, 927	101. 7
1961	4, 448	100. 0
1962	6	75. 7
1963	698, 953	124. 5
1964	62, 315	99. 1
1965	559, 675	139. 9
1966	620, 799	133. 1
1967	430, 444	111. 1

aIncludes 44205, Nomenclatura Brasileira de Mercadorias.
Figures are given in thousands of metric tons.
b1961 equals 100.

Source: Exports, SEEF, Ministério da Fazenda, Rio de
Janeiro; prices, see text.

perfectly, the ratio of world and domestic prices will remain
constant over time, and yet, exports will take place.

2. The prices used are averages over different grades
(in some cases), over an entire year; thus, considerable variance in relative prices within this timespan may be concealed
and the influence of short-term movements in relative prices
on exports lost. To what extent this happens depends on the
speed of market reaction on the part of exporters and the paths
of both price series involved over the year in question.

3. The prices available for empirical testing may not be
perfect reflections of the prices actually confronting exporters
because they represent specific grades or mixes of grades of
commodities at specific locations, neither of which is always
the most relevant from a theoretical point of view. For example, international transport costs may vary with the aggregate demand for shipping services, so that if the international
price chosen is that prevailing in another exporting country,
or in a major importing country, this international price will
not be a perfect proxy for the price obtainable by Brazilian
exporters.

4. Because the total supply of exportable commodities
might respond to current prices in future years, even though
it is relatively inflexible in the current year, only a shortrun
"elasticity" would be estimated. Yet, it is generally the case
that longrun elasticities are considerably higher. [19]

Given these problems, it is questionable exactly what
meaning may be attached to a relative price coefficient if it
should be significant in empirical tests of the model. Rather
than an elasticity, it may be said to be a measure of the extent
to which the export bureaucracy, domestic transportation
costs, imperfect information, and other frictions impede the
functioning of the market mechanism. On the other hand, if
the "frictions" are taken as relatively constant except when
exports are completely forbidden, it might be expected that
the efforts of exporters to overcome them would be positively
associated with the financial incentive with which they are
confronted (i. e., the higher the export price relative to that
available on the domestic market). It is the latter hypothesis
that will be tested in this section, subject to the caveats concerning the significance of the price term set forth above.
In particular, the estimated "price elasticity of exports" must
be considered as a lower bound, given the biases inherent in
its estimation.

The following procedure will be adopted for each export
product being studied. First, a price ratio is formed with

the international price or price index described in the first
section of this chapter, converted to a cruzeiro value (hypo-
thetical in the case of indexes), at the effective exchange rate
for the product in question as the numerator, and the domestic
price as the denominator.   To avoid problems regarding units,
both of these series are converted into indexes with the 1961
value of each taken as 100.   The resulting ratio is then multiplied by 100 so that it too is in index form with 1961 relative
prices equal to 100.

Next, an examination is made of the annual export quanta
for each product, and a critical value of the price-ratio index
is determined below which exports were severely reduced if
not eliminated.   Using the critical price ratio as a criterion,
the postwar years are separated into two groups--those in
which the international to domestic price ratio was "favorable"
and those in which it was "unfavorable" from the point of view
of exporters.

The unfavorable years for rice and corn included years
in which operações vinculadas were important. [20]   These years
were separated from the others.   If there was one other year
which had abnormally high exports in spite of the unfavorable
price ratio, although for no known reason, it too was separated.
The favorable years were divided into those in which, so far
as it was possible to determine, exports were relatively free,
and those in which there was reason to believe that direct export controls were operative during a substantial portion of
the year.   If there was any single year with unexplainably high
exports, it was separated from the rest.   Table 16 gives the
number of years in each group, favorable and unfavorable,
and the various subgroups, together with the average volume
of exports, maximum exports in a single year, and minimum
exports in a single year.

Finally, export-supply functions were estimated.   The
general form of the functions used was:

$$X_t = a_o + a_1 P_t + a_2 C_t + a_3 V_t + u_t$$

where P is the ratio of international to domestic prices, C is
the variable indicating the presence of direct controls, and V
indicates the presence of compensation agreements (operações
vinculadas) if any were carried out for the product in question.

TABLE 16

Brazilian Exports of Fresh, Chilled, Frozen, and Canned Beef
and Veal According to Domestic and International Market Conditions, 1947-67

Group	Number of Years in Group	Average Price Ratio Index	Thousands of Metric Tons		
			Average Exports	Maximum Exports	Minimum Exports
Favorable	15	107.8	30.5	51.3	14.1
Favorable and Free[a]	11	107.8	34.7	51.3	17.6
Favorable and Controlled[b]	4	107.8	20.0	26.4	14.1
Unfavorable[c]	6	83.8	4.9	11.1	0.1

[a]Includes 1947-50, 1957-59, 1961, 1962, 1965 and 1966.
[b]Includes 1960, 1963, 1964, and 1967.
[c]Includes 1951-56.

Source: See Table 12.

Beef

Two steer price series for Rio Grande do Sul were available, the net price paid per metric ton live weight for steers purchased by the Swift packing plant at Rosário do Sul and the average price per ton live weight for the entire state of Rio Grande do Sul obtained from INSTICARNE. Both provided the same discrimination between favorable and unfavorable years when converted to ratio form. However, in export functions, the INSTICARNE price was considered more successful in explaining exports. Only data based on the INSTICARNE series are presented here. The critical value chosen for the price ratio was 86 in index form, with 1961 equal to 100. This number has no significance other than serving as a criterion for separating favorable and unfavorable years because it is an index itself, and that index was calculated as the ratio of an index multiplied by an effective exchange rate divided by the price of a raw material (steers). On this basis, only the years 1951-56 were unfavorable. Average exports in unfavorable years were only 14.1 percent of the average for favorable and free years. Controls were important in four years--1960, 1963, 1964, and 1967. On August 13, 1960, CACEX suspended export licenses for meat on the grounds that meat prices in the domestic market were rising rapidly.[21] For 1963, we were unable to find a written source confirming the presence of controls, but various interested observers stated their existence to us verbally. In 1964, SUNAB prohibited many types of beef exports, and licensing procedures were very difficult.[22] Severe but ineffective domestic price controls were in effect throughout most of the year. In 1967, we know from firsthand accounts that direct controls were in effect; one of the mechanisms was the requirement that packing plants promise to slaughter a certain quota of cattle in the entresafra period before any exports would be permitted.[23]

Using direct-control variable values of 2 for 1960 and 1 for 1963, 1964, and 1967, the following export-supply function was estimated for the entire period 1947-67:

Beef exports = -62.458 + .8672 P - 7.823 C $\bar{R}^2$= .581
(1,000 MT)   (3.839)   (5.377)   (1.843)
                    Durbin-Watson Statistic (DW) = 1.601

The direct-controls variable was significant only at the 10 percent level; however, the price variable was highly

significant and implies an "elasticity" of 3.78 at the point of
means. The values in parentheses are t ratios. As in Table
12, this data is for fresh, chilled, frozen, and canned beef
and veal.

The number of cows slaughtered for shipment outside the
state five years prior to the export year was entered as an
independent variable because it had been successful in helping
to explain the number of cows and steers slaughtered. (See
Appendix.) It was not significant in the export function.

Rice

Rice is the product for which the best data are available,
because it is the only product being studied for which a fairly
broad, organized market exists at the wholesale level in Rio
Grande do Sul. In one year, 1962, no prices were quoted on
the Bôlsa de Mercadorias in Pôrto Alegre. This year was
completely abnormal in all respects due to crop failures in
large parts of Brazil and imposition of heavy-handed controls
on all stages of rice marketing. Maximum prices were fixed
in Rio Grande do Sul in March, although even for January and
February, there were no transactions on the Bôlsa de Mercadorias. [24] In November, the government went so far as to
disappropriate all existing stocks of both milled and rough
rice in Rio Grande do Sul. [25] Therefore, 1962 has been separated from the rest of the period as a special case.

The critical value of the rice price ratio index was 64,
the numerator being the international rice price index multiplied by the effective exchange rate for rice, and the denominator an index based on the cruzeiro price per metric ton of
medium-grain blue rose especial rice, with 15 percent brokens
taken as an annual average of monthly averages.

Of particular interest in Table 17 are the years 1950 and
1951, in which compensation agreements were responsible
for substantial exports in spite of price ratios well below the
critical level. In seeking to document these operations in
published sources, several interesting accounts were found
which we quote in part because they are indicative of Brazil's
export philosophy at that time.

In 1948 and 1949, it was reported that large crops in São
Paulo resulted in:

> an enormous increase in exportable surpluses
> which, in turn, created serious problems for the

TABLE 17

Brazilian Rice Exports According to Domestic and International Market Conditions, 1947-67

Group	Number of Years in Group	Average Price Ratio Index	Thousands of Metric Tons		
			Average Exports	Maximum Exports	Minimum Exports
Favorable	12	92.7	107.1	289.3	0.1
Favorable and Free[a]	7	95.9	191.7	289.3	101.4
Favorable and Controlled[b]	5	88.2	19.4	51.6	0.1
Unfavorable	8	49.7	14.2	118.1	0.0
Operações vinculadas[c]	2	58.1	106.9	118.1	95.7
Others except 1962[d]	6	56.3	1.0	2.8	0.0
1962[e]	1	n.a.	43.7	43.7	43.7

[a]Includes 1947-48, 1952, 1956, 1961, and 1965-66.
[b]Includes 1958-60, 1964, and 1967.
[c]Includes 1950-51.
[d]Includes 1949, 1953-55, 1957, and 1963.
[e]Domestic prices are not available for 1962 because the Bôlsa de Mercadorias was closed.

Source: See Table 13.

farmers.   This happens just when the largest crop
in history is expected . . . .   In the month of May
[1950] exportable stocks in the port of Santos
reached 165,000 tons.   The government therefore
resolved to free the export of rice, recommencing
the compensation trade. [26]

In January, 1952, the same publication noted that "planters
in the producing states showed themselves apprehensive, as
the existence of excess supplies menaced the economic out-
come of the 1951-52 crop in progress, in which a fall in prices
would bring serious losses." [27]   A lack of warehouse space
was also cited as a reason for facilitating exports.   In one
transaction alone, executed at the beginning of December,
1951, IRGA sold 44,000 tons to Japan.   Most of this rice was
not physically exported until the following year.
     In the six unfavorable years, when compensation agree-
ments were no longer supposed to be practiced, the average
export quantum was only 1,048 tons per year or 0.5 percent
of the average for the favorable years with relatively free exports.
     Considering the entire period of 1947-67, with the excep-
tion of 1962, for which no domestic price data were available,
the following export function was estimated:

$$\text{Rice Exports} = -159.2 + 3.408 \, P - 64.99 \, C + 33.24 \, V$$
$$(1,000 \text{ MT})\quad (3.730)\quad (6.386)\qquad (4.468)\qquad (1.392)$$

$$R^2 = .723 \qquad\qquad DW = 1.901$$

     The price variable was highly significant and implied an
"elasticity" of 3.2 at the point of means.   The direct-controls
variable was also highly significant, but the variable for
operações vinculadas was significant only at the 20 percent
level, although it had the expected sign.

                              Soybeans

     Soybeans and soybean products have been among Brazil's
most dynamic exports in the postwar period and increased
quite steadily throughout the period 1949-67.   The first year
in which exports occurred was 1949.   In that year, 18,704 tons
were exported; in 1967, the total was 429,931 tons, so the
period is dominated by a strong trend.   Direct-export controls

were important in two years, 1960 and 1964.[28] The influence
of the production trend and the direct controls overshadow the
price variable, which had the Chicago cash contract price in
the numerator and the only available domestic price series,
the SEP producer price, in the denominator. In fact, the
price variable was completely insignificant and had the wrong
sign.   The export function given here was therefore run without the price variable.   Production is measured in thousands
of metric tons.   The fairly low Durbin-Watson statistic falls
within the inconclusive range as regards the possibility of
autocorrelation of residuals.

Soybean exports = -20.08 + .5212 Production - 77.07 C
(1,000 MT)   (1.638) (12.86)   (3.027)

$$\bar{R}^2 = .904 \qquad DW = 1.173$$

Corn

Data for corn is very poor, and Rio Grande do Sul did not
participate in the export market.   Most corn exports come
from Paraná and São Paulo.   To obtain a domestic price to
compare with the export price, it was necessary to rely on
the only measure at hand, the average value of production
calculated from SEP data for the southern region of Brazil:
São Paulo, Paraná, Santa Catarina, and Rio Grande do Sul.
Nevertheless, even with this rather poor data, it was possible
to pick a critical price ratio index value of 94.   Table 18 shows
that exports in the unfavorable years averaged only 12,600
tons, whereas in the favorable years, the average was
259,500 tons.   The seven years classified as favorable and
free of direct controls had average exports of 411,700 tons.
The most bizarre year appears to be 1955, when exports took
place at a fairly substantial rate in spite of a very unfavorable
price.   No doubt there is some explanation for this event,
probably an operation similar to the compensation agreements
of the years 1949-52.
The export function was run for the entire period 1947-67.
The price variable was highly significant, and the direct-
controls variable was significant at the 5 percent level.   The
operações vinculadas dummy was completely insignificant
and was dropped.   There was significant autocorrelation of
residuals according to the Durbin-Watson statistic.   The price
coefficient indicates an "elasticity" of 3.95 at the point of
means.

TABLE 18

Brazilian Corn Exports According to Domestic and
International Market Conditions, 1947-67

Group	Number of Years in Group	Average Price Ratio Index	Thousands of Metric Tons		
			Average Exports	Maximum Exports	Minimum Exports
Favorable	11	118	259.5	699.2	0.0
Favorable and Free[a]	7	127	411.7	699.2	110.9
Favorable and Controlled[b]	4	102	19.2	62.3	0.0
Unfavorable	10	73.7	12.6	80.1	0.0
Operações Vinculadas[c]	2	83.0	17.1	22.4	11.7
Others except 1955[d]	7	72.0	1.7	11.7	0.0
1955[e]	1	63.3	80.1	80.1	80.1

[a]Includes 1947-48, 1951, 1963, and 1965-67.
[b]Includes 1959-61 and 1964.
[c]Includes 1950 and 1952.
[d]Includes 1949, 1953-54, 1956-58, and 1962.
[e]No explanation was found for the exports of 1955.

Source: See Table 15.

$$\text{Corn exports} = -398.0 + 6.012 \ P - 190.5 \ C$$
$$(1,000 \ \text{MT}) \quad (3.029) \quad (4.578) \quad (2.160)$$

$$\bar{R}^2 = .526 \qquad\qquad DW = 1.119$$

It may be concluded that exports of all four products were significantly influenced by the ratio of international to domestic prices and also by direct export controls. Furthermore, for all products except soybeans there appears to be a fairly well-defined point at which exporting becomes so unprofitable that it is very severely curtailed if not eliminated. This may be the result of either unfavorable exchange rates, low international prices, or a combination of the two factors, as well as the exclusion of imports in years when there was a shortage of the domestic product.

NOTES

1. Calculated from Food and Agriculture Organization (FAO), Trade Yearbook (Rome, 1966).

2. FAO, Agricultural Commodities: Projections for 1975 and 1985, Vol. 1 (Rome, 1967). This publication projects large deficits in world supply on the assumption that 1963 price levels will prevail. Similar conclusions for Brazil emerge from a study by the Fundação Getúlio Vargas, Projeções de Oferta e Demanda de Produtos Agrícolas para o Brasil (Rio de Janeiro, 1966).

3. This has not escaped the observation of the principal interested parties. Following is my translation of an excerpt from Leonidas Maia Alburquerque, "O Arroz Gaucho no Mercado Mundial," Congresso Estadual de Oriziicultura Anais (Pôrto Alegre, January, 1966), 179-82, which was a paper presented at the Rio Grande do Sul State Rice Conference in January, 1966: "The governmental policy of only exporting surpluses (excedentes) generally after one, two, or more years of storage, caused the offer of a product in the following conditions: (a) old (envelhecido), (b) outside the favorable season for exporting, and (c) burdened by prolonged storage costs."

4. Calculated from FAO, Trade Yearbook, 1966, op. cit.

5.   Henry Schact, "Different Cattle, Different Game, "
San Francisco Chronicle, April 11, 1969.

6.   Calculated from FAO, Trade Yearbook, 1966, op. cit.

7.   See Ruy Miller Paiva, "Bases de uma Política para a
Melhoria Técnica da Agricultura Brasileira, " Revista
Brasileira de Economia (June, 1967), 5-38. It must be added
that the extent of the error was probably reduced since a
series on average prices received by producers in São Paulo
state was used rather than a central market price, and sales
by producers are normally concentrated in the postharvest
period.

8.   The source most relied upon for a description of the
exchange system in the immediate postwar period was Donald
L. Huddle, "Balanço de Pagamentos e Contrôle de Câmbio no
Brasil: Diretrizes, Políticas e História, 1946-1954, " Revista
Brasileira de Economia (March, 1964), especially pp. 25-31.
Another useful reference covering a longer period but not
particularly helpful in learning about operações vinculadas is
Escritório de Pesquisa Econômica Aplicada (EPEA), Diag-
nóstico Preliminar, Setor de Comércio Internacional (Rio de
Janeiro, March, 1967).

9.   SUMOC, Directive 290, February 4, 1965, initiated
this tax, which was modified by SUMOC Directive 292, March
5, 1965, which set the rate of exchange retention at 30 percent
for Central Brazil and 20 percent for Rio Grande do Sul. This
may be interpreted as an indicator of the weaker competitive
position of Rio Grande do Sul beef in the Center-South market.
Resolution 17 of the new Central Bank eliminated the tax for
Rio Grande do Sul on February 17, 1966. The tax was not
removed in Central Brazil until May 12, 1967.

10.   Banco dó Brasil, CACEX, Comércio Exterior do
Brasil, 1954-63 (Rio de Janeiro, n. d.).

11.   The Brazilian wholesale price index was available
only as far back as 1939. It was linked to the Gunabara cost-
of-living index in 1939 to obtain an estimate of the 1938 value.

12.   The purchasing power parity concept has been attacked
by Bela Balassa, "The Purchasing Power Parity Doctrine:
A Reappraisal, " Journal of Political Economy (December,

1964), 584-96; and defended by James Holmes, "The Purchasing Power Parity Theory: In Defense of Gustav Cassel as a Modern Theorist," Journal of Political Economy (October, 1967), 686-95. See also Gottfried Haberler, A Survey of International Trade Theory (Princeton University Special Papers in International Finance, No. 1, July, 1961); and Bela Balassa and Daniel Schydlowsky, "Effective Tariffs, Domestic Cost of Foreign Exchange, and the Equilibrium Exchange Rate," Journal of Political Economy (May-June, 1968), 348-60. The approach to estimating an equilibrium exchange rate suggested in the paper by Balassa and Schydlowsky was followed by Joel Bergsman in estimating his "quasi-free trade rate," described below.

13.   Joel Bergsman, Brazil's Industrialization and Trade Policies (New York: Oxford University Press, 1970).

14.   Law No. 3244 was promulgated on August 14, 1957. Many tariffs were as high as 150 percent ad valorem; EPEA, Diagnóstico, op. cit., p. 74.

15.   These matters are discussed in some detail in Ivan Lakos, "The Effects of Brazil's Foreign Exchange Policy on the Value of Her Exports and on the Flow of Private Investment with Respect to Brazil's Economic Development: 1946-1962" (unpublished Ph. D. dissertation, Harvard University, March, 1962); and Nathaniel H. Leff, "Export Stagnation and Autarkic Development in Brazil, 1947-1962," Quarterly Journal of Economics (May, 1967), 286-301. See also Leff's more general discussion of the exportable surplus theory of trade, "The 'Exportable Surplus' Approach to Foreign Trade in Underdeveloped Countries," Economic Development and Cultural Change (April, 1969), 346-55.

16.   Leff, "Export Stagnation," op. cit., p. 289.

17.   Ignácio Tosta Filho, Fatôres Estruturais e Conjunturais do Comércio Exterior, Bank of Brazil, Rio de Janeiro; cited by both Lakos and Leff.

18.   "Foreign Trade--Still Reduced in 1960," Conjuntura Econômica (International Edition, February, 1961), p. 30.

19.   Some of these points are discussed in Arnold C. Harberger, "Some Evidence on the International Price

Mechanism," Journal of Political Economy (December, 1957), 506-21, which contains other relevant references. Most discussions in the literature have centered around import demand rather than the supply of exports. This is true for Brazil. A discussion of the literature on estimating import demand functions may be found in Samuel A. Morley, "Import Demand and Import Substitution in Brazil," in Howard S. Ellis, ed., The Economy of Brazil (Berkeley: University of California Press, 1969).

20. Though compensation agreements were supposedly eliminated in 1952, it seems that virtually the same kind of operation was practiced in other years, at least for rice. See "Pronunciamento do Dr. Mario de Lima Beck, Presidente do IRGA," Lavoura Arrozeira (January, 1965), 5-9, where such an operation executed by IRGA in the crop year 1964-65 is described.

21. "Brazilian Meat Outlook Good," Conjuntura Econômica (International Edition; October, 1960), p. 41. The same source observed that "without such restrictions exports would undoubtedly have reached quite substantial figures this year . . . ."

22. SUNAB Resolution 31, December 19, 1963, prohibited most fresh and frozen beef exports beginning January 1, 1964. Some exceptions were made, including canned beef. The other relevant SUNAB Resolutions are numbers 51, 86, 97, 106, 128, 132, 144, and 159, all applying to 1964.

23. SUNAB Resolution 327, February 9, 1967; and interviews at INSTICARNE, June, 1968.

24. Comissão Federal de Abastecimento e Preços (COFAP) Portaria No. 280, March 30, 1962. COFAP was the antecessor agency of SUNAB.

25. COFAP Portaria No. 989, November 20, 1962.

26. "Exportaremos Arroz," Conjuntura Econômica (June, 1950), pp. 7-8. My translation.

27. Ibid., (January, 1952), p. 16.

28.   "Foreign Trade--Still Reduced in 1960," loc. cit.; and SUNAB Resolution No. 42, January 23, 1964.   Later in 1964, other SUNAB resolutions authorized the export of some soybean meal and cake (Resolutions Numbers 79, 168, and 177).

4

IMPORT SUBSTITUTION
IN BRAZILIAN AGRICULTURE
AND WHEAT PRODUCTION
IN RIO GRANDE DO SUL

It has been official Brazilian policy to promote the expansion of domestic wheat output throughout the postwar period, and over 80 percent of Brazilian wheat has been produced in Rio Grande do Sul. Wheat was the only agricultural commodity imported in volume, and the attempt at import substitution for this product was the only one made within the agricultural sector. A study of Brazilian wheat production permits an analysis of the evolution of one of the very few positive agricultural policies pursued by Brazilian governments over a period of two decades.

First, a brief history of wheat production in Brazil will be presented. Then, the dual-price system for wheat and the massive "paper wheat" frauds to which it gave rise during the late 1950's are described. Third, the system of subsidies to domestic wheat producers and consumers which prevailed over the postwar period is examined. Fourth, the cost of wheat production in terms of purely domestic resources (i.e., net of import content), is estimated and compared with that of the four export products being studied. Using international prices for the five commodities in the year 1967, an estimate of the static efficiency of domestic-resource use in the production of each commodity is made. Fifth, reasons for the high cost of wheat production in Rio Grande do Sul are presented. Finally, a number of arguments which have been advanced favoring the production of wheat in Brazil despite the high costs involved are evaluated.

HISTORICAL BACKGROUND

The promotion of wheat production in Brazil has not been
restricted to the period following World War II.   Official
Brazilian government policy designed to stimulate wheat culture appears to date from 1534. [1]   Wheat was introduced to
Rio Grande do Sul in 1749 by colonists coming from the Azores.
The post World War II policies really had their roots in a
series of federal decrees in the late 1930's establishing financial incentives for wheat producers and a chain of federal
experiment stations designed to support and stimulate wheat
cultivation.   The state of Rio Grande do Sul also financed
wheat research relatively early and initiated an experiment
station in 1918. [2]   In January, 1944, the Serviço de Expansão
do Trigo (SET, Wheat Expansion Service of the Ministry of
Agriculture), was created with broad powers to stimulate domestic wheat production.   In 1945, Instituto Agronômico do Sul, now
known as Instituto de Pesquisa e Experimentação Agropecuárias
do Sul (IPEAS, Southern Institute for Agricultural Research
and Experimentation), was established in Pelotas, Rio Grande
do Sul.   One of its principal missions was wheat research.

In the immediate postwar period, import prices were
very high and domestic wheat was acquired freely by mills.
Decree Number 29,299 of January 26, 1951, made the purchase of domestic wheat by mills mandatory, and quotas were
set by the SET.   The prices paid by mills for domestic wheat
became increasingly greater than those for imported wheat
and gave rise to a dual-price system which suffered numerous
modifications but which still prevailed in 1969, with separate
prices for millers and producers, although the price to mills
of both domestic and imported wheat was unified in November,
1956.   During the mid- and late-1950's and early 1960's, this
dual-price system resulted in massive frauds (described below).   Nevertheless, in the 1950's, mechanized wheat production expanded extremely rapidly, principally on unfertile,
natural pasture land rented from cattle ranchers by agricultural entrepreneurs who often lacked even rudimentary knowledge of wheat culture.   This process was facilitated by the
granting of credit at rates of interest which were negative in
real terms and import subsidies for fertilizer and agricultural
machinery via a multiple and/or overvalued exchange-rate
system.

After a series of crop failures which appear to have been
in large part responsible for a substantial fall in the area under

wheat, production began a more healthy process of expansion
in the early 1960's which was accelerating through 1969, after
a slow start. This time, better support in terms of cultural
practices and marketing was supplied by a system of wheat
producer cooperatives, the formation of which was encouraged
by the Bank of Brazil's Domestic Wheat Purchase Commission
(CTRIN), which was made the sole domestic purchaser of
wheat in 1962.

Estimated area, production, yield, and real-producer
price for wheat are given in Table 19, which also contains a
brief explanation of the adjustments made on published data.

THE DUAL-PRICE SYSTEM AND
PAPER WHEAT FRAUDS

While wheat production has been encouraged by a minimum
price program throughout the postwar period, the price relationship between domestically produced and imported wheat
appeared to have been roughly that which would have prevailed
under any free-market system with a minimum-price program
during the years 1947-52. In November, 1952, in the face of
increasing incentives to millers to shun the domestic product
as fixed-exchange rates coupled with domestic inflation, and
falling international prices made foreign wheat increasingly
cheaper, the Bank of Brazil became the sole supplier of imported wheat to mills. The mills in turn were required to use
at least 25 percent of domestic wheat in their operations unless
this percentage was not available. With the intensification of
the wheat-expansion program and the initiation in October,
1953 (SUMOC Directive 70) of the system of multiple-exchange
rates under which wheat was imported at the lowest import
rate (custo de câmbio), a dual-price system was established
in which mills paid different prices for imported and domestic
wheat. The custo de câmbio rate was essentially the weighted,
average-export rate prevailing, plus a tax of as much as 38
percent ad valorem, but this tax was often waived for wheat.
Even though the auction system was abolished in 1961 (SUMOC
Directive 204), wheat continued to receive special treatment
until 1966, along with certain other imports considered to have
high political and economic significance, principally newsprint
and petroleum products. As described in Chapter 1, there
were several moves to reduce or eliminate these subsidies
beginning in 1961.

TABLE 19

Area, Production, Yield, and Real Producer Price
of Wheat in Rio Grande do Sul, 1947-68

Year	Area In Hectares	Production In Metric Tons	Yield in Kilograms per Hectare	Real Producer Price per Metric Ton[*]
1947	145,826	129,534	888	275
1948	205,388	143,364	698	324
1949	239,638	143,863	600	305
1950	245,570	187,879	767	277
1951	278,570	155,378	558	244
1952	302,486	251,845	833	216
1953	341,754	289,932	848	260
1954	427,982	349,512	817	267
1955	491,242	450,918	918	310
1956	359,144	341,666	951	265
1957	474,772	307,100	647	246
1958	614,377	203,654	331	252
1959	489,046	209,813	429	277
1960	470,555	266,168	566	303
1961	416,088	198,832	478	267
1962	249,272	301,597	1210	327
1963	306,765	113,951	371	312
1964	299,110	248,184	830	326
1965	357,930	260,646	728	328
1966	377,818	325,599	862	297
1967	536,456	373,591	696	293
1968	748,000	654,500	875	315

[*]Prices given in new cruzeiros of January 1, 1968.

Source: Area, production, and yield, 1947-61, SEP data,
but area and production are taken as 50 percent of the published
figures, 1962-68, Comissão Central de Levantamento e
Fiscalização das Safras Trit́icolas (CCLEF), but area and production are taken as 10 percent greater than published to take
account of production which was not sold. CCLEF estimated
that it covered 90 percent of production in these years. The
SEP data was revised downward on the basis of comparisons between SEP and CCLEF data for years in which both were available. Real prices based on official prices for bulk wheat at
interior locations plus any bonuses and inflated by an average of
the Pôrto Alegre cost of living index (Conjuntura Econômica,
State Index 13) and the Brazil wholesale price index, excluding
coffee (Conjuntura Econômica, National Index 45).

Miller purchase of domestic wheat was supposedly enforced through a nationwide system of quotas, under which a
mill could not purchase foreign wheat until it had obtained a certain quantity of the domestic product, and the proportion varied
from year to year, depending on the size of the domestic wheat
crop. This immediately produced severe distortions, as mills
far from the producing regions were required to mill a quota
of domestic wheat, and resulted in an uneconomic, spatial
distribution of domestic-wheat consumption. This phenomenon,
in which domestic wheat often needlessly clogged national ports
and other transport facilities, was dubbed the wheat excursion
(passeio do trigo), by Brazilian observers, who were quick to
point out the inefficiencies involved.

To avoid this problem, a system was instituted in which
northern and central Brazilian mills could exchange their
quotas with southern mills located close to the production
areas.[3] Such arrangements, called permutas, were executed
by private agreements between mills. While eliminating one
distortion, this system aggravated the "paper wheat" frauds
(described below).

Until the crop year 1956-57, mills received their quotas
of domestic and foreign wheat at different prices, and the
Ministry of Agriculture fixed the price to be paid to national
producers. On the other hand, foreign wheat was delivered
to the mills at the price of acquisition (at the custo de câmbio
exchange rate), plus a tax used to cover marketing expenses
and subsidize domestic producers.

The large differential between domestic and foreign wheat
prices which arose from this system encouraged substitution
of foreign for domestic wheat wherever possible. Delays in
the acquisition of the domestic product (which was also often
spoiled due to an inadequate system of storage and transportation), bribery of SET officials, and the clandestine importation
of foreign wheat, called "wheat nationalization," were some
of the means adopted by millers to avoid purchasing the
domestic product. With the producer price often well above
the import price, even at black market exchange rates, there
was also a strong incentive in the mid-1950's for both domestic
"producers" and millers located conveniently close to the
Argentinian and Uruguayan frontiers to become "nationalizers."

To eliminate the incentive for such frauds on the part of
millers, Federal Decree Number 40,316 of November 8, 1956,
determined that financial operations for the sale of national
wheat as well as foreign wheat would be carried out by the
Bank of Brazil. The price paid to the producer was thus

separated from the price paid by mills, just as the price of
foreign wheat had already been divorced from its import costs.
The mill still purchased the domestic wheat directly from
domestic producers, but the producers were to be paid via
the Bank of Brazil.

The idea behind this move was to make domestic wheat
cheaper to millers than imported wheat and thus stimulate the
absorption of the national product. This was achieved during
calendar year 1957, when millers paid somewhat more than
half of the producer price through the Bank of Brazil. The
rest of the price paid to the producer was financed by the Bank
of Brazil's sales of imported wheat to millers at prices above
those which the Bank paid for imports. The functioning of this
system is portrayed graphically in Figure 4.

Line SS' represents the supply curve of domestically
produced wheat, and DD' represents the demand curve of
Brazilian millers. In order to produce OQ_1 of wheat, the
producer price is set at P_p. At the subsidized wheat import
exchange rate, the Bank of Brazil can import wheat at price
P. However, if wheat were sold to the mills at price P, there
would be no profit on the transaction with which the Bank of
Brazil could subsidize domestic producers and cover its own
transactions costs. In essence, the problem of the government
was to determine the price to millers, P_m, such that the profit
on their sales of Q_1Q_2 of imported wheat, the rectangle WXYZ,
was approximately equal to the total subsidy paid to producers,
the rectangle P_mP_pUW, plus the operating costs of the program.
As should be clear from the extreme instability of wheat yields,
the entire operation involved considerable uncertainty. Line
P^* is the price of wheat which would prevail should an "equilibrium" exchange rate be adopted and the subsidy system
abandoned. In this case, expected domestic production would
be OQ^*, imports Q^*Q^{**}, and consumption OQ^*.

With the price to the Brazilian wheat producer divorced
from that paid by mills, a new opportunity for the lucrative
frauds known as the production of paper wheat (trigo papel),
was created. In 1957, a common technique for producing
paper wheat was as follows: The papeleiro miller simply
drew up a note of purchase in the name of a pseudoproducer.
The miller paid the Bank of Brazil the new, lower, millers'
price for domestic wheat, and the Bank of Brazil in turn paid
the pseudoproducer the full-producer price for domestic
wheat. After taxes and other small payments, the profit to
the enterprising papeleiro was on the order of 85 to 90 percent
of his outlay, assuming the pseudoproducer existed only

FIGURE 4

Multiple Price System for Imports, Production, and Consumption of Wheat in Brazil

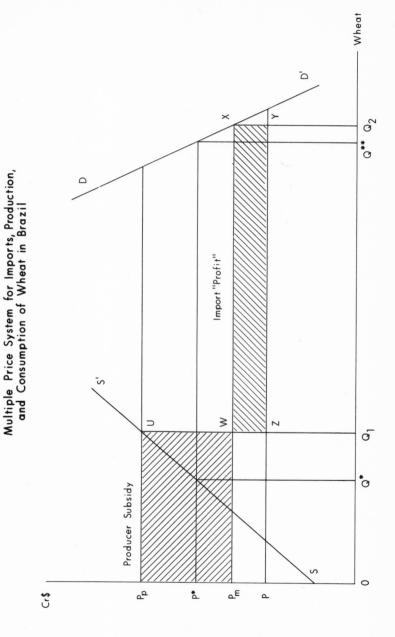

on paper. If side payments were necessary to secure the collaboration of an actual wheat producer (who nevertheless produced only paper wheat for this transaction), the profit was less, but still substantial.

The provision designed to avoid the passeio do trigo, allowing the exchange of domestic and foreign wheat quotas, was enlisted in this venture and made it still more profitable. Three parties were needed to perpetrate this version of the fraud: a mill in a northern or central state, a pseudo wheat farmer, and a mill in a producing state. First, the northern or central mill emitted a note of purchase in favor of a pseudoproducer in the South. The mill paid the Bank of Brazil the millers' price for domestic wheat, and the Bank remunerated the pseudo-producer. The profit was equal to the difference between the miller and producer prices for domestic wheat, minus some small transactions expenses and the turnover tax, again assuming no side payments to the pseudoproducer.

The second step was to "mill" the paper wheat. This is where the southern mill came in; it entered an agreement to exchange part of its quota of foreign wheat for a part of the northern mill's quota of domestic wheat. Theoretically, in this way, the imported wheat went directly to the northern or central mill, and the southern mill industrialized the domestic wheat. The mill in the north or center of the country remained with the greater quantity of foreign wheat at a price a little higher than that at which it could have been obtained through its own quota, but at any rate, at less cost than would have been incurred for domestic wheat. This was because, with the policy then in force of a single all-Brazil price for domestic wheat, northern and central millers were obliged to pay transport costs on the order of 25 percent of the official price to place the domestic product in their establishments.

Consequently, for the northern mill, beyond the profit on the "production" of paper wheat, there was an additional profit on the milling operation, only the second of which was subject to the corporate income tax. As for the southern mill, by relieving itself of its quota of foreign wheat, it participated in the profits of the fraud without having to mill anything but paper. If the southern mill's own quota of domestic wheat was also paper, its profits were even higher. Once "milled," the paper wheat was generally "sold," and the turnover tax and some other expenses were paid. The necessary bookkeeping adjustments did not present any problem for the inventive papeleiros. Attempts to prevent this kind of abuse of the permuta system were not very successful. One source

estimated that the production of paper wheat in 1958 was
probably about 200,000 tons, or roughly half the officially
estimated production of Rio Grande do Sul. [4]

It is not surprising that with the high rates of return prevailing on these operations, the number of small and inefficient
mills (in the technological sense), increased very rapidly during
this period. The exchange subsidy which existed for the import of milling machinery was hardly necessary to stimulate
investment in this sector because owning a mill was the key to
participating in the lucrative production of paper wheat. Between 1953 and 1957, the number of mills increased from 298
to 579, and rated capacity from 3.8 to 5.9 million metric tons
per year. [5] Consumption could hardly have exceeded 2.7
million tons, the sum of the highly exaggerated SEP production
estimate for 1956 and 1957 imports.

Not until 1962, when a strict and comprehensive system
of controls was established entirely managed by the Bank of
Brazil, which became the sole and direct purchaser of wheat
from producers or their cooperatives, were the frauds virtually
eliminated. Throughout the period 1953-60, fertilizer and
agricultural machinery was imported at the lowest exchange
rates and thus subsidized the use of manufactured inputs indispensable to the expansion of mechanized wheat production.
Bank of Brazil credit to wheat producers was also a source of
subsidies, since effective interest rates were almost invariably
below the rate of inflation.

SUBSIDIES AND CONSUMPTION

An evaluation of the net economic effect of the system of
producer and consumer subsidies in operation in any given
year during the postwar period is an extremely difficult under-
taking, given the rapidity with which policies were changing
and the varying but substantial rates of inflation prevailing
throughout the period. Nevertheless, even a cursory examination of the data available suggests certain unmistakable characteristics of the system.

Table 20 shows the average cost, insurance, and freight
(c.i.f.), import price Brazil paid for foreign wheat in U.S.
dollars per metric ton. Because Brazil imported the bulk of
her requirements in every year during the period 1946-67,
this series is considered the most relevant, especially since
only annual data are being considered. In the years since 1955,

TABLE 20

Average Prices Paid by Brazil for Wheat Imports,
1947-67

Year	Price*	Year	Price*
1947	153.49	1958	74.23
1948	195.89	1959	73.23
1949	129.35	1960	70.18
1950	88.28	1961	73.82
1951	99.14	1962	73.43
1952	114.43	1963	75.38
1953	105.90	1964	80.32
1954	89.27	1965	72.44
1955	84.32	1966	70.46
1956	76.32	1967	73.32
1957	72.31		

*Prices are given in U.S. dollar per metric ton and are
c.i.f. prices.

Source: SEEF, Ministério da Fazenda, Rio de Janeiro.

Public Law 480 imports from the United States have been
significant parts of the total, and wheat has also been imported
from Argentina under bilateral agreements. (These matters
are discussed below.)

As can be seen from Table 20, wheat prices were highest
in the immediate postwar period. Since 1955, there has been
no statistically significant trend in wheat import prices. While
the International Wheat Agreement of 1967 attempted to raise
the price floor, there is considerable doubt as to whether these
levels could be maintained in the face of rapid improvements in
wheat-production technology in many wheat-growing countries.
Thus, future prices may be expected to remain at close to
1967 levels or lower. In fact, Brazil paid an average of $67.67
per metric ton in 1968, compared with $73.32 in 1967.

Table 21 presents data on some of the different cruzeiro
wheat prices prevailing in Brazil during the years 1948-49
through 1966-67. The double-year denomination is used because wheat produced in the first year of each pair (year t-1)
is normally milled and consumed in the second year (year t).

TABLE 21

Various Prevailing Brazilian Wheat Prices and Estimated
Subsidies to Producers and Consumers as a Percentage
of the Opportunity Cost of Imported Wheat, 1949-67

Year t	Producer Price[a] (1)	Imports Effective Exchange Rate, c.i.f.[a] (2)	Imports Parity Exchange Rate, c.i.f.[a] (3)	Portaria Price to Millers[a] (4)	Average Price to Millers of Imported Wheat[a] (5)	Consumer Subsidy[b] (6)	Producer Subsidy[b] (7)
1949	2.417	2.419	3.359	2.417	2.540[c]	28.0	-13.7
1950	2.417	1.574	2.531	2.417	1.653[c]	37.8	14.6
1951	2.417	1.854	3.069	2.417	1.947[c]	39.6	- 5.5
1952	2.417	2.140	2.422	2.417	2.247[c]	11.6	19.7
1953	3.667	2.095	2.082	2.417	2.200[c]	- 0.6	39.3
1954	3.667	2.218	4.708	3.667	2.329[c]	52.9	- 6.5
1955	4.767	1.176	5.245	4.768	2.419	56.1	9.1
1956	6.667	2.331	6.616	6.668	3.238	53.4	20.9
1957	6.667	3.740	5.911	7.001	6.345	- 2.2	35.3
1958	7.000	4.798	6.787	5.334	6.160	13.6	23.8
1959	9.167	7.215	9.491	8.335	8.910	6.1	15.9
1960	12.830	7.018	12.120	8.335	8.960	29.6	27.1
1961	18.700	16.440	17.290	18.700	17.290	4.7	29.8
1962	23.120	26.260	26.720	23.120	26.000	7.3	5.6
1963	43.670	42.260	48.520	43.680	41.890	17.8	8.0
1964	73.000	89.080	93.570	52.500	92.300	6.1	- 6.4
1965	152.000	135.200	127.100	149.000	157.400	-17.9	42.9
1966	210.000	158.400	168.300	186.000	179.300	- 1.4	49.7
1967	265.000	190.300	221.300	176.300	213.900	7.9	43.7

[a]Prices given in cruzeiros per metric ton in Year t, except Column 1, which is given in Year t-1.

[b]Given in percent.

[c]Assumed equal to c.i.f. price of imports at effective wheat exchange rate plus 5 percent port and handling charges.

Source: Columns 1 and 4 taken from portarias closest to harvest in year t-1; also see text.

93

Comparison of prices is rendered more than normally difficult, as suggested above, because of the different timing in changes of the various, relevant prices. Nevertheless, the five basic prices presented in the table allow one to get a fairly accurate idea of the basic differences which existed. Column 1 gives the official producer price in new cruzeiros per metric ton for unsacked (bulk) wheat in the interior of Rio Grande do Sul, for the crop planted and harvested in the year t-1, plus any additional bonuses granted to wheat producers, as based on the official decrees (portarias), issued closest to the harvest date. Column 2 is the average c.i.f. import price for foreign wheat in the year t, at the average exchange rate which actually prevailed in that year. Column 3 gives the average c.i.f. import price as it would have been, had wheat been imported at the parity exchange rate. (See Chapter 3 for an explanation of the derivation of this exchange rate.) Column 4 is the price to millers at interior locations for domestic wheat as elaborated in the portaria issued closest to harvest time. Column 5 presents the average price to millers in port cities in the year t and weights each official price by the number of months it was in effect.

Using these prices, it is possible to get a rough idea of the extent to which producers and consumers were actually subsidized during this period. Column 6 presents the consumer subsidy as a percent of the opportunity cost to Brazil, estimated as the import price evaluated at the parity exchange rate plus an additional 5 percent estimated port and handling charges (5 percent is a conservative estimate of port and handling charges). This calculation is based on the assumption that consumer prices reflected the cost of foreign wheat to mills. Because domestic wheat was never more than 30 percent of total consumption and almost always less than 15 percent, given the existence of the paper wheat frauds at the time of maximum domestic production, and taking into consideration that a single price for domestic and foreign wheat prevailed after 1956, this assumption would not appear unreasonable. If anything, it probably underestimates the subsidy in the years after 1957, because the parity exchange rate does not take into account major changes in the tariff system which came into operation late in that year.

On this criterion, the real subsidy to wheat consumption has varied considerably over time, but four fairly distinct periods may be distinguished. The subsidy averaged 23.3 percent in the calendar years 1949-53, 54.1 percent in 1954-56, 10.4 percent in 1957-63, and -3.8 percent in 1964-67. The last period was that in which the "revolutionary" military governments of Castello Branco and Costa e Silva were in power.

Turning to the extent of the real cost of domestic wheat production to the Brazilian economy, virtually the same opportunity cost measure, the average c.i.f. cost of imported wheat calculated at the parity exchange rate, is used. Port charges are not added, however, as they would be the same for foreign and domestic wheat. The producer price paid at the harvest beginning late in year t-1 is increased by 20 percent to provide a conservative estimate of the cost of placing Brazilian wheat c.i.f. in non-Rio Grande do Sul ports, because marginal changes in wheat production would increase or decrease imports there, rather than in the principal producing state. This no doubt understates the cost of providing domestic wheat to mills, because wheat is normally purchased from farmers at the end of the year t-1 and the beginning of year t and is milled sometime in year t. Given the inflationary conditions prevailing and the fact that wheat is normally stored for some time prior to milling, often at government expense, storage costs could reach considerable proportions. Even if all domestic wheat is consumed in the first quarter of the year, the comparison with imported wheat is made at the average parity rate for the entire year, which tends to inflate the opportunity cost of foreign wheat. All of this suggests that the cost to Brazil of providing domestic wheat to mills is, if anything underestimated in these calculations.

The difference between the estimated domestic cost calculated in this fashion and the opportunity cost of wheat imports is expressed as a percentage of the opportunity cost of imports and is an indicator of the extent of the real subsidy Brazil paid the production, marketing, and transportation system in order to be able to consume domestic rather than foreign wheat. Further refinements on this measure would include adjustments for the subsidized agricultural credit and subsidized imports of manufactured inputs used in wheat production; however, the basic picture is quite clear from the unadjusted measure.

Again, the period 1948-49 through 1966-67 may be divided into four subperiods which to a large extent overlap with those for consumption subsidies. Between 1948-49 and 1953-54, the average subsidy was 8 percent, and in three of these years, the subsidy was negative. In the period 1954-55 through 1960-61, the average rate of the subsidy was 23.1 percent; in 1961-62 through 1963-64 (a period of high political instability and recurrent budgetary problems), 2.4 percent; and in the last

period, 1964-65 through 1966-67, production subsidies were
at the high level of 45.4 percent.   The same military governments which eliminated the consumption subsidy raised producer subsidies to alltime high levels and reflected their
determination to make Brazil a major wheat producer, cost
what it might.

It should be added here that the real cost of consumer and
producer subsidies during the period 1955-67 was greatly reduced by the availability of substantial Public Law 480 shipments of wheat and wheat flour under terms which in many
years amounted to a virtual grant. [6] Since April, 1966, however, with the signing of the Sixth Commodity Agreement, terms
became considerably stiffer, and loans were denominated in
dollars with real interest charges and shorter repayment
periods.   This reflects a basic change in the philosophy and
practice of U.S. foreign aid policy toward stimulating agricultural production in the less-developed countries.

Table 22 gives the dollar value of wheat and wheat flour
imports, the implicit exchange-subsidy ratio as measured by
the parity and quasi-free trade rates, the dollar value of the
wheat subsidy at each "equilibrium" rate, and the estimated
dollar value of Public Law 480 wheat and wheat flour imports,
considering these as a pure grant.   (See Chapter 3 for an explanation of the derivation of these exchange rates.) On this
assumption, Public Law 480 shipments were more than sufficient to finance the wheat import subsidies for every year
after 1958 except 1959 (parity rate subsidy only), 1960 and
1967 (by both parity and quasi-free trade rate measures of the
exchange subsidy).   On the other hand, in the years of highest
import subsidies, both in terms of rates and absolute values,
1952-56, only in the last year were Public Law 480 shipments
available in quantities which came anywhere near financing
the exchange subsidy.

THE EFFICIENCY OF DOMESTIC RESOURCE USE

For each of the five products being studied in this book,
available data on prices and the cost of production have been
utilized to prepare estimates of the efficiency of domestic
resource use by product for the crops harvested in 1967.

The measure of efficiency of domestic resource use
chosen is given as follows:

TABLE 22

Implicit Import Subsidies on Wheat and Wheat Flour
and the Value of Public Law 480 Shipments,
1947-67

Year	Value of Wheat and Flour Imports[a]	Implicit Import Subsidy Rate[b]	Implicit Import Subsidy Rate[c]	Value of Import Subsidy[b]	Value of Import Subsidy[c]	Value of Public Law 480 Wheat and Flour Imports[a]
1947	133,132	.290	--	38,622	--	--
1948	133,272	.284	--	37,823	--	--
1949	123,787	.353	--	43,635	--	--
1950	109,373	.348	--	38,040	--	--
1951	138,508	.396	--	54,849	--	--
1952	146,764	.481	--	70,391	--	--
1953	164,663	.501	--	82,463	--	--
1954	152,523	.605	.346	92,261	52,773	--
1955	161,682	.590	.553	96,848	89,410	2,239
1956	115,254	.582	.567	67,078	65,349	39,787
1957	107,559	.367	.362	39,474	38,937	31,320
1958	116,191	.297	.323	34,520	37,530	33,169
1959	131,944	.241	.377	31,799	49,743	36,924
1960	142,673	.421	.524	60,065	74,761	35,548
1961	139,471	.051	.365	7,141	50,907	112,000
1962	161,585	.034	.350	5,462	56,555	66,176
1963	164,892	.129	.325	21,288	53,590	57,875
1964	210,688	.047	.347	9,944	73,109	115,134
1965	136,967	-.064	.322	- 8,821	44,103	15,366
1966	172,182	.071	.207	12,173	35,642	39,417
1967	184,653	.147	.169	27,052	31,206	25,016

[a]Given in thousands of U.S. dollars, c.i.f.
[b]Parity.
[c]Quasi-free trade.

Source: Imports, SEEF, Ministério da Fazenda, Rio de Janeiro; parity
rate and quasi-free trade rate, implicit tax rates, see Chapter 3.

$$E_i = \frac{V_i}{C_i} \cdot 100$$

where

$$V_i = P_i^* - \Sigma_j M_{ij} \qquad \text{for all } i$$

$$C_i = P_i^* - \Sigma_j M_{ij} - T_i \quad \text{for rice, soybeans,} \atop \text{and beef}$$

$$C_i = 1.2\ P_i^{(d)} - T_i \qquad \text{for corn}$$

$$C_i = 1.2\ P_i^{(d)} - \Sigma_j M_{ij} \qquad \text{for wheat}$$

P_i^* = the annual average f.o.b. export price for product i in dollars per metric ton (c.i.f. import price for wheat)

$P_i^{(d)}$ = the producers' price in the interior of the state for product i in dollars per metric ton at the official exchange rate

M_{ij} = the dollar value of direct and indirect imported input j to produce a metric ton of commodity i (c.i.f. price for $_j$)

and T_i = the dollar value of the value added tax per metric ton of commodity i, at the official exchange rate

V_i = the domestic value added at world prices for commodity i

C_i = the cost in domestic resources of this value added.

The measure E_i is closely related to the domestic cost of foreign exchange concept used by Michael Bruno and Anne Krueger.[7] In the absence of a uniform basis for estimating production, processing, and transport costs for all products studies, the basic assumption has been made that prices are equal to costs, with adjustments for taxes and imported inputs. The SEP estimate of the Rio Grande do Sul producer price rather than the export price was used for corn, which was not exported in significant quantities, and it was assumed that the cost of placing the corn in Rio Grande do Sul ports would add another 20 percent to producer prices. In the case of wheat, it was estimated that the cost of transporting wheat to Rio Grande do Sul ports, loading it into ships, and transporting it to non-Rio Grande do Sul ports where it replaced foreign imports was 20 percent of the official producers' price. This must be considered a conservative estimate, even though the marketing system for wheat is considerably more efficient than that for corn.

For wheat and rice, import content was estimated from data on production costs published by Federação de Cooperativas Triticolas do Sul (FECOTRIGO, Federation of Wheat Cooperatives) and IRGA, respectively, both of which are based on weighted average production costs obtained through a statewide survey of producers. For soybeans, the information available was not as comprehensive or reliable; however, several estimates of production costs presented at a meeting of soybean producers in January, 1968, were utilized to prepare estimates of import costs for intensive fertilized and mechanized soybean production of the kind associated with wheat production in former natural pasture areas of the state. Costs for the nonmechanized soybean production practiced in colonial areas were generally lower. For corn and beef produced in Rio Grande do Sul in 1967, there was no import content. In calculating the direct and indirect import content of production costs for wheat, rice, and soybeans, it was assumed that 40 percent of the fertilizer costs and 80 percent of the depreciation and amortization charges for self-propelled combines were the only import costs. These estimates are based on markups in prices above the c.i.f. price of imports which are essentially distribution and, in the case of fertilizer, packaging charges, all of which can be assumed to be void of import content. Tractors are manufactured almost entirely from components produced in Brazil, and while a small percentage of fuel and lubricant costs represent imported petroleum products, these items were ignored.

The value-added tax (ICM, Imposto de Circulação de Mercadorias), was calculated at 15 percent of the f.o.b. value (or its estimate in the case of corn). Wheat is exempt from this tax, as are manufactured inputs used in the production of all five commodities. The first incidence of the tax, however, is on the full producers' price of the commodity in question; thus, at that stage, it amounts to a turnover tax. In 1968, the rate of the ICM was reduced for exports of rice, soybeans, and beef, in order to stimulate exports of these products. The ICM replaced a turnover tax, (IVC, Imposto de Vendas e Consignatções), which was the principal tax prevailing before 1967. The IVC and associated taxas ranged from 3.3 to 6 percent over the period 1955-66. From 1947 to 1955, there was a state export tax of 5 percent which was diminished by 1 percent per year in 1956-58 and then abolished by Federal Law Number 3,601 of December 1, 1958. The higher rates of the IVC prevailed in the years after the elimination of the export tax. Assuming at least two incidences of the turnover tax during the marketing process, the total rate of the principal explicit taxes on production has probably remained fairly constant over the period 1947-67, at about 12 to 15 percent of the f.o.b. value of exports.

Thus estimates of the domestic resource cost of production are based on the assumption that governmental expenditures financed by the value-added tax in no way benefit the producers of the commodities being studied. In a static, marginalist approach, this is probably an appropriate assumption. The state's secretary of agriculture received only 2.1 percent of the total state budget in 1967.[9] In short, the tax is considered as a transfer payment rather than as a cost of production.

Looking at Table 23, it can be seen that the index of static efficiency of domestic resource use, E_i, is much lower for wheat than for any of the other four products. This means that in 1967 it cost Brazil $2.20 worth of domestic resources to save one dollar's worth of wheat imports, whereas the comparable cost to earn a dollar was 85 cents for beef, 84.6 cents for rice, 82.3 cents for soybeans, and 86.7 cents for corn. These figures are obtained by taking the inverse of the efficiency ratio, that is C_i/V_i, which is the cost in domestic resources of one dollar in foreign exchange. In 1968, the comparable figure for wheat was even higher, $2.43, due to a higher producer price for wheat and lower import prices.[10]

REASONS FOR HIGH PRODUCTION COSTS

The answers to the question of why wheat production in Rio Grande do Sul is so costly are relatively simple. Marginal wheat production (a) takes place on land of low natural fertility and high acidity, (b) requires relatively expensive manufacture inputs, (c) comes from varieties which are inefficient utilizers

TABLE 23

Estimated Efficiency of Domestic Resource Use in the
Production of Five Agricultural Commodities in
Rio Grande do Sul, 1967[a]

Item	Beef	Rice	Wheat	Soybeans	Corn
Export price in $/MT f.o.b.	589.65	171.51	140.88[b]	96.02	51.23 (52.25)[c]
ICM at 15 percent	88.45	25.73	--	14.40	7.83
Dollar import cost of average fertilizer consumption per MT of commodity	--	3.92	10.37	7.98	--
Import component of estimated depreciation and amortization on combine	--	--	6.80	6.46	--
Domestic resource cost per MT of commodity	501.20	141.86	123.71	67.18	44.42
Domestic value added at world prices	589.65	167.59	56.15[d]	81.58	51.23
Efficiency of domestic resource use	117.6	118.1	45.0	121.4	115.3

[a]All prices and costs converted to U.S. dollars at official exchange
rates.
[b]Estimated cost of Rio Grande do Sul wheat c.i.f. non-Rio Grande do
Sul ports.
[c]There were no corn exports from Rio Grande do Sul. Estimated f.o.b.
cost.
[d]Average c.i.f. price of imports minus import content of domestic production.

of nitrogen, (d) suffers from difficult climatic conditions, and
(e) has obtained insufficient scientific and technical support.
Each of these assertions is discussed briefly below. The
juxtaposition of all these factors resulted in low and highly
unstable yields and the high unit costs of production which have
characterized Rio Grande do Sul wheat production.

Poor Lands. The former, natural pastureland best suited to
mechanized wheat production is, for the most part, highly
acid, often with high aluminium content; thus, it requires
heavy liming to secure maximum yields. Acidity is even more
harmful for soybean production, as it impedes the activity of
nitrogen-fixing bacteria associated with this crop. Mechanized
wheat land is also very low in natural fertility and makes chemical fertilizers a virtual necessity. [11]

Expensive Manufacture Inputs. Price data for some principal
fertilizers and items of agricultural machinery are presented
in Table 24 for both Rio Grande do Sul and the United States.
With the surprising exception of tractors, which are produced
in Brazil in six factories, all of which operated at extremely
low percentages of their rated capacity in 1967, all inputs were
costing Rio Grande do Sul farmers at least 46 percent more
than the average prices paid by farmers in the United States. [12]

Varieties Under Heavy Fertilization. Unlike the semidwarf,
stiff-strawed varieties developed in Mexico at the International
Corn and Wheat Improvement Center and now being used in
many other countries, all Brazilian varieties available in
1967 were incapable of efficiently using large quantities of
nitrogen. When the quantity of nitrogen exceeds about 80 kilograms per hectare, even the best varieties yield less than at
lower levels of fertilization, and the economically optimum
level of nitrogen fertilization in 1967, given the prevailing
product and factor prices and fertilizer-response function of
the best available wheat, was approximately 17 kilograms per
hectare, according to calculations presented in Chapter 6.
Economically optimum fertilization levels for nitrogen well
in excess of 100 kilograms per hectare are common in India
and Mexico where the more modern varieties are being used.

Difficult Climatic Conditions. This is perhaps the factor that
science will have the most difficulty correcting. Rio Grande
do Sul has a rather instable climate. Late frosts, the possibility of strong rains in the critical periods of flowering and

TABLE 24

Price Comparisons for Rio Grande do Sul and U.S.
Manufactured Inputs Used in Agricultural Production, 1967
(Exchange Rate of NCr$2.70 per U.S. Dollar)

| Location | Prices in U.S. Dollars per Metric Ton | | | | | In U.S. Dollars | |
	Ammonium Sulphate	Normal Super-phos-phate	Triple Super-phos-phate	Potassium Chloride	Lime	Tractor of 50-60 Horse-power	Combine
Rio Grande do Sul	90.74	62.04	120.07	85.40	11.11	5657	11,234
United States	52.75	42.10	82.25	52.20	5.18	5445	7,045
Ratio of Rio Grande do Sul to U.S. Price	1.72	1.47	1.46	1.64	2.14	1.04	1.59

Source: For fertilizers, Rio Grande do Sul, average price per year published in Lavoura Arrozeira, November-December, 1968, minus 10 percent estimated interest charges for deferred payment plus $7.41 estimated average transport costs from Pôrto Alegre to wheat production regions; for United States, average of April 15 and June 15 (average) prices to farmers from USDA, Statistical Reporting Service, Agricultural Prices (1967 Annual Summary). Tractor and combine prices for Rio Grande do Sul are those given in FECOTRIGO, Trigo, Safra 1967-1968: Estudo do Custo de Producão no Rio Grande do Sul (Pôrto Alegre, July, 1967); for United States, average of March, June, September, and December prices from USDA, Statistical Reporting Service, Agri-cultural Prices (June, 1969, Supplement 2, Revised Data).

103

harvest, and hot springs which favor the development of wheat rusts and other diseases were conditions which could not be altered with the technology available as of 1969. John W. Gibler, formerly an associate director of the International Corn and Wheat Improvement Center, is of the opinion that disease-resistant, fertilizer-intensive spring wheat varieties could be developed which would help to circumvent some of the worst climatic and disease problems described. However, the problem of summer droughts would then have to be faced. [13]

Insufficient Scientific and Technical Support. While the advances made by Brazilian wheat breeders, soil scientists, climatologists, and other scientists are far from insignificant, the fact remains that they did not succeed in increasing Rio Grande do Sul wheat yields significantly over the period 1947-67. (See Chapter 5.) Nor did they always manage to stay ahead of the development of new rust strains, although in the 1960's, there was distinct progress on this front (as discussed in Chapter 5).

This situation should be contrasted with the successes achieved in other countries, such as Mexico and India. In these countries, the strategy of research has been different from that applied in Brazil. Instead of seeking varieties which can produce best under conditions of low natural fertility, researchers in these countries have been seeking varieties which respond most efficiently to complete and massive fertilization. The results obtained following this approach have been impressive. Instead of increasing productivity per hectare 20 to 50 percent over traditional varieties, they have obtained increases of 200 to 500 percent. In 1943, the average productivity of Mexican wheat fields was 773 kilograms per hectare. By 1966, it had risen to 2,441 kilograms per hectare, or by a factor of 3.2.

The success of Mexico, a Latin American country, which left its position as a traditional wheat importer to become an exporter (Brazil imported Mexican wheat in 1967 and 1968), is worth noting. This achievement was not the work of an individual, but of a large team of researchers and extensionists, among whom were some of the best international experts. They were supported by the application of financial resources appropriate to the task undertaken, which was nothing less than the total transformation of wheat-production technology. [14]

More important than the sum of money spent in this effort was its continuity. The success was the result of more than fifteen years of uninterrupted work. In Brazil, ambitious

plans were not lacking, but financial and human resources
were. It was common for researchers at the institutes of the
Brazilian Ministry of Agriculture and also at the state research organizations not to receive their salaries, which were
quite low in any case, for long periods. It was sometimes
necessary for experiments, if they were to continue, to be
financed from the pockets of these same researchers. The
continuity of research also suffered greatly from abrupt changes
in leadership at the institutes, and these changes were more
related to the political affiliations of the directors than to their
technical qualifications. Under these conditions, the best
minds were not attracted to research, and, of those who entered, many left after a bitter experience. Not only was the
level of salaries in these research institutes low and unstable
in real terms (due to the effects of rapid inflation), but the
salary structure did not encourage specialization through post-
graduate training. [15]

ARGUMENTS IN FAVOR OF
DOMESTIC WHEAT PRODUCTION

The arguments in favor of domestic wheat production in
Brazil can be grouped into three basic categories--economic,
political, and romantic. Of these, only the first two need be
taken seriously as arguments. At best, the third involves
harmless poetry and, at worst, conscious exploitation of un-
tutored popular sentiments to further personal gain.
The romantic school of wheat enthusiasts is prone to at-
tribute religious and spiritual values to wheat. It is, according
to them, the king of cereals, the staff of life, a necessity in
peace and war, and a political symbol. These terms are used
literally in a publication of the Brazilian Ministry of Agriculture, a particularly florid segment of which is reproduced
below:

> Instinctively or intuitively, the peoples of the world
> struggle for the conquest of bread--white, fluffy, and
> delicious--so that, as if by fate, it were their inex-
> orable destiny, or because in it they sense the basis
> of their physical and spiritual force. [translation
> mine][16]

When we turn to the more respectable economic arguments,
the most pervasive by far is the assertion that wheat imports

consume valuable foreign exchange which should be reserved
for more "essential" imports considered vital to Brazil's
growth. Some of those putting forward this argument, who
can be called the exchange-shortage school (falta de divisas),
also favor raising the real price of wheat to the consumer; thus,
they would shift demand toward other cereals produced at lower
cost in Brazil. In fact, as was shown above, this philosophy
has prevailed since the Revolution of March, 1964. The majority in the past, however, generally favored the consumption
subsidy for political reasons, namely, to secure the electoral
support of working-class and low middle-income urban groups
in the period when Brazilian politics was sensitive to their
opinions. The military governments, committed to eliminating
or reducing distortions in the price system and not dependent
on popular political support, have considered themselves free
to do what was attempted sporadically in the past, i.e., eliminate the wheat-consumption subsidy. In one year, 1965, they
even went so far as to impose what amounted to a consumption
tax on wheat. [17]

While the falta de divisas school generally acknowledges
the importance of wheat research, the quantity of resources
allocated to the organization and execution of this activity has
been dwarfed by that spent on producer subsidies. It was
apparently felt that the latter were more effective in attaining
shortrun results, however high the cost, given the long time
lags involved in research. This school has never, to our
knowledge, produced any empirical studies of the opportunity
costs of its policies; the present work is an attempt to remedy
this oversight.

A more defensive argument in favor of domestic wheat
production is that resources have been invested in machinery,
marketing structures, warehouses, and the learning of wheat-
production technology, and that this investment, as well as the
people who depend on it for their livelihood, should not be
abandoned, as the resources involved are far from perfectly
mobile. In our opinion, this argument has considerable weight.
When we visited wheat cooperatives in the production zone of
Rio Grande do Sul in June, 1968, one of the questions we always put to local leaders was, "What would happen if wheat
prices were to fall by 50 percent?" The answer was inevitably
that the overwhelming majority of natural pastureland under
wheat would revert to natural or possibly artificial pasture,
and that the social effect would be catastrophic.

This argument, however, cannot be used to justify the
further increase of land, labor, and capital devoted to wheat

production. An associated argument is that wheat production,
being technologically demanding, results in substantial improvements in cultural practices. Technologies, nevertheless,
are useful only insofar as they produce a surplus of benefits
over costs. To calculate only benefits with no attention to
costs is an error very common in Brazil, perhaps in part
because the calculation of real cost was made extremely difficult by the rapid rate of inflation prevailing in the postwar
period, and large numbers of distortions existed in the price
system.

It is perfectly possible to calculate costs for the joint

Another economic argument is that the efficiency of wheat
production cannot be considered separately from that of other
crops, particularly soybeans. This is true for a substantial
part of mechanized soybean cultivation, which would no doubt
be reduced if the mechanized wheat area were to fall. Of
course not all mechanized wheat is produced in rotation with
soybeans.

It is perfectly possible to calculate costs for the joint
production of wheat and soybeans, and in effect this was done
in the soybean and wheat calculations presented in this chapter.
The depreciation and amortization charges for the self-propelled
combine were based on a useful life assumption, which in turn
reflected an assumption that the machine would be used for both
crops. If we use the assumed yields of 960 kilograms per
hectare for wheat and 1,380 kilograms per hectare for soybeans, weights of 0.5897 for soybeans and 0.4103 for wheat
may be applied to the efficiency indexes estimated for the two
products in 1967 to obtain the efficiency index for their joint
production. A more thorough analysis would depend on experimental data which is not yet available concerning yields of
both crops grown in rotation over a number of years. If we
use these rougher estimates, the combined index of efficiency
is 89.6 for wheat-soybeans as opposed to 121.4 for soybeans
alone and 44 for wheat alone. Thus, while the consideration
of mechanized wheat and soybean production as a single activity
results in a more efficient use of resources than the production
of wheat alone, it is not sufficient to make resources as productive as they would be in any of the other products considered.

A final economic argument is that foreign countries, including some of Brazil's major suppliers, subsidize wheat
production. Therefore, it is asserted, the Brazilian producer
must be subsidized if he is to compete with "unfair" foreign
exports. However, the question again is whether Brazilian
production should compete--if other nations are willing to
subsidize Brazilian wheat consumers, that represents a net
gain for Brazil.

It may be concluded that the only valid economic argument is that wheat production should not be rapidly reduced, because this policy would involve a waste of resources already committed to wheat or wheat-soybean production as well as considerable social costs. A third alternative, the joint production of wheat, soybeans, and beef on artifical pastures in a system of rotation, is not investigated here for lack of suitable data. No valid economic arguments exist for increasing wheat production further until research and extension have drastically altered the efficiency with which resources can be employed in this activity.

The political arguments for domestic wheat production are based on the supposed value of economic autarky. Strategic considerations such as the possibility of a world war which would make it difficult or impossible to supply the Brazilian market with U.S., Canadian, European, and other foreign wheat enter here. Such arguments should be familiar to students of the oil-depletion allowance and numerous other protective devices used in the United States. In such calculations, the chance of a war between Argentina and Brazil, which would eliminate the most important traditional source of imports, usually enters. That it would also no doubt be fought in the principal producing regions is not mentioned. The avoidance of economic pressures from the United States is also cited as a reason for reducing dependence on U.S. wheat imports. Another consideration is the possibility of a rise in wheat prices in the international market, although, as has been shown, the trend would appear to be downward if a trend exists.

It should be remembered, however, in weighing these essentially noneconomic arguments, that wheat is not indispensable and that the production of many low-cost substitutes could be rapidly increased in the event of a future emergency. The possibility of a future rise in wheat prices is better prepared for by research designed to reduce production costs than by the production of expensive wheat in the present.

Furthermore, if a policy of self-sufficiency in wheat were to be pursued, it must be remembered that in the years 1965-67, 52 percent of Brazil's wheat imports came from Argentina and socialist countries in Eastern Europe and was purchased through bilateral agreements in exchange for coffee, cocoa, and other Brazilian tropical products. Argentine imports represented 34 percent of Brazil's exports of manufactured goods in this same period. If Brazil ceased buying Argentine wheat, it is likely that Argentina would retaliate by ceasing to buy the products of Brazil's industry. A policy of autarky would also

be inimical to the spirit and slender substance of Latin American
economic integration.

NOTES

1. For a detailed account of the history of public policies
through the late 1950's, two standard references are Cunha
Bayma, Trigo (Two volumes); (Rio de Janeiro: Serviço de
Informação Agrícola, Ministério da Agricultura, 1960); and
Edgar Fernandes Texeira, O Trigo no Sul do Brasil (Grafica
Editôra Linotype, 1958). Summary versions with greater
analytic content may be found in Luiz Mendonca de Freitas
and Antonio Delfim Netto, O Trigo No Brasil (Associação
Comercial de São Paulo, 1960); and by Francis R. Bethlen,
"Effects of Brazilian Economic Development and Price Policy
on Brazilian Wheat Imports," Ph. D. dissertation, Purdue
University, January, 1962, mimeographed. Of these, the
work by Freitas and Netto is the best published reference on
the wheat scandals of the 1950's described below. As such,
I rely heavily on it together with official documents of the
Serviço de Expansão do Trigo for my account of these phenomena.
Peter Greenston of the University of Minnesota was preparing
a Ph. D. dissertation, "The Impact of P. L. 480 on Wheat Production and Consumption in Brazil," at the time that this volume
was in preparation. He has generously made available useful
price series and I wish to acknowledge the helpful exchange of
information, criticism, and suggestions which has been possible.

2. Ady Raul da Silva, Melhoramento das Variedades de
Trigo Destinadas as Diferentes Regiões do Brasil (Rio de
Janeiro: Serviço de Informação Agrícola, Ministério da
Agricultura, 1966), pp. 10-11.

3. Decree Number 40,316, November 8, 1956.

4. Freitas and Netto, op. cit.

5. Ibid.

6. In many years, repayment was permitted in cruzeiros
over a forty-year period without an exchange rate correction
factor. A complete account of the terms on which Public Law

480 wheat was made available to Brazil is contained in Greenston, op. cit.

7. See Michael Bruno, Interdependence, Resource Use and Structural Change in Trade (Jerusalem: Bank of Israel, 1963); and Anne Krueger, "Some Economic Costs of Exchange Control: The Turkish Case," Journal of Political Economy (October, 1966), 466-80. The relationship of this measure to the effective protective rate is discussed by Bela Balassa and Daniel M. Schydlowsky "Effective Tariffs, Domestic Cost of Foreign Exchange, and the Equilibrium Exchange Rate," Journal of Political Economy (May-June, 1968), 348-60.

8. FECOTRIGO, Trigo, Safra 1967-1968, Estudo do Custo de Produção No Rio Grande do Sul (Pôrto Alegre, July, 1967); and IRGA, Departamento de Obras e Assistência Técnica, "Estimativa do Custo de uma Quadra Quadrada de Arroz, Safra 1966/1967" (Pôrto Alegre, 1967).

9. Governo do Estado do Rio Grande do Sul, Balanço Geral do Estado do Rio Grande do Sul, 1967, Pôrto Alegre, 1967.

10. Calculations were made by the same method as used for 1967. Fertilizer and depreciation and amortization costs for self-propelled combines were estimated from data in FECOTRIGO, Safra 1968-1969 op. cit., (July, 1968).

11. On these points, see Raul Edgard Klackmann, et al., Regiões do Trigo no Brasil; and Raimundo Costa de Lemos, et al., O Solo na Cultura de Trigo no Brasil Serviço de Informação Agrícola, Ministério da Agricultura, (Rio de Janeiro: 1965 and 1967 respectively).

12. The tractor prices given for the United States for 50 to 60 horsepower tractors were collected by the USDA's Statistical Reporting Service and included extra cost features, such as special transmissions and hydraulic control equipment, "most commonly purchased by farmers." Further, the average horsepower of the Brazilian tractors priced was 53, whereas the U.S. tractors were probably more evenly distributed over the range of 50 to 60 horsepower. Brazilian tractor factories operated at about 18 percent of capacity in 1967 on a two-shift basis. Data from IPEA, Setor de Agricultura, was originally from Sindicato Nacional da Indústria de Tratores. The estimated index of nationalization (percentage

of domestically produced components) was 95 percent by
weight.

13. Interview, Pôrto Alegre, December 13, 1968.

14. See E. C. Stakman, Richard Bradfield, and Paul G.
Mangelsdoff, Campaigns Against Hunger (Cambridge, Mass.:
The Belknap Press of Harvard University Press, 1967), for
a description of the organizational effort which produced the
new Mexican wheats.

15. The organization of research and extension in Rio
Grande do Sul is discussed at length in Chapter 7 of the
Portuguese language version of this book, Peter T. Knight,
Agricultura, Tecnologia e Comércio Internacional: Estudos
da Realidade Brasileira (Rio de Janeiro: Editôra APEC, 1971).
A less complete English version is contained in a mimeographed
paper the author prepared for USAID/Brazil, "Agricultural
Modernization in Rio Grande do Sul, Brazil," May 28, 1969.

16. Ministério da Agricultura, "Contribuição ao
Planejamento da Política Brasileira do Trigo" (Rio de Janeiro,
May 26, 1965).

17. Based on the calculations presented in Column 6,
Table 21.

CHAPTER

5

PRODUCTIVITY STAGNATION
AND TECHNOLOGICAL CHANGE
IN RIO GRANDE DO SUL

This chapter has two principal objectives: to document the fact that land and herd productivity have stagnated in Rio Grande do Sul during the postwar period, and to establish what types of technological change have in fact taken place concurrently with this stagnation in productivity.

PRODUCTIVITY STAGNATION FOR
FIELD CROPS AND BEEF

There are many possible indexes of technological change in agriculture. The one most universally available, in spite of its faults, is the increase in yields per unit of land over some interval of time. Like all measures of output per unit of a single input, land productivity may not show any upward movement in spite of technological progress under fairly restrictive assumptions regarding factor and product prices. Pronounced differences in weather and/or disease incidence between periods may make intertemporal comparisons of land productivity unreliable. This problem is more severe the smaller the area over which the change is measured. The difficulty may be reduced by taking averages over a number of years or, better, by fitting regressions of yield on time over the period being considered.

Given that the price of land relative to capital and labor can be expected to rise due to population growth, one would expect to see an upward trend in yields per hectare as more capital and labor are applied to "raw land," even if

technological change were not constantly being embodied in
better and often cheaper machinery, pesticides, weed-control
measures, seeds, irrigation systems, and, perhaps most
importantly, in the farmers themselves in the form of increased skills and knowledge.

Table 25 presents yield data for Brazil, Rio Grande do
Sul, and a number of other major producing countries and
regions for the four annual crops--rice, wheat, soybeans,
and corn. Brazil and Rio Grande do Sul rank poorly by the
measure selected, i.e., the percentage increase in land
productivity over a ten-year period. The base is the five-
year average for 1952-56. The inclusion of several particularly bad years in the second period tends to bias the Rio
Grande do Sul productivity index downward for soybeans. As
a further test, regressions of yield on time were run for the
twenty-one-year period 1947-67 for all four products. In no
case was there any significant upward or downward trend in
yields. There was a slight indication of a downward trend in
soybean yields, but this was statistically insignificant.

The over-all picture, then, was one of yield stagnation
for these four crops. Any yield-increasing technological
change or movements along production functions appears to
have been offset by declining soil fertility and the extension
of cultivation to more marginal lands. The importance of this
finding is heightened when it is observed that there were highly
significant upward trends in real producer prices of wheat
and soybeans on the order of 2 or 3 percent per year over the
period 1950-67. In the case of wheat, however, the over-all
upward trend conceals a notable cyclical movement which reflects changes in government policy. For the other two crops,
rice and corn, there was no significant trend in real producer
prices. Yield and price regressions are presented in Table 26.

Simple indicators of technological change are, if anything,
more difficult to calculate for beef. Productivity per hectare
in terms of live-weight gain would be a measure comparable
to yield per hectare for annual crops. However, due to the
shifting nature of extensive grazing operations and the possibility of grazing sheep, horses, and goats on the same land
as beef cattle, aggregate land-productivity statistics are not
very reliable even when available.

The best generally available measure of herd productivity
is meat production (beef and veal) per head of cattle in the
herd. This measure is about as unbiased as possible, given
the statistics available, although growing herds will naturally
show lower "productivity" in this sense than stagnant or

TABLE 25

International Comparisons of Yields and
Yield Changes of Four Commodities
For Selected Years
(in Kilograms per hectare)

Product and Country	Average Yield 1952-56	Average Yield 1962-66	Index
Rice			
U.S.A.	3000	4566	152
Japan	4340	5056	116
South Korea	3340	4120	123
Taiwan	2670	3598	135
Thailand	1350	1592	135
Burma	1500	1618	108
Asia	1540	1754	114
World	1820	2036	112
Brazil	1450	1558	107
Rio Grande do Sul	2740	2595	95
Wheat			
France	2170	2998	138
U.S.S.R.	910	1042	115
U.S.A.	1250	1732	139
Argentina	1330	1484	114
Mexico	1100	2286	208
Europe	1620	2154	133
Latin America	1200	1434	120
World	1080	1264	117
Brazil	880	788	90
Rio Grande do Sul	883	773	88

TABLE 25 - Continued

Product and Country	Average Yield 1952-56	Average Yield 1962-66	Index
Soybeans			
U.S.A.	1360	1632	120
Canada	1500	2068	138
Mainland China	800	798	100
World	1460	1662	114
Brazil	1457	1065	73
Rio Grande do Sul	1487	922	62
Corn			
France	2240	3408	152
Hungary	1920	3160	149
Rumania	1280	1922	150
U.S.A.	2650	4288	162
Argentina	1600	1834	115
Mexico	810	1072	132
Europe	1550	2990	159
Latin America	1260	1374	109
World	1700	2212	130
Brazil	1190	1292	109
Rio Grande do Sul	1334	1365	102

Source: All country data, FAO, Production Yearbook, 1967; Brazilian and Rio Grande do Sul data, SEP, Ministry of Agriculture. SEP data is that reported to FAO.

TABLE 26

Yield and Producer Price Trends of Four
Commodities in Rio Grande do Sul

Product		Constant	Time	$\bar{R}^2$	Standard Error of Estimate as Percent of Mean Yield or Price
Rice	Yield =	2,589.0 +	4.286 (.6999)	.000	6.131
	Price =	215.4 +	1.216 (.6441)	.000	17.261
Wheat	Yield =	755.9 -	4.271 (.5494)	.000	28.946
	Price =	247.0 +	.3813 (3.429)[a]	.388	8.148
Soybeans	Yield =	1,394.0 -	14.38 (1.545)	.065	19.862
	Price =	137.5 +	2.668 (2.6908)[b]	.269	12.634
Corn	Yield =	1,342.0 +	2.934 (1.1706)	.018	4.878
	Price =	117.9 -	.4454 (.5630)	.000	14.440

Note: Yields are in kilograms per hectare; prices are in 1967 new cruzeiros per metric ton; inflator is arithmetic mean of wholesale price index excluding coffee and Pôrto Alegre cost of living index. Annual averages, except for wheat where the December-January average was used for 1958-67 and the two-year moving average centered on December-January for 1950-58. Yields are for the period 1947-67; and prices are for the period 1950-67. Figures in parentheses are t ratios.

[a]Significant at the 1 percent level.

[b]Significant at the 2 percent level.

Source: Rice, IRGA, Anuário Estatístico do Arroz, vari-our issues; wheat: prices, official prices, bulk, interior points, including bonuses, yields, SEP, 1947-61, CCLEF, 1962-67; soybeans: yields, INSTISOJA, prices, SEP; corn: prices and yields, SEP.

declining ones. Two weaknesses which it shares with other
measures of herd productivity are as follows: Veal, steer,
and cow meat are considered as homogeneous, and changes
in the quality of meat over time or between countries are not
measured.

By the measure chosen, Rio Grande do Sul and Brazil
performed poorly over the period 1952-56 through 1962-66
compared with some of their principal competitors in the
international beef trade. The data are presented in Table 27.
Major factors affecting productivity statistics are differing
mortality rates, fertility rates, and age of slaughter between
countries and over time.

TABLE 27

International Comparisons of Meat Production
For Selected Years

Beef and Veal Production per Head of Herd	Kilograms per Head		Index
	1952-56	1962-66	
West Germany	66.88	86.04	129
United Kingdom	66.44	74.81	113
U.S.A.	68.09	80.20	118
Argentina	44.33	52.32	118
Australia	44.73	51.79	108
Canada	57.97	66.34	114
Brazil	16.52	14.73	89
Rio Grande do Sul	18.34	15.42	84
(Rio Grande do Sul)	(21.18)	(20.97)	(99)

Source: All countries except Brazil, FAO, Production
Yearbook, 1967; Brazil, SEP, Agricultural Censuses, and
PLANISUL, Table 19; Rio Grande do Sul, SEP; Rio Grande
do Sul in parentheses, PLANISUL and census projections.

It should be noted here that Brazilian beef production statistics are generally recognized as being subject to considerable margins of error. In particular, there is a marked discrepancy between herd size statistics based on agricultural censuses and those made by SEP of the Ministry of Agriculture. Therefore, two independent estimates of meat production per head of Rio Grande do Sul beef herd are provided. The first is based on SEP data, and the second on an interpolation and projection of the annual rate of growth of herd between 1950 and 1960 in agricultural census estimates. The independent production estimates were made by a consulting firm in Pôrto Alegre. [1] This source observed that even these estimates may be on the low side due to the operation of primitive, clandestine slaughterhouses which avoid taxation and sanitary regulations and thus also escape any statistical collection procedures. However, these clandestine operations were prevalent throughout the period, and while they may bias productivity estimates downward, they are unlikely to be responsible for trends in productivity. The SEP estimates indicate a drop in productivity on the order of 15 percent over the period 1952-56 through 1962-66, while the independent estimates show no trend. We believe the independent estimates are a more accurate reflection of reality.

To further test the hypothesis of declining productivity, regressions of meat yield per head of herd on time were run for both series--the SEP data for the years 1950-67 and the independent estimates for 1950-65. The SEP data had a highly significant downtrend at about 1.5 percent a year, while the independent estimates revealed no significant trend. (See Table 28.) These differences probably reflect the alleged overestimates of herd size by the SEP for the later years in the series.

It may be concluded that, even if herd-size figures are somewhat inflated for recent years, productivity in the Rio Grande do Sul beef sector has been stagnant or declining in the postwar period and reflects an absence of technological change. This stagnation occurred in spite of a strong upward trend, on the order of 3 percent per year, in real producer prices for beef cattle over the period 1950-67. This uptrend, however, was marked by cyclical fluctuations of varying amplitude and duration. Both price and yield regressions are presented in Table 28. Other observers confirm this impression of technological stagnation. A comprehensive report published in Pôrto Alegre in 1968 concluded:

TABLE 28

Trends in Meat Production Per Head of Beef Herd
and Producer Prices For Beef Cattle in
Rio Grande do Sul

Price or Productivity Measure	Constant	Time (Values in parentheses are t ratios)	$\bar{R}^2$	Standard Error of Estimate as Percent of mean productivity or price
1. Beef and Veal Production per Head in Beef Herd SEP data, 1950-66 kg/head	19.54	− .2585 (4.827)[a]	.582	5.902
2. Beef and Veal Production per Head in Beef Herd PLANISUL Estimated Production and Herd estimates based on Censi data, 1947-65 kg/head	20.48	+ .0168 (.1648)	.000	8.536
3. INSTICARNE Average Producer Price for Beef, 1967 NCr$ per metric ton. Annual Average of wholesale price index excluding coffee and Pôrto Alegre cost of living index is inflator 1950-67	336.8	+ 12.58 (4.131)[a]	.486	13.850
4. Average Net Price to Producers for Steers, Swift Packing Plant at Rosario, RGS, NCr$ per metric ton. Inflator same as above. 1950-67	269.0	+ 13.12 (3.639)[a]	.419	19.010

[a]Significant at the 1 percent level.

Source: SEP, PLANISUL, INSTICARNE, and the Swift Packing Plant.

> With the exhaustion of the economic frontier, the livestock sector found itself in a clear state of stagnation within the prevailing technological standard. There is only one way out--technological innovation, initiating a new stage in its history, a stage of intensive rather than extensive growth. [2]

There is indeed considerable evidence that the process of extensive growth of agricultural production which appears to have taken place in Rio Grande do Sul in the postwar period had reached its natural limits by the end of the 1960's. As was shown in Chapter 2, the area devoted to pastures fell over the period 1950-60, and this trend may be presumed to have continued as the cropped area expanded further in the 1960's. After reaching a peak of 442,619 hectares in the 1964-65 crops, the area in the state planted to rice did not again reach even 400,000 hectares as of the closing of the decade. It seems that rice area grew close to the limits of water resources of the traditional types. Wheat, soybeans, and corn can expand in area only if natural pasture area declines, and the best lands for these crops are already occupied. The conclusion which can be drawn from this section is that growth prospects via the incorporation of additional land area in Rio Grande do Sul are slim. Given the increasing population of the state, this also implies that without yield-increasing technological change, Rio Grande do Sul is not likely to contribute to the rapid rates of growth of minor agricultural exports which will be required in the 1970's to maintain a rate of growth of total exports consistent with planned rates of growth of GDP. Yield-increasing technological change offers the major opportunity for output increases and for reducing costs of production. Expanded fertilizer use and agricultural research and extension activities are particularly promising in this regard. Fertilizer use in Rio Grande do Sul is examined in Chapter 6. [3] But first, the types of technological changes which actually took place during the postwar period will be examined.

TECHNOLOGICAL CHANGE IN
THE POSTWAR PERIOD

This section presents evidence concerning three types of technological change which have taken place in Rio Grande do Sul during the postwar period--varietal improvement, mechanization, and soil recuperation programs. More detailed analysis of the profitability and extent of fertilizer use is presented in Chapter 6.

Varietal Improvement

This type of technological change, while requiring individual decisions on the part of agricultural entrepreneurs, depends to a large extent on organized and institutionalized activities carried on primarily in the public sector. In the present section, our focus is on the principal accomplishments of these organizations and the rate of adoption of new varieties by farmers.

Rice. Throughout the postwar period, IRGA's Rice Experiment Station has worked to select, and, more recently, to create new rice varieties. IRGA collects statistics on the rice varieties planted, and over time there have been substantial changes not only in the varieties planted, but also in the mix between short-, medium-, and long-grain rices, all of which suggests that producers adopt new varieties if they are available and perceived to be superior to those previously used. Data on the percentage of total area planted to various grain lengths and the average premiums for medium- and long-grain rice as a percentage of the price paid for short-grain rice on the Pôrto Alegre wholesale market for milled rice are presented in Table 29.

Except for the period 1950-54, when yields of short-grain rice were inferior to those of other grain lengths, there was no significant yield advantage for any grain length. Prices for long-grain varieties, however, were at a substantial premium over others at the wholesale level, although this premium seems to have fallen over time as long-grain rice plantings increased. Average producer prices by grain length were not available. The premium for medium- over short-grain rice, on the other hand, was much smaller or nonexistent. The increasing percentage of long-grain rice planted would appear to indicate that farmers responded to price differentials in favor of long-grained varieties.

Another example is provided by the expansion of area planted to variety EEA 404, developed by IRGA's Rice Experiment Station and first planted in significant quantities in 1964. This rice is a medium long-grain variety which appears to yield about 9 percent above the common long-grain variety

TABLE 29

Area Planted to Rice of Various Grain Lengths and Wholesale Price Premiums in Rio Grande do Sul, 1950-67

Years	Percentage of Total Area Planted			Average Wholesale Premium for Milled Rice as a Percent of Short-Grain Prices	
	Short Grain	Medium Grain	Long Grain	Medium Grain	Long Grain
1950-54	63.6	32.8	3.6	3.7	25.2
1955-59	44.7	40.6	11.7	4.5	20.6
1960-64	48.3	30.1	21.4	3.5[a]	12.9[a]
1965-67	37.7	18.1	44.2	1.5	11.2

[a]Four-year average, excluding 1962, which was a highly abnormal year with few transactions on the free market due to government price controls.

Source: Areas planted by grain length, IRGA, Anuário Estatístico do Arroz, Safra 1966-67, for years 1950-66; Lavoura Arrozeira, September-October, 1968, for 1967. Prices, annual averages, Bôlsa de Mercadorias de Pôrto Alegre.

called <u>Agulha</u> on the basis of the first three years' commercial results. However, those who first adopt a new variety
may be more progressive farmers than the average in other
respects, and this yield performance is insufficient to establish the superiority of EEA 404 in commercial plantings. Of
course, many qualities other than yield are important, among
them appearance, milling yield, resistance to shattering, and
precociousness. The data on area planted to EEA 404 is presented in Table 30, which indicates that within three years
after its commercial introduction, the variety accounted for
45.7 percent of long-grain area planted and 21.8 percent of
total area planted.

While this apparent progress is encouraging, two great
deficiencies of the varieties used as of 1968 must be noted.
First, and most important, none of the varieties appears to
be capable of efficiently using high levels of nitrogen fertilization. As stated in Chapter 6, experiments conducted in
1967-68 showed that the best rice variety yet released in Rio
Grande do Sul had a peak response to nitrogen at the level of
40 kilograms per hectare. The semidwarf, stiff-strawed
variety, IR 8, developed at the International Rice Research
Institute in the Philippines, does not peak until 120 kilograms
or more of nitrogen. At this level of fertilization, yields of
6,000 to 10,000 kilograms of rice per hectare have been obtained for a single crop. [4]

Unfortunately, it appears that under Rio Grande do Sul's
climatic conditions, IR 8's growth cycle is too long--on the
order of 175 days versus 135 days for EEA 406--so that the
IR 8 did not reach maturity before it had to be harvested.
In addition, the yield of whole grains was only 43 percent as
compared with 59 percent for EEA 406, and 67.9 percent for
EEA 404, grown under identical conditions, as is shown in
Table 31. Nevertheless, in the future it should be possible
to combine IR 8's fertilizer responsiveness with other desirable characteristics such as precociousness and milling yield,
which would be a major breakthrough in Rio Grande do Sul.

The other major problem, and one which was receiving
attention from both state and federal authorities in 1968, was
the generally poor quality of seed rice used in Rio Grande do
Sul. Most rice used for seed did not meet even rather loose
standards with regard to purity, germination rate, and the
content of red rice and weed seeds.

<u>Wheat.</u> Through 1966, the most common variety of wheat
planted was <u>Frontana</u>, created by the dean of Brazilian wheat

TABLE 30

Area Planted to One Rice Variety in
Rio Grande do Sul, 1965-67

Year of Planting	Area Planted to EEA 404	EEA-404 Area as a Percentage of Area Planted to Long-Grain Rice	EEA-404 Area as a Percentage of Area Planted to All Varieties
1964	3,671	2.9	0.9
1965	25,086	22.0	7.9
1966	70,227	45.7	21.8

Source: IRGA, Anuário Estatístico do Arroz, various issues.

TABLE 31

Average Yields Under High and Low Fertility
Conditions of Three Rice Varieties, 1966-68

Variety	High Fertilization	Low Fertilization
EEA 404	5,241	5,230
EEA 406	5,563	4,084
IR 8	4,765	5,191

Note: High fertilization was defined as the recommendation for a 5,000 kilogram per hectare yield; low fertilization was one half this quantity. Actual quantities of nutrients per hectare were not provided by the source.

Source: "Novas Variedades de Arroz," Lavoura Arro-zeira, November-December, 1968. Yields are two-year averages for four locations in Rio Grande do Sul.

breeders, Iwar Beckman, and first distributed to farmers in
1945. It is resistant to leaf rust but susceptible to several
principal varieties of stem rust.[5] By 1967, this variety had
been overtaken as the leader in area planted in Rio Grande
do Sul by IAS 20 (Iassul), a variety resistant to the strains of
rust prevalent until 1962, but susceptible to some new rust
types. It is an early maturing red wheat with moderate resistance to leaf rust and was first released to farmers in
1963. IAS 20 was created by a team headed by Ady Raul da
Silva working at the Instituto Agronômico do Sul (now known
as IPEAS).[6] In the 1968 harvest, it was discovered that this
variety shatters badly under humid harvest conditions. Table
32 gives an idea of the superiority of IAS 20 over the traditional
variety, Frontana. Over a seven-year period including three
normal, two good, and two bad years for wheat, IAS 20
averaged 37 percent higher yields in tests conducted on experiment stations in Rio Grande do Sul. This advantage was
more marked in the bad years, an average of 84 percent, and
somewhat less pronounced in the good years, an average of
27 percent.

Together with improvements in marketing, the development of rust-resistant wheats in the IAS series was an important factor in the renaissance of Rio Grande do Sul wheat
production after the debacle of repeated harvest failures in
the late 1950's. Table 33 documents the rapid rate of increase
in plantings of IAS 20 over the years since it was introduced.
(Data on areas planted by variety are not available for 1963.)
This rapid rate of adoption is an indication of the success
which has been achieved in the wheat seed production and distribution programs carried out through the wheat cooperatives
formed in the early 1960's. It is worth noting that the superiority of IAS 20 in commercial production fell as its use became
more widespread, as is indicated in Table 32. In view of the
lack of a similar phenomenon in the data from tests conducted
on experiment stations, it is likely that the first adopters of
the new variety were progressive with regard to practices
other than the use of improved varieties.

As in the case of rice, however, none of the wheats
available to Brazilian farmers as of 1968 were capable of
efficiently using heavy nitrogen fertilization. (See Chapter 6.)
This can be attributed to a failure in wheat-research strategy.
Brazilian wheat breeders appear to have devoted more attention to developing varieties which extract the maximum
possible from the generally phosphorous-deficient and acid
soils of the state than in seeking to create varieties which

TABLE 32

Average Experimental and Commercial Yields of
Two Wheat Varieties in Rio Grande do Sul, 1960-66

Year	Conditions	Frontana Experiment Stations	Frontana Commercial Production	IAS 20 Experiment Stations	IAS 20 Commercial Production	Index (Frontana = 100) Experiment Stations	Index (Frontana = 100) Commercial Production
1960	Normal	1,113	--	1,509	--	135.6	--
1961	Bad	365	--	707	--	193.7	--
1962	Good	1,485	--	1,719	--	115.8	--
1963	Bad	460	--	810	--	176.1	--
1964	Good	1,590	834	2,200	1,132	138.4	135.7
1965	Normal	1,100	717	1,510	832	137.3	116.0
1966	Normal	1,220	857	1,580	930	129.5	108.5
Average of normal years		1,144	785	1,533	881	134.0	112.2
Average of bad years		413	--	759	--	183.8	--
Average of good years		1,538	834	1,959	1,132	127.4	135.7
Over-all average, experiment stations 1960-66		1,048	--	1,434	--	136.8	--

Source: 1960-63, IPEAS, Setor de Fitotecnia e Genética; 1964-66, CENTRISUL, Trigo 67, Recomendações de Variedades e Epocas de Plantio (Pelotas, May, 1967).

126

TABLE 33

Area Planted to Two Wheat Varieties in
Rio Grande do Sul, 1964-67

Areas Planted in Hectares	1964	1965	1966	1967
Frontana	173,597	207,748	137,269	101,860
(% of total area)	(63.8)	(63.9)	(40.0)	(20.1)
IAS 20	249	29,988	109,260	254,837
(% of total area)	(0.1)	(9.2)	(31.8)	(52.3)
Total wheat area	271,918	325,391	343,471	487,688

Source: Comissão Central de Levantamento e Fiscalização das Safras Tritícolas, Levantamento das Lavouras
Tritícolas, 1964 and 1965; and Anuário Estatístico do Trigo,
1966 and 1967.

would provide optimum response under conditions of high
fertilization with suitably corrected soils. The latter strategy
was followed with great success in Mexico, and the results
obtained in that country and elsewhere were not unknown to
Brazilian wheat breeders. At the end of the decade of the
1960's, there was some evidence that the Mexican-style
philosophy of research was taking hold in Rio Grande do Sul,
albeit rather late in the day. [7]

Beef. The Rio Grande do Sul herd is composed largely of
European breeds, principally Herefords and Shorthorns,
with lesser numbers of Aberdeen Angus, Devon, and Charo-
lais stock. [8] The genetic quality of the herd is considered
high by both domestic and foreign observers. [9] An FAO-
ECLA publication noted, however, that "no cattle, however
good they may be from a genetic standpoint, can produce high
yields unless they are properly fed and sensibly cared for
and handled."[10]

There has been a rapid rise in the practice of artificial insemination with frozen semen provided by the Artificial Insemination Service of the state's Secretary of Agriculture. The Service was initiated in 1958, and by 1966, the number of inseminations per year had risen steadily to 23,902.[11] It must be remembered, however, that the total herd in Rio Grande do Sul numbered roughly 1.2 to 1.4 million head in 1966. In any event, most observers agree that the principal problem of the beef sector in Rio Grande do Sul is the winter-forage shortage described in Chapter 2 rather than the genetic quality of the herd.

Mechanization

Mechanization is a type of technological change which depends less on organized activities carried out by the public sector than upon the individual decisions of agricultural entrepreneurs. Subsidized credit for the purchase of agricultural machinery or overvalued exchange rates for imports of the same may, of course, affect the speed of adoption, and both have been used for this purpose in Brazil. The consequences of these policies in terms of agricultural employment in some regions of Brazil have received little study.[12]

As in the case of other agricultural statistics, those for mechanization of rice production are the most complete. Table 34 presents data on average horsepower per tractor, number of hectares in rice per tractor, and number of hectares in rice per combine for Rio Grande do Sul rice farms of over 9 hectares during the period 1949-66. It is clear that mechanization of rice production increased throughout this period; the most rapid change took place during the period 1953-60, when exchange rates for agricultural machinery imports were particularly favorable.

IRGA estimates that 60 percent of rice land is ploughed by tractor.[13] For other operations, such as disking, this figure may be considerably higher. For reasons mentioned in Chapter 2, mechanization of the harvest has proceeded much more slowly.

For wheat, some information is available on the years 1962-66 and is summarized in Table 35. The extremely small average size of the nonmechanized farm (4.4 hectares compared with 55.4 for mechanized wheat farms), suggests that mechanization has already proceeded about as far as possible for this crop. The principal regions of the state in

TABLE 34

Mechanization of Rice Production in
Rio Grande do Sul, 1949-66

Year	Horsepower per Tractor	Hectares per Tractor	Hectares per Combine
1949	28.7	152.5	2677
1950	30.6	133.4	2451
1951	31.2	109.9	2144
1952	32.4	97.1	1876
1953	32.8	87.3	1437
1954	33.1	70.7	820
1955	33.7	62.5	677
1956	33.6	61.9	658
1957	33.6	59.3	633
1958	33.6	57.3	611
1959	33.6	54.8	633
1960	33.6	50.4	554
1961	33.6	46.0	475
1962	33.6	45.6	482
1963	39.8	42.7	443
1964	39.8	44.0	509
1965	39.7	40.2	425
1966	39.6	38.6	413

Source: IRGA, Anuário Estatístico do Arroz, various issues. Equipment and area data are for rice farms of over 9 hectares in the rice zone of Rio Grande do Sul.

which wheat area can expand are natural pasturelands where
the mechanized technique, using tractors and self-propelled
combines, is almost universal.

Soil Recuperation Programs

In July, 1966, the first step was taken in a program
which appears destined to make a major impact on agricultural
productivity in Rio Grande do Sul. Alarmed at the low fertility
and progressive exhaustion of the agricultural soils of the
state, graduate students at the Faculty of Agronomy and
Veterinary Science (FAV), of the Federal University of Rio
Grande do Sul (UFRGS), with the cooperation of state and
local authorities, initiated a program of large-scale soil
tests in selected municípios. The program became known as
Operation Armadillo (Operação Tatú), a name inspired by the
digging up of thousands of soil samples in farmers' fields.
In the following year, 2,300 soil samples from Santa Rosa
County were analyzed, and an action program was begun
which involved the application, supervised by specially trained
extension workers, of a package of improved agricultural
practices, with strong emphasis on soil recuperation, and
was financed with medium-term agricultural credit. The
term "soil recuperation" refers to a combination of: (a) correction of soil acidity with lime, and (b) heavy use of chemical
fertilizers, including both "corrective" and subsequent
"maintenance" components. The lime and fertilizer dosages
are individually prescribed on the basis of the soil analyses
carried out on samples taken from each participant's fields
and the nutrient requirements of crops which are to be grown.
The results achieved by the producers--mostly small
colono farmers producing soybeans, corn, and wheat--aroused
exceptional interest both in the Santa Rosa region and elsewhere in the state. By the 1968-69 crop year, there were
nine Operação Tatú programs in operation, with a total 1,249
farmers participating and 3,181 hectares recuperated. By
1969-70, the program had become the State Program for the
Improvement of Soil Fertility and involved six state or federal
organizations plus a large number of local governmental and
producer entities. Detailed plans for involving a total of 3,337
farmers on a total of 8,643 hectares were prepared. [14]
Table 36 shows the dramatic results achieved by a sample
of the farmers participating in the 1968-69 program. For
two of the three crops on which data are available, production

TABLE 35

Mechanization of Wheat Production in
Rio Grande do Sul, 1962-66

	Mechanized	Nonmechanized
Number of establishments	3,777	18,119
(Percent of total)	(17.3)	(82.7)
Hectares planted to wheat	209,321	79,932
(Percent of total)	(72.4)	(27.6)
Average area per establishment, in hectares	55.41	4.41

Source: Comissão Central de Levantamento e Fiscalização das Safras Tritícolas. Figures are averages for total
period, not averages of annual averages.

TABLE 36

Yields Obtained by Farmers Participating in
Operação Tatú Soil-Recuperation
Programs, 1968-69

Crop	Corn	Soybeans	Wheat
Number of producers in sample	41	27	14
Average yield in kilograms per hectare on recuperated land	4,230	2,340	1,700
Average yield on unre- cuperated control land	1,500	1,440	770

Source: Plano Estadual de Melhoramento da Fertilidade
do Solo.

per hectare of recuperated land was more than double that
of untreated control plots on the same farms. Soybean
yields were increased by only 62 percent, in part due to a
drought during a critical part of the soybean growth cycle.
While the fact that participation in the program was voluntary
may have biased results upward, and given that the more
progressive farmers were likely to have enrolled, it should
be noted that control plots were on the same farms. Thus,
the ratio of yields on recuperated and control plots might be
expected to be relatively unbiased.

In a personal communication to the author, Marvin T.
Beatty of the University of Wisconsin Department of Soil
Science, which has been instrumental in developing the
Operação Tatú program via its AID-financed graduate pro-
gram at UFRGS, stated why he believes that the data presented
here are "firm and very favorable."

1.   They come from a large number of farms in 13
      municípios.
2.   They represent actual farm rather than experi-
      mental plot situations.
3.   The farmers could expect to produce 3 to 5 crops
      during the loan period, while one crop will re-
      pay the major share (80 percent or more) of the
      investment at present prices.
4.   More than one kind of crop gives favorable cost/
      benefit ratios at prevailing prices.
5.   Physical yield responses are large enough to be
      dramatic and easily apparent to the farmer and
      his neighbors.
6.   The yield responses show that sufficient techni-
      cal assistance, farmer skill, and responsive
      varieties exist to produce positive results when
      they are properly combined in the package. [15]

It is still too soon to say that such programs have had an
impact on crop yields at the state level. However, the very
substantial impression that they have made at the local level
and the eagerness with which they are being sought by additional municípios suggest that in Rio Grande do Sul, as elsewhere in the world, where financial incentives are combined
with proper technical assistance, major breakthroughs in
agricultural productivity can be obtained.

CONCLUSIONS

In the period 1947-67, such technological change as
occurred in Rio Grande do Sul was not sufficient to result in
any statistically significant increase in land or herd productivity at the state level for the commodities studied. When research institutions have developed superior varieties of wheat
and rice, these have been adopted fairly rapidly, although no
notable breakthroughs have been achieved by researchers.
The results of the soil-recuperation programs initiated toward
the end of the 1960's suggest that most farmers have lacked
sufficient technical knowledge and medium-term credit to
realize the full potential of existing varieties of wheat, corn,
and soybeans through adequate fertilization and correction of
soil acidity. What agricultural credit has been available has
been almost exclusively confined to short-term loans for
financing current production.

Mechanization, on the other hand, has proceeded very
rapidly in wheat, soybean, and rice production, at least on
farms which are large and flat enough to make it economically
attractive.

Continued productivity stagnation in Rio Grande do Sul,
given the exhaustion of possibilities for further extensive expansion of output, could have adverse affects on Brazil's
balance of payments and would thus help to perpetuate a
foreign-exchange constraint on the over-all rate of economic
growth. For example, both the FAO and the Fundação Getúlio
Vargas projections showed Brazil moving from that of a net
exporter to a net importer of beef in the 1970's.[16] Yet, Rio
Grande do Sul is a natural exporter of all of the products
under study except wheat, due to her geographical separation
from the largest consuming areas of Brazil and could certainly make a strong, positive contribution to the balance of
payments if sharp increases in productivity were achieved.

The same FAO report referred to above projected strong
international demand for beef, rice, corn, and fats and oils
over the decade of the 1970's. Although protective policies
in developed countries and rapid increases in production by
traditional major importers of rice could cloud this rather
rosy picture, the outlook for Rio Grande do Sul's export
products is about as favorable as that for any agricultural
commodity traded internationally. Even if international markets do not develop as projected, domestic demand could
absorb large increases in output from Rio Grande do Sul if

productivity increases were not generalized to all major producing states. Improvements in income distribution and a
rapid rate of over-all economic growth would also increase
effective domestic demand for these commodities, given the
low nutritional levels prevailing in large parts of Brazil.

As for wheat, the production of which depends on substantial subsidies, Brazil appears committed to a substantial
increase in domestic output. In fact, the 1969 crop was estimated at over 1 million tons, or more than a 100 percent
increase since 1967. [17] In Chapter 4, it was estimated that
the net cost in domestic resources to save one dollar's worth
of wheat imports via domestic production in 1967 was $2.20.
If Brazil is determined to push ahead with wheat-expansion
plans, it is important that productivity in this crop be raised
and costs lowered; otherwise, a future government, searching
for a way to cut expenditures, is likely to reduce subsidies
to wheat sharply and thus cause severe economic dislocations
and social unrest in the wheat-producing areas. For wheat,
of course, demand is no problem, as over 85 percent of consumption requirements have traditionally been imported.

Increased use of chemical fertilizers and lime, as well
as substantial achievement in the fields of agricultural research and extension, could contribute significantly to raising
productivity and lowering costs. The following chapter
examines the question of fertilizer use in some detail.

NOTES

1.   PLANISUL, "Estudo Econômico Sôbre A Bovinocultura No Rio Grande do Sul" (Pôrto Alegre, July 30, 1968,
mimeographed), p. 72.

2.   Ibid., p. 42, my translation.

3.   I have analyzed the organization and financing of
agricultural research and extension in Rio Grande do Sul in
Chapter 7 of my book, Agricultura, Tecnologia e Comércio
Internacional: Estudos da Realidade Brasileira (Rio de
Janeiro: Editôra APEC, 1971). An earlier and less complete
version of this material in English may be found in my paper
prepared for USAID/Brazil, "Agricultural Modernization in
Rio Grande do Sul, Brazil," May 28, 1969, mimeographed.

4.   International Rice Research Institute, <u>Annual Report</u>, 1966.

5.   Ady Raul da Silva, <u>Melhoramento das Variedades de Trigo Destinadas às Diferentes Regiões do Brasil</u> (Rio de Janeiro: Servico de Informação Agrícola, Ministério da Agricultura, 1966), pp. 16-17.

6.   <u>Ibid</u>. , p. 20.

7.   See, for example, "Ata da II<u>ª</u> Reunião Anual da Cultura do Trigo" (Pelotas, 1968, mimeographed); and John C. McDonald, "Brazil's National Wheat Campaign Begins" (Rio de Janeiro: U.S. Department of Agriculture, Foreign Agricultural Service, November 6, 1969, mimeographed).

8.   Adolfo Antônio Fetter, "Pecuária Bovian de Corte no Rio Grande do Sul, " <u>Lavoura Arrozeira</u> (September-October, 1968), p. 148; and FAO-ECLA, <u>Livestock in Latin America: Status, Problems, and Prospects, Volume II, Brazil</u> (New York: United Nations, 1964), p. 16.

9.   FAO-ECLA, <u>loc. cit.</u>; IPEAS-CENTRISUL, <u>Pastagens na Zona Fronteira do Rio Grande do Sul</u>, Circular No. 32 (Pelotas, February, 1967); and Miguel Cione Pardi and Ruy Brandão Caldas "Plano Nacional de Combate à Febre Aftosa" (Ministério de Agricultura, unpublished typescript, no date, probably 1966 or 1967).

10.   FAO-ECLA, <u>op. cit.</u> , p. 35.

11.   Fetter, <u>op. cit.</u> , p. 49.

12.   For a general discussion of the employment implications of rapid mechanization, see Bruce Johnston and John Cownie, "The Seed-Fertilizer Revolution and Labor Force Absorption, " <u>American Economic Review</u> (September, 1969), 569-82.

13.   IRGA, "Estimativa do Custo de uma Quadra de Arroz, Safra 1967/68" (Pôrto Alegre, January, 1968, mimeographed).

14.   Universidade Federal do Rio Grande do Sul, Facul-
dade de Agronomia e Veterinária, Ministério da Agricultura,
Instituto de Pesquisa e Experimentação Agropecuárias do
Sul, Superentendência da Região Sul, Secretaria dos Negócios
da Agricultura, Instituto Rio Grandense do Arroz, Associação
Sulina de Crédito e Assistência Rural, Plano Estadual de
Melhoramento da Fertilidade do Solo (Pôrto Alegre, 1969).
All data quoted in this section without specific citation were
obtained from this document.

15.   Letter from Professor Marvin T. Beatty, dated
September 3, 1969.

16.   FAO, Agricultural Commodities: Projections for
1975 and 1985, Volume I (Rome: United Nations, 1967); and
Fundação Getúlio Vargas, Projeções de Oferta e Demanda
de Produtos Agrícolas Paro o Brasil (Rio de Janeiro, 1966).

17.   CCLEF, Anuário Estatístico do Trigo, Safra 1967/
68. This publication has semiofficial estimates of the 1968-69
and 1969-70 crops.   On the official commitment to increase
wheat production, see Ministério de Planejamento e Coordenação Geral, Programa Estratégico de Desenvolvimento:
Areas Estratégicas I e II, Agricultura, Abastecimento (Rio
de Janeiro, January, 1968), 73-75.

6

FERTILIZER USE
IN RIO GRANDE DO SUL

There is nothing mysterious about the sources of technological progress in agriculture. Technological progress inevitably implies qualitative changes in inputs used in the production process, either human, or physical, or both. Human changes are the product of educational processes, both formal and informal. Qualitative improvements in physical inputs are, ultimately, the product of research and development activities and are rarely undertaken by farmers themselves in the modern world.

Technological progress in the input-producing industries, even when it does not lead to qualitatively better inputs for agriculture, may reduce the price of previously existing inputs and thus induce price-responsive farmers to use them in greater quantities. Strictly speaking, this is not technological change in the agricultural sector; rather, it is a movement along a production function in response to a factor-price change. In the real world, the result of radical factor-price changes is often to stimulate learning processes, which means technological change. An example is a fall in fertilizer prices which may stimulate farmers to undertake soil analyses and learn how to use fertilizers scientifically. There is nothing about factor-price changes which compels such learning processes, at least in the shortrun, and especially in economies which are protected from outside competition by natural barriers and/or by conscious policy.

---

*Unless specific major nutrients are referred to, in the discussion which follows, the term "fertilizer" is understood to include lime for the neutralization of excess soil acidity.

In most cases, a higher level of agricultural technology
requires higher levels of skills within the agricultural sector
and greater support from outside that sector, defined narrowly
as those economic units involved in the production of agricultural commodities. A higher level of technology normally
means increasing control by the agricultural producer over
his natural environment. The higher the stage of development,
the greater the degree to which the uncertainty normally
associated with agriculture is removed. This refers principally to output or yield uncertainty, although individual farmers
can reduce the impact of price uncertainty by constructing
storage facilities and by learning how to take full advantage
of existing marketing facilities.

The natural fertility of the soil and climatic conditions
become less important, and manufactured inputs more so.
For example, the creation of semidwarf, stiff-strawed,
photoperiod-insensitive varieties of rice and wheat which are
resistant to many diseases and capable of efficiently utilizing
large doses of chemical fertilizers for the formation of grain
rather than straw is probably the most dramatic accomplish-
ment of modern agricultural science. Together with the
pronounced fall in the cost of nitrogenous fertilizers which
has occurred due to technological breakthroughs in the synthesis and transportation of ammonia, it is the heart of the
agricultural revolution which was transforming the world
grain outlook in the late 1960's. Here is a case where a new
input (in this case, better seeds), makes more efficient use
of an existing input (nitrogenous fertilizer), than did previously
existing varieties; thus, there is an increasing demand for
nitrogen even at unchanged prices. The profitability of the
fertilizer-responsive varieties is further enhanced by the fall
in nitrogen prices. To the extent that disease resistance is
also bred into the seeds, a source of yield uncertainty is
removed. Higher yields per unit of land may also render
economic the use of additional manufactured inputs such as
pesticides, weed killers, and the like.

THE CASE FOR INCREASING FERTILIZER USE

A strong case can be made for using fertilizer as a
"leading edge" in the process of agricultural modernization
in Rio Grande do Sul, even though fertilizer-intensive grain
varieties suitable to the region have not yet been developed.

The arguments presented here are probably also valid for
many other areas of Brazil and indeed elsewhere in the
developing world.

Profitability. Even without special subsidies and with the
use of presently available varieties of rice, wheat, soybeans,
corn, and forages, fertilization rates substantially in excess
of the averages which appear to have prevailed in the 1960's
are highly profitable for a fairly wide range of commodity
and nutrient prices. Evidence to show that this is so is presented below.

Rate of Adoption. A package of improved practices, of which
scientific fertilization based on soil tests is the principal
element, usually results in a quantum jump in output which
becomes highly visible in a short period of time and thus has
a pronounced demonstration effect upon neighboring farmers
and facilitates very rapid adoption. The readily apparent
effects of scientific fertilization stimulate farmer interest in
other modern technology and thus help to shift him off the
traditional production function. Some evidence to support
these statements in the case of Rio Grande do Sul was presented in Chapter 5.

Scale Neutrality. Fertilizer is an input which is scale neutral,
that is, the fertilizer response of crops is independent of the
size of the agricultural enterprise employing the new technology. Its use can benefit small farmers as well as large.
Thus, it might be called a "democratic" innovation.

Outmigration of Agricultural Labor. Unlike the introduction
of mechanization, which may have the undesirable side effect
of stimulating the migration of agricultural labor to already
overcrowded cities where employment opportunities for un-
skilled (with regard to manufacturing or service industries)
persons are limited, fertilizer use increases labor requirements per hectare even while decreasing the labor/output
coefficient. This is because more labor is required to apply
the fertilizer, and the increased output also results in the
use of more labor in the harvesting process if mechanization
of the harvest is not simultaneously introduced where it is
not already present. Of course, increased fertilizer may
contribute indirectly to the mechanization process through
increasing profits in the agricultural sector and thus facilitate
the purchase of tractors and combines. But compared, for

example, with the often suggested (largely by tractor companies) policy of subsidizing tractor purchase, expenditures
on the promotion of increased fertilizer use are far less likely
to create unemployment.[1]

Topography Neutrality. Fertilizer response does not appear
to depend on the topography of the land on which the nutrients
are applied, at least within reasonable limits. In Rio Grande
do Sul, the great majority of family farms are relatively
small and are located in hilly terrain where soil fertility was
initially higher than in the flat or gently rolling natural pasture
areas. However, yields have decreased as the natural fertility
was exhausted. Thus, this is a point with important social
and political implications. Such areas do not lend themselves
to intensive mechanization. In the absence of soil-recuperation
programs, they would eventually be abandoned. Owners would
either migrate to the cities, to the now virtually exhausted
agricultural frontier in western Santa Caterina, Paraná, or
still further to Goiás, Mato Grosso, or even Paraguay in
search of virgin lands where they would repeat the traditional
process which is best described as "soil mining."[2] During
recent years, both rural-urban and rural-rural migration
from these colonial areas have become increasingly common,
as agricultural frontier land in Rio Grande do Sul no longer
exists in significant quantities. Such movements pose problems typical of declining areas in all countries—the existing
social infrastructure deteriorates, and investments in similar
facilities must be made in the new areas. In Brazil, at the
end of the 1960's the agricultural frontier was so far from
major consuming centers that the export of surplus production
was rendered very precarious due to high transport costs.

Relative Crop Neutrality. Fertilizer is a relatively crop
neutral input—most crops in Rio Grande do Sul will respond
significantly to fertilization, although it must be admitted
that the intensity of the effects differs somewhat between crops.
The principal point here is that a decision to spur fertilizer
use does not directly imply a decision to push one crop at the
expense of others. More specifically, it does not mean favoring the import substitute, wheat, at the expense of export
products such as rice, soybeans, and beef. The relative
stimulus to different products will depend on their relative
responsiveness to nutrient applications, given any price
structure, and this is subject to change as new varieties, with
differing capacities to utilize fertilizer, are developed.

In view of these considerations, it is clear that fertilizer can play a central role in the process of technological change in agriculture. It is the critical element in moving from an extractive activity to a modern agriculture dependent on manufactured inputs for an increased output.

This chapter deals with past and potential fertilizer use in Rio Grande do Sul. The first section examines the available evidence concerning the profitability of fertilizer use with the varieties of rice, wheat, and corn available in Rio Grande do Sul in the late 1960's. The second section analyzes the past demand for fertilizer in the state and includes evidence on the responsiveness of farmers to shortrun changes in nutrient to crop-price ratios. In the third section, the question of what determined fertilizer prices during the period 1955-67 is taken up, and the potential for future reductions in fertilizer prices to farmers is examined. The final section makes use of the results presented earlier in the chapter to project future demand for fertilizers under alternative assumptions concerning prices to farmers and achievements in plant-breeding programs.

THE PROFITABILITY OF FERTILIZER USE

Optimal fertilization rates for any specific agricultural product and locality depend on nutrient-to-product price ratios, the natural fertility of the soil, the response capacities of varieties planted, tenancy conditions, the availability of capital, and, in the presence of capital constraints and/or interaction effect, the prices of other factors such as land, labor, pesticides, and agricultural machinery.

The analysis which follows is based on fertilizer-response functions estimated from experiments carried out in the late 1960's in Rio Grande do Sul, most of them on private farms rather than in experiment stations. The rice fertilization experiments were conducted as part of a joint project between IRGA's Estação Experimental do Arroz and FAV/UFRGS, with technical assistance from the University of Wisconsin. They were conducted in thirteen locations throughout the rice region of Rio Grande do Sul during the 1967-68 crop year and used the variety EEA 406. The wheat and corn experiments were conducted by FAV/UFRGS in cooperation with the Secretaria de Agricultura and the Convênio UFRGS-University of Wisconsin, in the 1966-67 crop year for wheat at five

locations in the northern plateau wheat region, using the
variety C-3 Cotiporã, and at four locations in 1965-66 and
1966-67 for corn, using an unspecified variety.

We were able to obtain data for only one or, at the most,
two years, and the trials were conducted with only one variety
for each crop. Therefore, although the results are generalized to the entire period for which fertilizer consumption
estimates are available, it would be an error to place great
confidence on the accuracy of the coefficients estimated.

Furthermore, the fertilization trials on which the response
functions are based leave much to be desired in the matter of
experimental design, so far as the determination of economically optimum fertilization levels is concerned. Nevertheless,
we believe that the general order of magnitude, especially for
the nitrogen coefficients, is correct.

The methodology adopted can be applied to give a much
more accurate analysis once additional fertilization experiments specifically designed for this purpose have been carried
out in a large number of locations. Similarly, scientific
sampling methods could be applied to the problem of determining actual fertilization rates by crop and region and would
thus allow more accurate comparisons between economically
optimal and observed applications.

The technique used to estimate fertilizer response was
multiple regression analysis, using quadratic terms for nutrients applied at more than one nonzero level in multi-location
experiments. The basic model was of the following form:

$$Y = a_1 L_1 + a_2 L_2 + \ldots a_m L_m + b_1 N + b_2 P \qquad (1)$$
$$+ b_3 K + b_4 C + b_5 T + b_6 N^2 + b_7 P^2 + b_8 K^2 + u$$

where

Y = yield in kg/ha

$L_1 \ldots L_m$ = dummy variables for each of m locations set
equal to unity if the observation was at that
location, and zero if it was not

N = nitrogen applied in kg/ha

P = P_2O_5 applied in kg/ha

K = K_2O applied in kg/ha

C = dummy variable for lime application equal to
one if lime was applied, and zero otherwise

T = dummy variable for trace elements set equal to
unity if trace elements were applied, and zero
otherwise.

Interaction terms were included in some regressions run, but in no case did they have significant coefficients. This is likely to be a problem caused by experimental design and/or insufficient geographical dispersion of experiments, as nitrogen-phosphorous interactions have been found in some cases for experiments conducted in other countries. Much work of this kind conducted recently in India, however, showed a lack of nitrogen-phosphorous interactions.[3] Observations at all locations, and in the case of corn, crop years, were pooled. Dummy variables for each location were used to give independent estimates of the intercept. Thus, the influence of differences in natural soil fertility and other factors which may have systematically influenced the level of yields between locations was reduced. Where more than one repetition of a given treatment was made at any location, the mean for all repetitions was used as the treatment observation for that location to avoid singularity of the $X'X$ matrix.

Had there been a greater number of fertilization levels at each location, a preferable method of statewide aggregation would have been the estimation of separate functions for each region, defined in terms of soil types and other agronomic criteria to be as homogeneous as possible, and then combined into an average function for the state, using as weights the arable land area in each region. Separate functions for different locations were estimated in the case of wheat, where sufficient degrees of freedom were available.

No lime was applied, nor was there more than one non-zero potassium level, in the rice experiments. Therefore, the C and K^2 variables were not included for this crop. Two lime levels were included in some wheat experiments, so an additional dummy variable was included for lime in the aggregate wheat-response function and set equal to one if the extra lime was applied, and zero otherwise.

The estimated response functions, together with the t ratios of their coefficients, are reported in Table 37. The coefficients for the dummy variables representing separate locations are not given here, although they were always statistically significant, and differed considerably. Figures 5, 6, and 7 are graphs of the nitrogen and phosphorous-response functions for rice, wheat, and corn, derived from the regression results.

In general, the five following observations can be made concerning the functions estimated. First, for all three crops, there are statistically significant diminishing returns to nitrogen applications. The estimated-yield curve turns

TABLE 37

Coefficients from Fertilizer Response Functions for Rice, Wheat, and Corn in Rio Grande do Sul

Rice, irrigated
13 locations
130 observations
$\bar{R}^2 = .9907$

$$20.39N + 12.63P + 1.446K + 54.78T - .2537N^2 - .0752P^2$$
$$(2.123)[a] \quad (1.496) \quad (.8602) \quad (.4041) \quad (2.399)[a] \quad (.9594)$$

Wheat
5 locations
184 observations
$\bar{R}^2 = .9806$

$$5.610N + 6.025P + .3197K + 233.7C_1 + 64.71C_2 - 17.85T - .0360N^2 - .0156P^2 - .0015K^2$$
$$(5.243)[b] \quad (10.53)[b] \quad (.5586) \quad (6.659)[b] \quad (2.629)[b] \quad (.3828) \quad (3.985)[b] \quad (5.133)[b] \quad (.5070)$$

Corn
4 locations
92 observations
$\bar{R}^2$ .9859

$$19.29N + 5.422P + .7085K + 461.10_1 + 7.673T - .0865N^2 - .0187P^2 - .0013K^2$$
$$(5.661)[b] \quad (1.346) \quad (.1346) \quad (4.066)[b] \quad (.0333) \quad (2.650)[b] \quad (.5735) \quad (.0241)$$

Note: Location variables not reported. Values in parenthesis are t ratios.
[a]Significant at greater than the 5 percent level
[b]Significant at greater than the 1 percent level

FIGURE 5

Nitrogen and Phosphorous Response Curves for Irrigated EEA-406
Rice in Rio Grande do Sul, 1967-68

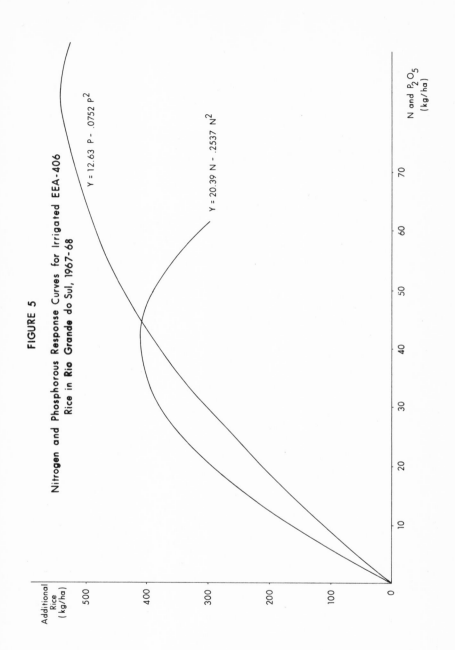

$$Y = 12.63\ P - .0752\ P^2$$

$$Y = 20.39\ N - .2537\ N^2$$

Additional
Rice
(kg/ha)

N and P_2O_5
(kg/ha)

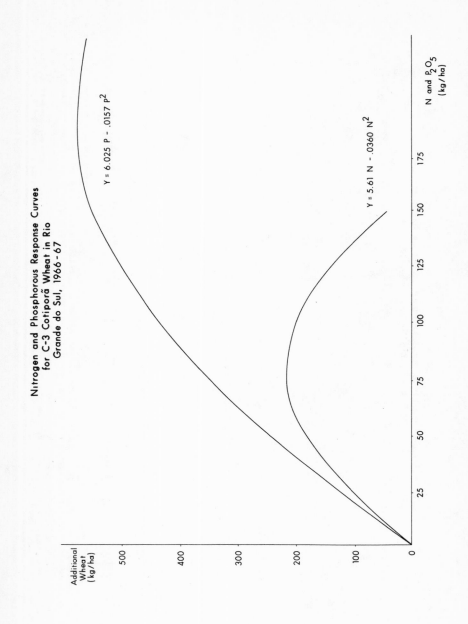

Nitrogen and Phosphorous Response Curves
for C-3 Cotiporã Wheat in Rio
Grande do Sul, 1966-67

$Y = 6.025 \, P - .0157 \, P^2$

$Y = 5.61 \, N - .0360 \, N^2$

Additional
Wheat
(kg/ha)

N and P_2O_5
(kg/ha)

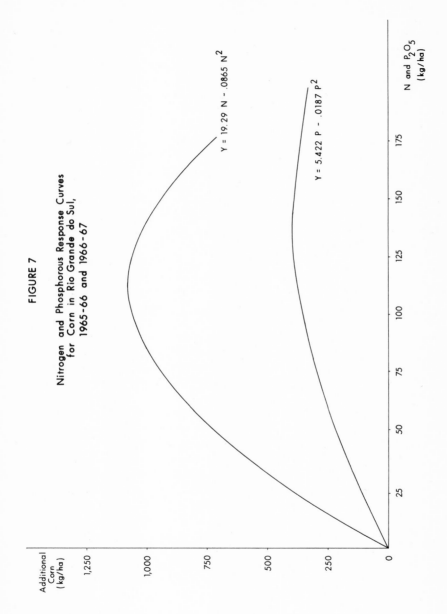

FIGURE 7

Nitrogen and Phosphorous Response Curves
for Corn in Rio Grande do Sul,
1965-66 and 1966-67

$Y = 19.29 \, N - .0865 \, N^2$

$Y = 5.422 \, P - .0187 \, P^2$

N and P_2O_5
(kg/ha)

Additional
Corn
(kg/ha)

1,250

1,000

750

500

250

0

25   50   75   100   125   150   175

147

down for wheat, however, at much lower additional yields and higher nitrogen levels than in the case of rice or corn.

For the purpose of comparison, Figure 8 presents the nitrogen-response curve for wheat in Rio Grande do Sul and two curves obtained from Indian experiments with Mexican wheats developed at the International Maize and Wheat Improvement Center. The lower of the two Indian curves was fitted by B. S. Minhas and T. N. Srinivassan to data from the 1964-65 All-India Wheat Trials.[4] The higher curve was constructed by taking the average coefficients from response curves for the same wheat, Lerma Rojo, fitted to data from seven separate locations in the 1966-67 All-India Coordinated Wheat Trials by Ralph W. Cummings, Jr., Robert W. Herdt, and S. K. Ray.[5] Figure 9 presents a comparison of nitrogen-response curves of IR 8, a photoperiod-insensitive, stiff-strawed rice developed at the International Rice Research Institute in the Philippines with EEA 406, the best variety yet developed by IRGA's experimental rice station as of 1968. Data on IR 8 are for the rainy season at the Maligaya Rice Research and Training Station in the Philippines. Nitrogen response in the sunnier dry season was considerably greater.[6]

These curves are a graphic demonstration of the fact that Rio Grande do Sul wheat and rice breeders have not yet enjoyed much success in creating varieties capable of using nitrogen efficiently. In international comparisons of response functions, however, care must be taken in interpretation. The response functions estimated in this chapter are for all major nutrients, lime, and trace elements simultaneously. Those most commonly reported, for example in India and the Philippines, are for nitrogen alone. It may be assumed that all other nutrients were supplied in fairly high dosages. This latter approach eliminates some of the multicollinearity problems arising from poorly designed experiments which use multiple levels of all elements, although such problems are, to a considerable extent, avoidable if the experiment is properly planned. Adequate finance may also be a factor. However, it would certainly tend to overestimate the response to nitrogen to the extent that there is any interaction between nutrients.

Another problem in comparisons of fertilizer response from different experiments concerns the extent of use of pesticides, weeding, and other special care which may influence the yield. Most of the Rio Grande do Sul data were obtained from experiments laid out in corners of farmers' fields rather than in experiment stations, whereas data from India and the Philippines were from experiment stations. This is likely

FIGURE 8

Comparison of Nitrogen Response of Lerma Rojo Wheat in India
with C-3 Cotiporã Wheat in Rio Grande do Sul

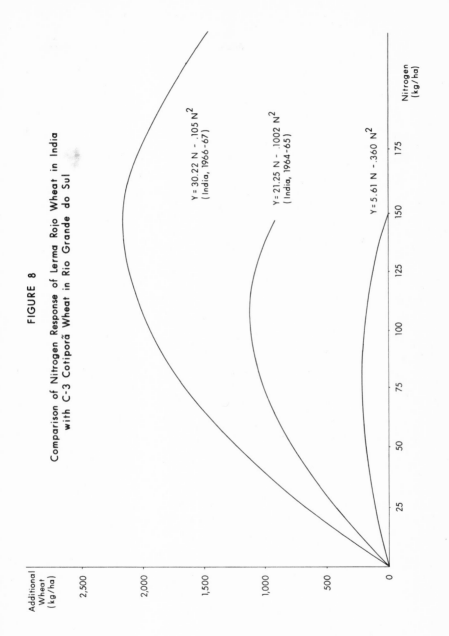

$Y = 30.22 \, N - .105 \, N^2$
(India, 1966-67)

$Y = 21.25 \, N - .1002 \, N^2$
(India, 1964-65)

$Y = 5.61 \, N - .360 \, N^2$

Nitrogen
(kg/ha)

Additional
Wheat
(kg/ha)

2,500

2,000

1,500

1,000

500

0

25   50   75   100   125   150   175

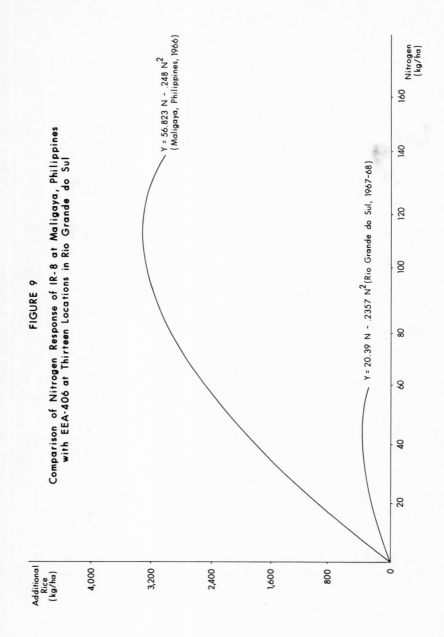

FIGURE 9

Comparison of Nitrogen Response of IR-8 at Maligaya, Philippines
with EEA-406 at Thirteen Locations in Rio Grande do Sul

$Y = 56.823 \ N - .248 \ N^2$
(Maligaya, Philippines, 1966)

$Y = 20.39 \ N - .2357 \ N^2$ (Rio Grande do Sul, 1967-68)

Additional
Rice
(kg/ha)

4,000

3,200

2,400

1,600

800

0   20   40   60   80   100   120   140   160

Nitrogen
(kg/ha)

150

to result in higher yields, ceteris paribus, in India. Nevertheless, at least the nitrogen terms for wheat and rice seem
to be consistent with results obtained for traditional varieties
(those not bred for fertilizer response) in other parts of the
world, that is, declining yields above about 40 to 50 kilograms
of nitrogen per hectare due to lodging.

Second, the curves for P_2O_5 show much less pronounced
diminishing returns over the range of nutrient levels studied.
The level of significance for phosphorous coefficients was
much lower than that for nitrogen in the case of rice and corn.
For corn, this appears to be due to the selection of atypical
locations for experiments. According to a statewide study
conducted in 1967, available phosphorous in 74 percent of the
samples tested was rated as "very low," and another 12 percent were classified as "low." Only 10 percent had "good"
ratings.[7] The corn experiments were conducted in areas with
high amounts of naturally available phosphorous. For rice,
multicollinearity between the N and P terms ($r_{N.P}$ = .881) due
to an unfortunate experimental design may be part of the explanation, but the results are nevertheless perplexing in view
of the reported heavy use of phosphorous in rice culture and
generally high yields obtained in the rice-fertilization trials.
On the other hand, in the wheat trials, both the P and P^2 terms
were highly significant in the aggregate function as well as
for four separate functions estimated for specific locations.

Third, in no case was a significant response to potash
observed, except in one location for wheat, and there the
influence was negative. This suggests that the value of potassic
fertilizers is low in Rio Grande do Sul for these crops under
present fertility conditions. As yields are pushed higher
through more intensive use of other fertilizers and improved
varieties, more potassium may be withdrawn from the soil.
Thus, in the future potash fertilization may well become profitable. This evidence would appear to support the findings of
the above-cited survey that 70 percent of the soils tested
throughout the state had "good" or "medium" levels of available
potassium.[8]

Fourth, the lime response of wheat and corn is highly
significant. There are diminishing returns to applications
above the levels recommended by the State Secretary of Agriculture, so far as wheat is concerned. With corn, no conclusions can be reached as to the value of additional liming, as
only one lime level was employed in the experiments.

And fifth, under present conditions, the addition of trace
elements does not appear to be necessary in Rio Grande do Sul.

In no case was the response for any crop significantly different
from zero. As in the case of potassium, this situation could
change in the future.

By using the response functions estimated, it is possible
to calculate average optimum fertilization levels subject to
the reservations discussed above. In particular, it should be
pointed out that the aggregate functions are not designed to
make specific recommendations for any one area, but rather,
to give some idea of the average response throughout the state.
The objective is to compare realized fertilizer consumption
under the price conditions which prevailed in the past. It
must be acknowledged that this is a partial equilibrium approach
to a complex problem in general equilibrium with dynamic
elements.

The lack of significant interaction between nutrients makes
it possible to estimate optimum fertilization levels for nitrogen and phosphorous separately, although if significant interaction had been found, optimum levels of all nutrients could
be established by the solution of a set of simultaneous equations. Optimum phosphorous levels for corn were not estimated in view of the atypical locations at which the experiments
were conducted. For rice, the coefficients obtained in the
aggregate-response function were used because, while not
significant, they appeared to be reasonable in magnitude in
the opinion of agronomists consulted. Since potash did not
appear to have any positive influence on the output of the crops
studied, potassic fertilization was not analyzed.

Given no capital constraints, the optimum nitrogen and
phosphorous applications can be determined by setting the
partial derivatives of the response functions, with respect to
each of these nutrients, equal to the ratio of nutrient to expected product prices, and solving the resulting linear equations independently. This method amounts to assuming that
variable costs associated with fertilizer use are negligible
and that the farmer either owns his land or pays a rent which
does not vary with output. If variable costs associated with
fertilizer use are proportional to output, say some fraction
v of the value of output, and a system of sharecropping exists
in which the landlord does not make any contribution to cultivation costs, a general expression for the optimum nutrient
application from the view of the tenant, x*, is given by the
following:

$$x^* = \frac{(1 - v - s)b - R}{2(1 - v - s)c} \qquad (2)$$

where the response function is of the form $a + bx - cx^2$, s is
the fraction of output paid to the landlord, and R is the ratio
of delivered nutrient to expected farmgate-product prices.
This expression was obtained by differentiating a profit function
with respect to nutrient application. More explicitly,
  profit = gross returns - costs

$$= (a + bx - cx^2)P_c - F - P_x x - (v + s)P_c (a + bx - cx^2) \quad (3)$$

where P_c is the expected price for the commodity being
fertilized, P_x is the price of fertilizer for payment at harvest
time (including interest charges over the growing season),
and F is fixed costs associated with cultivation. Setting the
partial derivative of this function with respect to x equal to
zero, rearranging, and dividing through by P_c, and calling
R the ratio of nutrient to expected product prices, the expression given above may be derived. If the landlord pays the
same share of fertilizer costs as he receives of the output,
the expression for x* becomes:

$$\frac{(1 - v - s)b - R + sR}{2c(1 - v - s)} \quad (4)$$

and if the landlord also pays the same proportion of all
variable expenses associated with fertilizer use as he receives
in output, the optimal fertilization level from the point of view
of the tenant becomes:

$$\frac{(1 - v + vs - s)b - R + sR}{2c(1 - v + vs - s)} \quad (5)$$

    Using equation (2) and the response functions estimated,
the optimal fertilizer application may be found for alternative
values of v, s, and R. Of course, this method collapses into
that described above when both v and s equal zero. In any
case, the optimum fertilization rates obtained are those which
equate marginal costs of fertilizer application to the tenant
with marginal returns to the tenant evaluated at the expected
sales price. Under Brazilian conditions (rapid inflation), care
must be taken to price the nutrient and the product at the same
point in time. The best means of doing this is to include four
or five months of credit charges in the prices of the fertilizers.
    Two limiting assumptions concerning the formation of
producer commodity price expectations are investigated. The
first, a pessimistic one, is that farmers expect the prices
which prevailed in the last harvest to continue. This will be
called the one-period hindsight assumption. The second
assumption is that the farmer accurately predicts the average
producer price for the current crop year. This may be called
the perfect-foresight assumption. The numerator of the price
ratio is the same in either case. To test the sensitivity of the

optimum fertilization rates to differing hypotheses concerning price-expectations formation, the optimizations are carried out for $s + v = 0$ and for $s + v = 0.3$.

For the years 1967, 1965, and 1960, Table 38 gives the delivered nutrient to product price ratios (R) and optimum fertilizer-application rates for rice, wheat, and corn under four combinations of price-expectations formation assumptions and values of $s + v$. The years chosen bracket a wide range of R values. The year with the highest nutrient-to-product price ratios in the 1960's was 1965; 1960 had the lowest average R values (it was the last year of subsidized exchange rates for fertilizer imports), and 1967 occupied a middle ground in this respect. Fertilizer prices include interest charges and estimated average transportation costs to interior points in the state. Nitrogen is priced in the form of ammonium sulphate; phosphorous prices are simple averages of prices for P_2O_5 in the form of triple superphosphate, normal superphosphate, and ground phosphate rock (hiperfosfato). The potash price is for K_2O in the form of potassium chloride. [9] Product prices are the best available estimates of prices actually received by producers. [10]

Estimated optimum fertilization levels for each crop under the assumption that the R prevailing in 1968 were to be reduced by 25 percent are also included in Table 38. The table indicates that the optimum nitrogen level for wheat is quite sensitive to R, s, and v in the range investigated. Only if the wheat grower has accurately forecast the producers' price and been free of the sharecropping system and/or heavy variable costs associated with the use of fertilizer (neither application expenses nor harvest costs are likely to increase proportionately with output when production is fully mechanized), would it have been profitable to apply nitrogen in all three years. This is likely to be part of the explanation for the low consumption of nitrogen in Rio Grande do Sul in spite of highly subsidized wheat prices. Even with no marginal, variable costs associated with nitrogen use and no unfavorable sharecropping arrangements, the use of nitrogen is uneconomic at values of R above 5.61. This statement applies, of course, only to varieties of wheat available as of 1968, which were extremely inefficient users of nitrogen.

Nitrogen/corn price ratios have been more favorable to nitrogen use (although fertilization of corn is rare in Rio Grande do Sul), and in the case of rice it would require an R value of 14.27 to make nitrogen use unprofitable even with $s + v$ equal to 0.3. Thus, even under the most unfavorable price ratio, tenancy conditions, and variable-price assumptions analyzed (R = 10.58, s + v = 0.3), it still would have been profitable to use 10.4 kilograms of nitrogen per hectare. This is because the nitrogen-response curve for rice, while it presents sharply negative returns above 40 kilograms per hectare, rises steeply in the region from zero to about 30 kilograms per hectare. (See Figure 5.)

It was much more generally profitable to use phosphorous for wheat and rice over the values of R, s, and v tested. Corn did not show phosphorous response for the reasons given above. This suggests that the observed predominance of phosphatic fertilizers in aggregate consumption has a firm agronomic and economic rationale.

The question remains why potash is used at all, given the absence of significant response in any of the functions fitted for any crop. In part, it may be explained by the relatively low price of this nutrient and the lack of technical sophistication on the part of farmers who may tend to buy "nutrients" as an aggregate based on the average price for all nutrients in a blend rather than the specific ones required for the soil and crops involved. It is also likely, however, that the experimental design or the location of the experiments was a factor.

The relatively high nitrogen applications indicated for corn are significant in view of the fact that fertilizers are known to be relatively little used in the production of this crop in Rio Grande do Sul. This supports the experience of participants in Operação Tatú. (See Chapter 5.) As mentioned above, phosphorous fertilization was found to be quite profitable in most locations in spite of the experimental results for the trials used to calculate response functions.

Table 39 compares the actual imports of nitrogen and phosphorous for all crops in the same three years (1967, 1965, and 1960), with the estimated optimal consumption of fertilizers for rice and wheat alone under four combinations of assumptions regarding price-expectation formation and values of s + v. Estimates of optimum consumption were derived by multiplying the optimum applications by the area actually planted in each crop in the years indicated. Estimated optimal consumption for these two crops alone is compared with total imports, and because some fraction of the latter surely was used for other crops, on this count the estimate is the highest possible assumption with regard to the level of fertilization of rice and wheat.

Furthermore, Table 39 indicates, on the perfect-foresight

TABLE 38

Optimum Fertilizer Applications for Rice,
Wheat, and corn in Rio Grande do Sul,
Selected Years
(in kilograms per hectare)

Crop	Year	F^a s+v=0	H^b s+v=0	F^a s+v=0.3	H^b s+v=0.3	R^c
			Opimum Nitrogen Application			
Rice	1967	30.5	28.40	26.2	23.3	4.95 F
						5.98 H
Wheat	1967	17.2	5.30	0.0	0.0	4.37 F
						4.89 H
Corn	1967	47.4	42.80	19.9	13.4	11.09 F
						11.88 H
Rice	1965	26.4	19.30	20.5	10.4	7.00 F
						10.58 H
Wheat	1965	9.2	0.00	0.0	0.0	4.95 F
						5.74 H
Corn	1965	28.7	0.00	0.0	0.0	14.33 F
						19.36 H
Rice	1960	33.0	31.82	29.9	28.2	3.65 F
						4.24 H
Wheat	1960	43.1	32.10	28.1	12.4	2.51 F
						3.30 H
Corn	1960	79.0	68.00	65.2	49.4	5.61 F
						7.52 H
Rice, 25 percent[d]		34.8	-	32.7	-	2.66
Wheat, 25 percent[d]		44.2	-	29.7	-	2.43
Corn, 25 percent[d]		77.1	-	62.3	-	5.96

TABLE 38 - Continued

| Crop | Year | Optimum Phosphorous (P_2O_5) Applications | | | | R^c |
		F^a s+v=0	H^b s+v=0	F^a s+v=0.3	H^b s+v=0.3	
Rice	1967	67.4	63.9	60.3	55.3	2.49 F
						3.02 H
Wheat	1967	122.0	108.2	72.0	5.8	2.64 F
						4.09 H
Rice	1965	59.1	46.4	48.4	30.4	3.73 F
						5.64 H
Wheat	1965	108.1	76.0	25.0	0.0	3.65 F
						4.67 H
Rice	1960	69.5	67.2	63.3	60.0	2.17 F
						2.52 H
Wheat	1960	144.9	85.8	125.0	92.1	1.48 F
						2.20 H
Rice, 25 percent[d]		73.1	-	68.5	-	1.63
Wheat, 25 percent[d]		144.9	-	110.4	-	1.80

[a]Perfect foresight hypothesis concerning price expectation formation. F indicates current crop year commodity price in denominator.

[b]One period hindsight hypothesis concerning price expectation formation. H indicates previous crop year commodity price in denominator.

[c]Ratio of delivered nutrient price to expected producers commodity price.

[d]Percentage lower R than in 1968.

assumption regarding farmers' price-expectations formation, in the absence of unfavorable sharecropping arrangements, with variable costs associated with fertilization assumed to be zero, and further assuming that all fertilizer was used on these two crops alone, that consumption of both nitrogen and phosphorous for wheat and rice was suboptimal in all three years, but that the degree of suboptimality had fallen notably since 1960. Roughly the same pattern of decline in suboptimality in more recent years is found under the alternative assumptions regarding R, s, and v, except that in 1967, nitrogen consumption was actually in excess of optimal for the cases of $s + v = 0.3$ under both price-expectations formation assumptions. Only under the most extreme assumption (hindsight and $s + v = 0.3$), was consumption of phosphorous "excessive" using this estimating procedure. This was true for both phosphorous and nitrogen in 1965 as well as for phosphorous alone in 1967.

The much greater suboptimality observed in 1960 as opposed to 1967, in spite of more favorable price ratios in the earlier year, is an indication that changes in factors other than price were important in increasing fertilizer consumption since 1960. Among the factors responsible for the improvement over time, probably the most important were the increase in agricultural credit granted by the Bank of Brazil, the development of a strong system of wheat cooperatives with elements of a built-in extension system, and the longer-run learning effect. In the years since 1965, falling real-fertilizer prices were probably also significant in accelerating the learning process.

Unfortunately, there is no disaggregated data on costs and returns in the Operação Tatú programs. However, from the aggregate data for 1968, the cost of corrective liming and corrective-plus-maintenance fertilization worked out to NCr$363 per hectare. At 1968 prices, the average value of the increase in yields for recuperated land was NCr$357 for wheat, 343 for corn, and 246 for soybeans.[11] To calculate the returns on the investment more accurately, it would be necessary to have data on the cost of maintenance fertilization and product prices for at least three more years, as the corrective liming and fertilization would be effective for at least that long.

It is the opinion of research workers in the field of soil science that the correction of soil acidity through liming is one of the practices which could make the most substantial contributions to increasing agricultural productivity in

TABLE 39

Comparison of Estimated Optimum Nutrient
Consumption for Wheat and Rice With Observed
Total Nutrient Imports of Nitrogen and
Phosphorous in Rio Grande do Sul, Selected Years

	1967	1965	1960
Rice area[a]	383,328	352,285	358,150
Wheat area[b]	536,456	357,930	470,555
Nitrogen imports[c]	13,089	5,981	6,481
Phosphorous imports[c]	51,485	21,555	24,395

R and s + v	1967		1965		1960	
Assumptions[d]	N*	P_2O_5*	N*	P_2O_5*	N*	P_2O_5*
F 0.0	20,919	91,284	12,593	59,512	32,400	93,075
	(160)	(177)	(211)	(276)	(500)	(381)
H 0.0	13,730	82,539	6,799	43,549	26,501	64,441
	(105)	(160)	(114)	(202)	(409)	(264)
F .3	10,043	61,740	7,222	25,999	23,931	81,490
	(77)	(120)	(121)	(121)	(369)	(334)
H .3	8,932	24,309	3,664	10,709	15,935	43,338
	(68)	(47)	(61)	(50)	(246)	(178)

[a]Area is for crop planted in given year, in hectares.
[b]In hectares. Also see Source below.
[c]In metric tons.
[d]F is perfect-foresight price expectations formation
assumption, and H is one-period hindsight price expectations
formation assumption; s + v is the sum of share of crop paid
to landlord and ratio of variable costs associated with fertilizer
use to crop value.

*Optimum consumption in metric tons calculated from
fertilizer response functions given in table 37, assuming
profit maximization by farmers operating under conditions
specified, considering only the area under wheat and rice as
specified in footnote a. Figure in parentheses is optimum
consumption as a percent of observed imports.

Source: Rice area for 1967 from Lavoura Arrozeira,
November-December, 1968; 1965 and 1960 data from IRGA,
Anuário Estatístico do Arroz, Volume 23. Wheat areas for
[1967 and 1965 from CCLEF, Anuário Estatístico do Trigo,
Safra 1966-67, increased by 10 percent to include estimate
of unregistered area; 1960 area from SEP, reduced by 50
percent.]

Rio Grande do Sul. In the following paragraphs, the profitability of investments in lime, often alleged to be low in
view of the rather high prices prevailing for this input in
Rio Grande do Sul, is investigated by using the response
functions estimated above.

The price of lime varies considerably within the state
due to the heavy influence of transport costs for this item.
Unfortunately, most of the known lime deposits are located
in the central depression or southern portions of the state,
while lime is needed most in the northern and southern plateau
regions. Irrigated rice, which is the predominant crop in the
central depression and the litoral, does not appear to require
soil correction because the pH rises when the lands are flooded
for irrigation.

In June, 1968, lime prices were running from NCr$30 to
NCr$37 in the wheat and corn areas in the north of the state.
The price was taken as NCr$35 for purposes of calculations.
Assuming six months' interest charges at 2.5 percent per
month, the price at the first harvest after application (i.e.,
for payment six months after purchase), is roughly NCr$40
per metric ton. This was equivalent to about $10 at the ex-
change rates of early 1969. The average price of lime in the
United States as of December 15, 1967 was $5.18 per ton,
which is equivalent to $5.71 per metric ton. The U.S. price
includes spreading, whereas that for Rio Grande do Sul does
not.

For the purpose of calculating the present value of investments in lime, it is assumed that the estimated 1968 crop
prices are maintained in future years at the same real levels,
and that an extremely high real discount rate of 25 percent is
used to find the present value of the future benefits of lime
investments. Only one crop per year is assumed to be grown
on the land, a very conservative assumption for wheat land,
which is often also used for soybeans, as described in Chapter
2. Soybeans are one of the crops which most benefit from the
neutralization of excess soil acidity. The effect of lime is
considered to last, undiminished, for four years. Given these
assumptions, is the present value of output increases attributable to lime greater than its costs, all evaluated in terms
of prices at the time of first harvest?

This question will be asked for wheat at the specific
locations of Chapada and Giruá, and for corn in the aggregate-
response function. Due to the form of the wheat experiments,
it is not as easy to interpret the aggregate lime coefficients
for this crop--recommended (and applied) lime treatments
varied according to the soil at each location.

Wheat at Giruá was as follows:
>Cost: 2 tons of lime per hectare at NCr$40 per ton
>= NCr$80
>Additional output due to lime: 309.9 kilograms per
>hectare for four years (t ratio on this coefficient was
>6.958)
>Product price: NCr$383 per metric ton, bulk,
>interior points
>Present value of increased output for four years:
>   NCr$118.69+ 94.95 + 75.96+ 60.77 = 350.37

The investment can pay for itself in the first year. An additional three tons of lime would cost NCr$120 and produce an in-
crement of 153.6 kilograms of wheat per year per hectare for
a December, 1968, value of NCr$173. This additional invest-
ment would pay for itself within three years. However, the
coefficient in the response function for the second lime application is significant only at the 25 percent level, so this result
must be considered uncertain.

Wheat at Chapada was as follows:
>Cost: 2.5 tons of lime at NCr$40 per ton = NCr$100
>Additional output due to lime: 94.64 kilograms (t
>ratio of this coefficient was 3.144, significant at the
>1 percent level), for four years
>Product price: NCr$383 per metric ton, bulk,
>interior points
>Present value of increased output for four years:
>   NCr$36.24 + 28.99 + 23.19 + 18.55 = 106.97

The investment is just barely profitable with a discount rate
of 25 percent. An additional 5 tons of lime produces an
additional yield of 101.6 kilograms of wheat per year. This
investment would clearly not be profitable at any positive discount rate, given the assumption made as to the life of the
investment.

Corn, with aggregate results for Giruá, Santo Angelo,
Guiaba, and Santa Rosa, was as follows:
>Cost: 4 tons of lime at NCr$40 per ton = NCr$160
>Additional output due to lime: 461.1 kilograms per
>hectare (t ratio for this coefficient was 4.066, signi-
>ficant at the 1 percent level), for four years
>Product price: NCr$125 per metric ton
>Present value of increased output for four years:
>   NCr$57.63 + 46.11 + 36.88 + 29.50 = NCr$170

The investment is just profitable with a discount rate of 25 percent. The conclusions which may be drawn from this exercise, assuming that the yield increases due to lime are roughly representative of the lime response for these crops in Rio Grande do Sul, are first, that the admittedly high price of lime in itself cannot be responsible for the low lime consumption said to prevail, and second, it does not appear to be necessary to use subsidized interest rates to stimulate investment in lime. The Bank of Brazil is understandably hesitant to grant long- and medium-term agricultural credit at rates of interest which are negative in real terms. It would appear, however, that moderate real rates of interest could be charged for three- or four-year loans and still leave an ample margin of profitability for investments in lime.

In the discussion to this point, beef has not received any attention. Nevertheless, fertilizer and lime are among the most important costs in the formation of artificial pastures. Table 40 compares the output and rate of return achieved on artificial and natural pastures in an experiment conducted at the IPEAS experimental ranch, Cinco Cruzes, at Bagé. The exact method by which the returns were calculated is unclear, but estimated to be 30-35 percent on artificial pastures compared with 3.5-5.0 percent on natural pastures.

In February, 1967, the costs for forming one hectare of artificial pasture of ryegrass, white clover, and cornichão of the type used in the Bagé experiments were those reported in Table 41. These costs included depreciation on equipment. Steers were selling at $374 per metric ton live weight at Rosário during the "harvest" extending from March through June, 1967, and prices are generally higher in the period between harvests. At these prices, an annual gain per hectare of 403 kilograms, which was achieved in the Cinco Cruzes experiments, would more than pay the cost of pasture formation in one year and leave sufficient margin to pay transport expenses by truck to the packing plant. Of course, this calculation leaves out expenses for normal operations of a ranch. Personnel at Cinco Cruzes assert that the artificial pastures in which these experimental results were obtained were in better condition in 1968 than when they were first used, back in 1961. Only small additions of phosphorous were required at two-year intervals. Proper management of artificial pastures requires the learning of new techniques which differ considerably from those used in the traditional, extensive system.

Most Rio Grande do Sul soils require liming to correct soil acidity as well as fertilizer to achieve the best results.

TABLE 40

Comparative Productivity of Natural and Artificial Pasture
in Fattening Newly Weaned Steers, Bagé, Rio Grande do Sul

Productivity Measure	Pasture Artificial	Natural
Age at slaughter in months	24	54
Months from weaning to slaughter	15	45
Gain in live weight per head	252	312
Gain in live weight per year, per hectare	403	48
Return on investment, in percent	30-35	3.5-5

Source: IPEAS-CENTRISUL, Pastagens Na Zona Fronteira do Rio Grande do Sul, Circular No. 32, February, 1967.

TABLE 41

Costs of Forming One Hectare of Artificial Pasture
at Bagé, Rio Grande do Sul, February, 1967

Item	NCr$	Percent of Total Cost
Ploughing	15.29	11.6
Disking	22.94	17.4
Sowing	6.64	5.0
Seeds	34.00	25.8
Fertilizer	35.10	26.6
Distribution of Fertilizer	.75	.6
Miscellaneous	17.21	13.0
Total	131.93	100.0

Source: IPEAS-CENTRISUL, Pastagens NA Zona Fronteira do Rio Grande do Sul, Circular No. 32, February, 1967.
The exchange rate in February, 1967, was NCr$2.7 per U.S.
dollar.

In a detailed examination of the profitability of fertilized, artificial pastures planted in rotation with rice, one study found an annual profit on investment of 28 percent.[12] This study was meticulous in including such costs as liming, additional fencing for better control of grazing, and a number of others which appear to have been omitted in the experimental data from the Cinco Cruzes experiments. To obtain the most favorable results, the pastures must be carefully managed and the cattle sold in the between-harvest period (entresafra) when prices are highest.

THE DEMAND FOR FERTILIZER

In this section, the factors influencing fertilizer demand in Rio Grande do Sul over the period 1955-67 are analyzed. In particular, evidence concerning farmers' reactions to changes in expected nutrient-to-crop price ratios is sought, because changes in fertilizer and (in the case of wheat) commodity prices were one of the principal tools of agricultural policy during the period being studied. The exchange system was used to subsidize fertilizer consumption, especially in the years 1956-61, when the average fertilizer rate was below even the effective rates for beef, rice, soybeans, and corn. At the very end of the period, subsidized credit was also used, and all interest and service charges on many fertilizer loans were paid by special fund.

There are no data on fertilizer consumption disaggregated by major plant nutrients for Rio Grande do Sul. To estimate total annual consumption, imports of major nutrients (N, P_2O_5, and K_2O) were calculated from disaggregated import data for Rio Grande do Sul ports for the period 1955-67 by using standard coefficients to convert each fertilizer compound into nutrient equivalents. The resulting time series are presented in Table 42. This method of estimating total consumption has two principal sources of error: Some nutrients may enter the state by land, or by coastal shipping from other points in Brazil, thereby escaping inclusion in the import statistics, and nutrients imported in a given year may not necessarily be consumed in the same year.

With regard to the first possible source of error, overland shipments were minimal, and so far as we have been able to determine, imports via coastal shipping were negligible. Phosphate fertilizers are produced in Rio Grande do Sul, but the phosphate rock containing all the phosphorous in such fertilizers is imported. The second problem may be more serious, particularly since abrupt changes in exchange rates may have been anticipated by importers and may have resulted in abnormal import patterns. Since monthly data on fertilizer imports were not available, it was not possible to correct for this. At any rate, the two principal selling seasons for fertilizer are April-June and August-October, the first being for wheat, the second for rice and other summer crops. To avoid holding expensive stocks, it is normal for importers to schedule imports only a few months ahead of expected sales. This would place the normal import pattern squarely within the calendar year for the crops planted (but not necessarily harvested) during that year.

Table 42 shows that apparent consumption of the major nutrients increased strikingly over the period 1955-68. (All 1968 data are for January through September, as fertilizer imports are normally concentrated in this period.) There are no data available on lime consumption or production. Almost all lime consumed in Rio Grande do Sul is produced within the state. The average annual compound rate of growth was 15.6 percent for nitrogen, 7.1 percent for P_2O_5, and 11.4 percent for K_2O. These figures conceal the unevenness of the growth. For all nutrients, imports increased very rapidly in the period 1955-58 and then declined until 1962, although only in the case of P_2O_5 were the imports for that year lower than in 1955. With the exception of a brief lapse in 1964, imports of each nutrient increased steadily, starting in 1963, and the increases were particularly sharp in 1967 and 1968.

Even in 1968, apparent consumption of nutrients per hectare of arable land (not including pastures) was very low in comparison with that prevailing in European and high-productivity Asian countries, as is shown in Table 43. Phosphorous consumption in Rio Grande do Sul is high relative to that of other major nutrients, particularly nitrogen. This fact is probably explained by the following: (a) the low phosphorous content of most Rio Grande do Sul soils, (b) the existence of a protected, domestic phosphate industry, (c) the high price of nitrogen relative to other nutrients, (d) the lack of technical sophistication of Rio Grande do Sul farmers, and (e) the relatively low capacity of currently available wheat and rice varieties to support high nitrogen applications without lodging. Nevertheless, Rio Grande do Sul consumption of fertilizers per hectare of arable land is second only to São Paulo, and from 50 to 200 percent above Brazilian averages, depending on the nutrient.

TABLE 42

Imports of Major Nutrients, Rio Grande do Sul,
1955-68

Year	N Metric tons	N Index[a]	P$_2$O$_5$ Metric tons	P$_2$O$_5$ Index[a]	K$_2$O Metric tons	K$_2$O Index[a]
1955	2,534	100	22,721	100	6,396	100
1956	5,391	213	32,184	142	6,840	107
1957	7,671	303	38,468	169	15,688	245
1958	8,693	343	41,476	183	15,755	246
1959	6,371	251	21,354	94	8,873	139
1960	6,481	256	24,395	107	13,110	205
1961	6,285	248	16,816	74	9,578	150
1962	5,889	232	16,565	73	9,324	146
1963	7,562	298	32,084	141	12,904	202
1964	5,874	231	20,068	88	8,691	136
1965	5,981	236	21,555	95	11,701	183
1966	7,213	285	16,661	73	11,046	173
1967	13,089	517	51,485	227	17,529	274
1968[b]	16,674	658	55,294	243	25,928	405

[a]1955 equals 100.
[b]January-September.

Source: Calculated from detailed import data for ports
of Pôrto Alegre and Rio Grande, SEEF, Ministério da Fazenda,
Rio de Janeiro, using standard nutrient content coefficients.

TABLE 43

International Fertilizer Consumption Per Hectare
of Arable Land

Country*	N	P_2O_5	K_2O
Belgium	130.42	135.28	173.30
West Germany	95.06	95.72	143.30
United Kingdom	79.51	61.85	57.95
Denmark	55.62	46.01	67.20
France	41.31	59.73	46.55
Ireland	23.46	88.43	70.84
Greece	34.06	26.13	3.84
Italy	26.38	26.17	8.90
Spain	17.68	15.15	4.43
East Germany	79.66	67.08	109.39
Hungary	29.67	19.67	11.37
Poland	24.65	20.66	25.26
U.S.S.R.	7.67	5.60	6.19
United States	22.56	17.88	13.86
Japan	120.59	84.78	96.44
Taiwan	156.11	41.23	40.65
South Korea	76.79	64.91	18.17
India	3.15	0.91	0.39
U.A.R.	97.53	16.14	0.34
Cuba	34.52	38.07	25.38
Mexico	11.13	2.17	0.29
Rio Grande do Sul	4.09	13.58	3.68
Brazil	2.05	4.10	2.56

*Data for all countries, given in kilograms per hectare,
are for 1964-65. Data for Rio Grande do Sul and Brazil are
1968 estimates.

Source: FAO, Fertilizers: An Annual Review of World
Production, Consumption and Trade, 1966 (Rome, 1967),
except Brazil, estimated from January-September imports,
estimated domestic production, estimated October-December
imports, and results of 1960 agricultural census.

Aggregate apparent-consumption figures do not permit meaningful evaluations of the degree to which economic optimality has been approached in fertilizer-application rates. As noted in the previous section, optimum fertilization rates depend on a number of economic and physical variables.

In Rio Grande do Sul, there are no time series available for nutrient consumption by crop, much less by location. However, according to all reports available, the vast majority of fertilizer consumed in the state is used on wheat and rice. Because it was impossible to separate out consumption of nutrients for any single crop with any accuracy, it was decided to assume that all nutrients imported in a given year were used in the same year for the wheat and rice crops planted the same year. It was the consensus of the fertilizer-marketing personnel with whom we spoke in Pòrto Alegre and also in the interior of the state that relatively small amounts of fertilizer were used on other crops, particularly until the mid-1960's. Mechanized soybean producers often rely on the residual effect of wheat fertilization, planting the soybeans immediately after the wheat harvest. Only in the last few years of the period did colono producers begin to fertilize soybeans and corn. As explained in Chapter 4, the wheat area is a very dubious statistic, but the same area estimates presented there and in Chapter 2 are used here. Table 44 gives the estimated per hectare consumption of major nutrients for land under wheat and rice for the period 1955-67.

The simplest possible model for explaining fertilizer consumption is to assume that farmers use each nutrient in fixed proportions, that the percentage of area in each crop using fertilizer has not changed over time, and finally, that approximately the same dosages are used for wheat and rice. It turns out that roughly 50 to 60 percent of the variance in nutrient imports can be explained by this model, expressed mathematically as follows:

$$N_t = a_o + a_1 A_t + u_t \tag{6}$$

where

N_t = imports of a given nutrient in year t

A_t = the sum of wheat and rice area planted in year t

u_t = random-disturbance term.

If time trends are included for nitrogen and potash, $\bar{R}^2$'s rise and Durbin-Watson statistics move into the range indicating no significant autocorrelation of residuals. The time trend may pick up the effect of declining nitrogen and potassium prices (they have declined significantly over the time period

TABLE 44

Apparent Nutrient Consumption Per Hectare of Land Under
Rice and Wheat in Rio Grande do Sul, 1955-68

Year	N^a	Index[b]	$P_2O_5{}^a$	Index[b]	K_2O^a	Index[b]
1955	3.2	100	29.1	100	8.2	100
1956	8.5	266	51.0	175	8.8	107
1957	10.1	316	50.5	174	20.6	251
1958	9.4	294	44.8	154	17.0	207
1959	7.7	241	25.8	89	10.7	130
1960	7.8	244	29.4	101	15.8	193
1961	8.3	259	22.3	77	12.7	155
1962	9.6	300	26.9	92	15.1	184
1963	11.1	347	46.4	159	18.7	228
1964	7.9	247	27.1	93	11.7	143
1965	8.4	263	30.4	104	16.5	201
1966	9.8	306	22.7	78	15.2	185
1967	14.2	444	56.0	192	19.0	232
1968	15.2	475	50.3	173	23.6	288

[a]Data in kilograms per hectare.
[b]1955 equals 100.

Source: Rice area, IRGA, Anuário Estatístico do
Arroz, Volume 23, 1955-66; Lavoura Arrozeira (November-
December, 1968) for 1967; and IRGA estimate for Wheat area,
SEP data reduced by 50 percent, 1955-61; CCLEF data plus
10 percent, 1962-68, 1968 preliminary estimate. For ap-
parent fertilizer consumption, see Table 42, above.

covered) and associated learning on the part of farmers, but
it should be noted that there have not been significant trends
in the ratio of delivered nitrogen, phosphorous, or potassium
prices to rice and wheat prices. The regressions for the
simple model are presented below.

$$\text{Nitrogen} = -8,875 + 17.39 \text{ A} + 364.8 \text{ T} \quad R^{-2} = .750 \quad DW = 1.503$$
$$\phantom{\text{Nitrogen} = -8,875 +}(4.358) \quad\quad (2.984)$$

$$P_2O_5 = -28,161 + 73.06 \text{ A} \quad\quad\quad\quad R^{-2} = .485 \quad DW = 1.682$$
$$(3.642)$$

$$K_2O = -12,909 + 28.61 \text{ A} + 369.0 \text{ T} \quad R^{-2} = .689 \quad DW = 1.946$$
$$(4.341) \quad\quad (1.828)$$

Nutrients are in metric tons, area in thousands of hectares,
and the figures in parentheses are t ratios of the coefficients.

The ratios of nutrient to wheat and rice prices were used
as independent variables to explain nutrient imports per hectare
of land under wheat and rice, alone, with a time trend, and
in a distributed lag-adjustment model. Three different assumptions were made concerning the denominators of these price
ratios, the expected producer price: (a) that the farmer
accurately predicted the price he would receive for his wheat
or rice at harvest; (b) that he made his prediction pessimisti-
cally, assuming that he would receive the same money price
as in the harvest prior to planting with no correction for inflation; and (c) that he accurately forecasted the rate of inflation, applying the appropriate correction factor to the price
received in the last harvest to make his estimate of the price
he would receive for the crop he was planting. Nutrient
prices used included interest charges for payment at the time
of harvest and thus brought the numerator and denominator of
the ratio to approximately the same point in time. Nutrient
prices included estimated average transport costs to the farm
from Pôrto Alegre basing points. The basic price was for
nitrogen in the form of ammonium sulphate, phosphorous in
a mixture of three equal parts of triple superphosphate, normal superphosphate, and ground phosphate rock, and potassium
in the form of potassium chloride. Estimated transport costs
included the cost of transporting inert materials associated
with the nutrients in the specified forms. Base prices were
the annual average of monthly prices prevailing for deferred
payment in Pôrto Alegre as collected by IRGA and published
in Lavoura Arrozeira. In no case did the price ratio variables
contribute significantly to the explanation of variance.

These somewhat surprising results must be interpreted
with care. None of the statistical series used is flawless --in

fact, all of them involve assumptions. For example, on the price side, it may be that the prices used were not the relevant ones; in other words, the farmer may not buy "nutrients" (the effective part of fertilizer), but rather "fertilizer" in some vaguer sense. While it is possible to price the nutrient content of mixed fertilizers quite accurately by using regression analysis, or, more crudely, by calculating the equivalent price for the same nutrients in straight form, it is possible that the farmers did not make even the cruder calculations. Furthermore, the absence of fertilizer-consumption estimates by crop forces the aggregation of wheat and rice area and the exclusion of other crops. The absence of significant price variables may be evidence that farmers' decisionmaking does not vary from year to year so as to pick up annual changes in output and fertilizer-price configurations. Favorable ratios may well have to be sustained for several years to obtain significant farmer response.

Returning to the question of time trends, it may well be that part of the significant uptrend in consumption of nitrogen and potash per hectare in the absence of any trend in any of the formulations of price ratios may be explained by the spread of fertilizer use to crops other than rice and wheat. In the last years of the series, soybeans, Irish potatoes, and even corn received some fertilizer, although it is impossible to say how much. At any rate, the analysis would appear to cast some doubt on the efficacy of stimulating fertilizer sales by shortrun price manipulations.

In 1967, a program under which interest charges and associated bank costs on fertilizer loans for food crops to be financed by a special fund was established as part of a program linked to a fertilizer loan to the Central Bank of Brazil by AID. This fund is the Fundo de Estímulo Financeiro ao Uso de Fertilizantes e Suplementos Minerais (FUNFERTIL). Inspection of the time series on nutrient imports per hectare of wheat and rice land suggested that the FUNFERTIL program and associated efforts to stimulate fertilizer consumption may have caused a significant increase in nutrient consumption in 1967 and 1968. A similar program under an earlier loan was operative in 1965 and possibly part of 1966. To test the significance of the apparent increases, four different dummy variables were set up with zeros for all years except (a) 1965-68, (b) 1966-68, (c) 1967-68, and (d) 1965 and 1967. As was suspected, the best results were obtained with variable c. The years 1955-68 for all nutrients are as follows:

$$N = 8.490 + 6.204 \, D \qquad \bar{R}^2 = .578 \qquad DW = 1.279$$
$$ (15.69) \ (4.332)$$
$$P_2O_5 = 33.86 + 19.26 \, D \qquad \bar{R}^2 = .266 \qquad DW = 1.504$$
$$ (11.10) \ (2.388)$$
$$K_2O = 14.40 + 6.901 \, D \qquad \bar{R}^2 = .290 \qquad DW = 1.993$$
$$ (13.86) \ (2.511)$$

The dependent variables are measured in kilograms of nutrient imports per hectare. In no case did the introduction of a linear time trend contribute significantly to the explanation of variance. Thus, it would appear that there was a significant (at the 5 percent level for P_2O_5 and K_2O and at the 1 percent level for nitrogen) improvement in the last two years, although it is unlikely that any single program, such as FUNFERTIL, is entirely responsible for this phenomenon.

Turning now to the statistics on fertilizer use on rice farms over nine hectares in size, some additional results may be obtained. This data are for total fertilizer consumption, including inert materials, with no average analysis specified. If one is willing to use only nonprice variables, a time series covering the years 1949-66 is available. The first notable fact is that a single, independent variable, the total area planted to rice on farms over nine hectares in the rice zone of Rio Grande do Sul, explains over 88 percent of the variance in the series on total fertilizer consumption on such farms. This statistic probably overestimates the influence of area alone, since there is a simple correlation of 0.868 between the area series and time, and strong evidence that the rice area which is fertilized has been rising over time, while the amount of fertilizer used per unit of rice land fertilized has not shown any significant trend. If time is included along with area planted to rice to explain total fertilizer consumption on rice, the $\bar{R}^2$ rises to 0.945. The relevant regressions are given below; values in parentheses are t ratios.

Total fertilizer used on rice (thousands of metric tons)	=	-17.55 0.2166 A (11.45)	$\bar{R}^2$ = 0.945 DW = 1.843
	=	-0.7247 1.070 T 0.1180 A (4.334) (4.503)	$\bar{R}^2$ = 0.945 DW = 1.583
Fertilizer per hectare planted to rice (kilograms)	=	120.0 3.167 T (7.414)	$\bar{R}^2$ = 0.760 DW = 1.628
Fertilizer per hectare fertilized (kilograms)	=	273.9 0.6409 T (1.362)	$\bar{R}^2$ = 0.048 DW = 1.571

Price data were available to investigate the influence of price on fertilizer consumption per hectare fertilized and per hectare planted to rice, but only for the period 1955-66. Fertilizer prices were estimated by taking a geometric, weighted average of prices for N, P_2O_5, and K_2O, using as weights the ratio of each nutrient to total nutrients in the "average mixture" sold by a major fertilizer distributor in the summer of 1967. The mixture was 4-21-7 (percentages by total weight of N, P_2O_5, and K_2O, respectively. The prices for individual nutrients were the same used for analyzing the data on nutrient imports. The weighted geometric average fertilizer price was divided by each of the three estimated expected rice prices in the same manner as described above.

No significant relationship between fertilizer consumption per hectare and fertilizer to expected rice price ratios was found. However, when fertilizer consumption per hectare planted to rice was the dependent variable, an elasticity of -0.378 to the ratio of fertilizer prices to rice prices for the crop actually fertilized (perfect-foresight hypothesis) was found, but this elasticity was significant only at the 10 percent level. There was also a small but highly significant time trend. When the trend term was not included, the price ratio was not significant. For neither of the other two formulations of the price ratio was any significant relationship found.

Log fertilizer consumption
per hectare in rice
(kilograms) $= 5.062 -0.3779 \text{ Log R } 0.01686 \text{ T}$
                                              $(2.015) \qquad (3.324)$
$\bar{R}^2 = 0.472 \qquad DW = 2.495$

In view of the relatively low level of significance of the price-ratio term, not too much weight can be attached to the elasticity obtained. It would appear to indicate that a larger proportion of rice area was fertilized in years when the price ratio was lower, but in conjunction with the finding of no significant effect on the intensity of fertilizer use on the land actually fertilized, it would seem that farmers did not adjust the intensity of fertilizer use on the basis of year-to-year price changes. The adjustment model was tried, but neither the lagged consumption per hectare planted nor any version of the price ratio had significant coefficients.

THE PRICE OF FERTILIZER

This section examines some of the factors which have influenced the price of fertilizers in Rio Grande do Sul from 1955 through 1967 and the prospects for significant reductions in fertilizer prices to farmers in the early 1970's.

Given that virtually all major plant nutrients consumed in Rio Grande do Sul are imported, the price of a ton of any specified fertilizer compound may be expressed as follows:

$$P_f = \left[P_{cif}R(1+i) + U \right] (1+M) + T \tag{7}$$

where

P_f = price in NCr\$ per ton to farmer in the interior

P_{cif} = c.i.f. price in dollars in Rio Grande do Sul ports

R = the cruzeiro/dollar exchange rate

i = interest charges

U = port and handling charges

M = the transformation and distribution margin, including bagging if the product is not already bagged, blending if blending is performed, distribution costs, and the profits on all these operations

T = transport costs from factory or warehouse in the port to application point in the interior.

Tariffs were not imposed on fertilizer imports to Rio Grande do Sul in practice over the period studied. In what follows, several of the variables entering into the above equation are considered in some detail.

International Transport Costs

A comparison of the f.o.b. and c.i.f. values of fertilizers imported through Rio Grande do Sul ports in 1967 showed that transportation and insurance charges ran from 13.8 to 42.8 percent of the c.i.f. value in Pôrto Alegre, with an average of 24.1 percent for nitrogenous fertilizers, 17.7 percent for phosphatics (including diammonium phosphate), and 21.2 percent for potassics.[13] These charges are substantial, but virtually unavoidable, except by importing more relatively high analysis fertilizers. This would be the simplest method of reducing the burden. In fact, here has been a trend toward the importation of more urea (45 percent nitrogen), diammonium phosphate (18 percent nitrogen, 46 percent P_2O_5), triple

superphosphate (46 percent P_2O_5), and potassium chloride
(60 percent K_2O), and less fertilizers with lower nutrient
content, such as sodium nitrate (15 percent nitrogen), ammonium sulphate (20.5 percent nitrogen), Thomas slag (18 percent
P_2O_5), normal superphosphate (20 percent P_2O_5), and potassium
sulphate (49 percent K_2O). This trend could be encouraged by
financial incentives to importers.

Even if nitrogenous and phosphatic fertilizers were to be
produced in Rio Grande do Sul, the raw materials would have
to be imported. In the case of phosphatics, the production
process is a weight-reducing rather than weight-augmenting
one because phosphate rock contains about 34 percent P_2O_5
as opposed to 46 percent for triple superphosphate. Since
potassic fertilizers are really products of the mining industry,
and workable deposits have not been discovered in Rio Grande
do Sul or Brazil, the only possible saving on transport costs
by local production would be for nitrogenous fertilizers.

However, if nitrogenous fertilizers are to be produced
from scratch, that is, including the production of ammonia
from naptha (natural gas, the cheapest raw material for
ammonia synthesis, is not available in Rio Grande do Sul),
the minimum size for the economic centrifugal process is in
the neighborhood of 160,000 tons per year of nitrogen, or
over ten times the June-September, 1968, imports. The upper
range in plant size is about 400,000 tons a year. These two
sizes represented the extremes available within the engineer-
ing state of the art in 1969. In moving from the 160,000-ton
to the 400,000-ton plant, investment costs rise considerably
less than proportionally with capacity. But the really large
returns to scale are achieved with the switch from recipro-
cating to centrifugal compressors, which becomes possible
at the 160,000-ton per year level.

Returns to scale also exist in the production of sulphuric
acid, the principal raw material other than phosphate rock
for the production of phosphatic fertilizers, and in the production of diammonium phosphate. It is, however, really the
size of the ammonia production facility which puts a lower
limit on the size of an integrated plant with any chance of
competing on an economic basis with imports. [14]

Thus, if it is desired to produce ammonia within Rio
Grande do Sul rather than to import it, the development of
160,000 tons per year of nitrogen demand would be the target.
However, even if the demand existed, such a plant would have
to be based on naptha rather than natural gas as the feedstock,
which would put it at a considerable disadvantage compared to

plants of equal size located in Venezuela or Chile. A recent
study on industrial integration within the Latin American Free
Trade Area indicated that Brazil could be supplied most economically from one of these locations. [15]

This study, which was based on an analysis of returns to
scale and transport costs, showed that Venezuela had a small,
absolute-cost advantage over other producers, followed closely
by Chile, in supplying the Brazilian market with nitrogenous
fertilizers. Both Venezuela and Chile suffer from high-cost
structures which unfavorably affect their capacities to export
and ability to compete with lower-cost Latin American producers in many manufacturing industries other than those
based on their particular natural-resource endowments--in
the case under discussion, cheap natural gas. If high-cost
fertilizer plants proliferate over Latin America, which is
the current trend, it is difficult to foresee how such countries
as Venezuela and Chile will be able to export sufficient nitrogenous fertilizers to support optimum scale plants and to
purchase manufactured exports from such countries as Brazil,
Argentina, and Mexico.

Of course, there are other possibilities which would be
economic at lower scales if ammonia could be imported from
low-cost sources. The option of foregoing the production of
ammonia means that urea, the highest analysis dry nitrogen
fertilizer, could not be produced, since it requires carbon
dioxide, a byproduct of ammonia synthesis, as a raw material.
Various types of diammonium phosphate (DAP) as well as
ammonium nitrate could be produced from imported ammonia,
and the market for liquid ammonia (82 percent nitrogen content)
and/or aqua ammonia, could be developed. Liquid forms of
nitrogen require special handling and storage facilities on the
farm as well as at import terminals and also require the learning of new techniques.

Dollar Price of Nutrients

Over the period 1955-68, the dollar prices of nitrogen
and K_2O had statistically highly significant downward trends.
The price of P_2O_5 had no significant trend. In all cases,
there were substantial fluctuations about the trend value.
The trend estimate regressions were as follows:

Values in dollars, $P_N = 214.6 - 8.096\ T$ $\bar{R}^2 = 0.8178$
c.i.f. per metric   (7.704)
ton of nutrient $P_P = 121.9 - 1.500\ T$ $\bar{R}^2 = 0.0956$
                                       (1.541)
Figures in paren- $P_K = 151.3 - 3.954\ T$ $\bar{R}^2 = 0.5785$
theses, t ratios   (4.341)

These changes in prices were the result of changing supply-
and-demand conditions in the world fertilizer market, in
particular a marked expansion of production in the 1960's.

Table 45 presents the statistic 100 minus the c.i.f. dollar
price index (1955 = 100) for each of the major nutrients for
the years 1955-67. This provides a measure of the influence
of factors not directly controlled by Brazilian institutions on
the price of nutrients to fertilizer importers. (An exception
to this statement is changes in composition of fertilizer imports within major nutrient groups: There was a trend toward
higher analysis imports within each group, except for rock
phosphate, which was separated from other phosphate imports.)
Dollar import prices for nitrogen, P_2O_5, and K_2O were at
their low for the entire period in 1968, and the general consensus in the trade was that these levels or slightly lower
could be expected to prevail in the early 1970's.

Price Changes

As was explained in Chapter 3, a system of multiple-
exchange rates prevailed throughout most of the period under
consideration. The system underwent numerous changes,
and a trend toward simplification and unification of the rate
structure began in the late 1950's. In 1969, there was no
multiple-rate system, but export taxes (called exchange
retentions) amounting to multiple-exchange rates still existed
for coffee and cocoa. In essence, the exchange system subsidized fertilizer imports at the same time that it taxed agricultural exports and subsidized wheat consumption, as well
as a number of other privileged categories of imports such
as capital equipment, newsprint, and petroleum products.
The reader is referred to Chapter 3 for a graphic representa-
tion of the relationships between different exchange rates.
(See Figure 3.) The domestic fertilizer industry, which
principally produced phosphatic fertilizers, received direct
subsidies during the period of greatest subsidization of fertilizer imports, the objective then being to maintain low prices
for fertilizers in the domestic market.[16]

TABLE 45

Decreases in Dollar Import Prices For Four Categories
of Fertilizers Compared With 1955 Prices
in Rio Grande do Sul Ports,
1955-67

Year	Nitrogen in All Forms	P_2O_5 as Finished Fertilizer	P_2O_5 as Phosphate Rock	K_2O in All Forms
1955	0.0	0.0	0.0	0.0
1956	3.5	-15.2	-13.5	-0.9
1957	11.2	-22.2	-12.5	9.3
1958	19.8	-18.8	- 0.9	14.6
1959	27.1	-10.9	27.6	22.0
1960	29.9	- 7.3	19.0	30.5
1961	33.9	-17.7	13.6	10.6
1962	36.4	- 7.3	16.8	8.5
1963	42.2	- 2.2	16.1	22.3
1964	36.0	- 5.8	4.5	21.8
1965	27.9	- 4.9	2.5	17.1
1966	35.8	-10.7	7.9	23.7
1967	54.4	11.4	20.1	34.4

Note: Data represent percentage decreases, c.i.f.; 100 minus the price index for each year, with base of 1955 = 100.

Source: Calculated from import data supplied by SEEF, Ministério da Fazenda, Rio de Janeiro.

The influence of the exchange system on c.i.f. cruzeiro
fertilizer prices may be calculated by comparing the effective
fertilizer-exchange rates during the period 1955-67 with the
parity and quasi-free trade rates. (See Chapter 3 for a
description of the derivation of these estimates of "equilibrium"
rates.) Table 46 presents two estimates of the exchange
subsidy. As can be seen from this table, fertilizer imports
were heavily subsidized by the exchange system through 1961,
according to both estimates. Since 1965, the level of subsidy
has been much less than in earlier years and reflects a reform
of the exchange and tariff systems which has taken place since
the military takeover of 1964. There was little likelihood of
a real devaluation of the cruzeiro in the early 1970's. In
fact, if domestic production of nitrogenous fertilizers is undertaken to a greater extent, it is probable that tariff protection
will be increased.

Transformation and Distribution Margins

It was possible to estimate a breakdown of average costs
for late 1968, based on interviews with import managers of
two fertilizer companies located in Pôrto Alegre. On the basis
of these estimates and the average c.i.f. prices of imports
for the period January through September, 1968, gross overhead and profit margins prevailing in Pôrto Alegre in late
1968 were calculated. These results are presented in Table
47.

The estimated margins ranged from a low of 32.3 percent
for diammonium phosphate to a high of 43.8 percent for potassium chloride. On the basis of interviews with members of
the industry and consumers throughout the state, we believe
that these margins were near record-low levels, as it was
generally stated that competition had increased over the period
studied. Fertilizers were exempt from sales- and value-
added taxes throughout the period 1955-68. There were no
customs tariffs levied against fertilizer imports (unmixed)
until the tariff revision of 1966, and then only on phosphatic
fertilizers. These were subject to a complicated system of
exemptions. Port and handling charges, however, appeared
extremely high and ran from 21 to 32 percent of the c.i.f.
price. There are probably considerable opportunities for
cost reduction within this category.

Table 48 presents a comparison of interior prices in
Rio Grande do Sul and São Paulo for the three most common,

TABLE 46

Two Estimates of Fertilizer Exchange Subsidies in
Rio Grande do Sul, 1955-67

| | Exchange Subsidy (in percent) | |
| | Parity Criterion | Quasi-Free Trade Criterion |
Year		
1955	29.94	23.54
1956	38.42	36.18
1957	45.83	45.33
1958	35.00	37.44
1959	30.64	43.66
1960	40.76	51.29
1961	45.52	63.54
1962	9.3	40.02
1963	19.87	37.86
1964	20.79	45.72
1965	-.63	29.40
1966	8.66	22.07
1967	14.35	16.61

Source: Observed average exchange rates for fertilizer imports to Rio Grande do Sul calculated from dollar and cruzeiro value of imports data supplied by SEEF, Ministério da Fazenda, Rio de Janeiro. For derivation of parity and quasi-free trade exchange rates, see Chapter 3. Subsidies were calculated as 1 minus the effective rate divided by the parity or quasi-free trade rate times 100.

TABLE 47

Estimated Gross Margins For Overhead and Profits of Basic Fertilizer Materials Sold in Pôrto Alegre, December, 1968

Product	(1) Average Import Price	(2) Port Fees and Taxes, Unloading, and Freight to Factory	(3) Interest charges[a]	(4) Total Cost[b]	(5) Cash Payment Price, Retail	(6) Gross Margin Over Cost	(7) Gross Margin as percent of Cost
Amonium sulphate	120.21	38.47	12.02	170.70	227.88	57.18	33.5
Diamonium phosphate	229.75	64.16	22.98	316.89	419.15	102.26	32.3
Urea	290.26	59.75	29.03	379.04	514.60	140.56	37.1
Triple superphosphate	164.41	48.53	16.44	229.38	313.25	83.87	36.6
Potassium chloride	111.22	31.70	11.12	154.04	221.55	67.51	43.8

Note: Columns 1-6 given in new cruzeiros per metric ton.
[a]Represents interest charges at 2.5 percent per month for four months (working capital).
[b]Addition of columns 1, 2, and 3.

Source: Average c.i.f. import prices for January–September, 1968, SEEF, Ministério da Fazenda, Rio de Janeiro. All other figures based on interviews with import managers of two fertilizers companies, their posted prices for cash transactions, and known port taxes (Taxa de Renovação da Marinha Mercante e Taxa de Renovação dos Portos). Where estimates of costs and/or prices differed between the two sources, the simple arithmetic average of the two figures was used.

straight fertilizer materials in 1967. Two specific companies
which are considered to be low-cost distributors and which
publish price lists were selected --Ultrafertil for São Paulo
and Companhia Riograndense de Adubos (CRA) for Rio Grande
do Sul. Ultrafertil was a newcomer to the São Paulo market
and was engaged in building Brazil's first, large-scale, integrated fertilizer plant near the port of Santos. It was also
opening up a system of fourteen distribution centers in the
interior of São Paulo, of which five appeared to be in operation
in 1967. Ultrafertil's biggest problem at the time was to
increase nitrogen consumption in the São Paulo market area,
as the output of its naptha-based plant, when it came on stream,
was expected to be considerably larger than demand. Its pricing policy appeared geared to this end in 1967. Whether
Ultrafertil was selling ammonium sulphate below cost as a
market-penetration tactic cannot be determined with the data
available. At any rate, even after correcting for the higher
average import costs in Rio Grande do Sul as opposed to the
rest of Brazil (mostly Santos in the case of fertilizers), CRA's
estimated interior price, including estimated average transport costs for ammonium sulphate, was over 20 percent higher
than average Ultrafertil prices at five interior points in São
Paulo. For triple superphosphate, the difference was only
10 percent, and for potassium chloride it was negligible.

Assuming Ultrafertil had the most aggressive and modern
fertilizer-distribution system in Brazil as well as the advantage of operating in the more concentrated São Paulo market,
where it must have reaped some returns to scale in distribution
costs, it may be concluded that CRA prices compared relatively
favorable for these straight products, with the exception of
ammonium sulphate.

A large proportion of the nutrients consumed in Rio Grande
do Sul reach farmers in the form of NPK blends rather than
as straight materials such as ammonium sulphate, triple superphosphate, and potassium chloride. Interviews with farmers,
cooperative directors, and sales directors of fertilizer companies indicated that farmers were willing to pay for the con-
venience of prepared blends. The question arises: How much
were they paying?

It is difficult to answer this question with any certainty,
but two different estimation techniques were utilized. The
first was to evaluate the nutrient content of the different blends
at the price of the cheapest form of each nutrient at the factory, in the form of straight materials. This was done for
representative mixtures sold by three companies operating
out of Pôrto Alegre, and the results are presented in Table 49.

TABLE 48

Comparison of Average List Prices of Ultrafertil, S. A.

Item	Ammonium Sulphate	Triple Super- phosphate	Potassium Chloride
(1) CRA Pôrto Alegre list prices for cash trans- actions, NCR\$/MT	230. 56	309. 76	208. 56
(2) Estimated average road transport costs to in- terior points of Rio Grande do Sul	18. 00	18. 00	18. 00
(3) Estimated interior price, CRA fertilizers, Rio Grande do Sul (1)+(2)	248. 56	327. 76	226. 56
(4) Average list prices for 5 interior cities in São Paulo, Ultrafertil fertilizers, cash trans- actions	201. 82	294. 32	219. 55
(5) Difference between 1967 average c. i. f. costs in Pôrto Alegre and rest of Brazil	4. 93	4. 67	5. 99
(6) Estimated CRA interior price minus c. i. f. cost differential (3)-(5) = corrected CRA interior price	243. 63	323. 09	220. 57
(7) Difference between Ultrafertil interior prices and corrected CRA prices (6)-(4)	41. 81	28. 77	1. 02
(8) Difference between Ultrafertil interior price and adjusted CRA interior price as a percent of Ultrafertil interior price (7)÷(4) x 100	20. 7%	9. 78%	0. 50%

Source: Import prices calculated from SEEF, Ministério da Fazenda import data. Ultrafertil and CRA prices from pub- lished price lists for cash transactions, late 1967. Transport costs in Rio Grande do Sul based on interviews with fertilizer sales personnel. Based on Pôrto Alegre prices of Companhia Riograndense de Adubos, late 1967.

Estimated Mixing Margins for NPK Fertilizers in Pôrto Alegre, December, 1968

FORMULA	(1) Retail Price at Factory for Cash Payments	(2) Equivalent Value of Nitrogen in Form of Ammonium Sulphate	(3)[a] Equivalent Value of non-water Soluble P_2O_5 as Ground Phosphate Rock	(4)[a] Equivalent Value of Soluble P_2O_5 as TSP	(5) Equivalent Value of K_2O as KCL	(6) Total Equivalent Cost	(7) Mixing Margin (1 - 6)	(8)[b] Mixing Margin as Percent of Equivalent Cost
3 - 21 - 9	167.45	32.08	83.07	--	32.59	147.74	19.71	13.4
5 - 22 - 10	266.05	53.47	7.91	136.11	36.22	233.71	32.34	13.8
5 - 23 - 10	290.50	53.47	--	156.52	36.22	246.21	44.29	17.99
10 - 20 - 10	311.25	106.94	--	136.54	36.22	279.70	31.55	11.28
2 - 23 - 6	241.36	21.39	--	156.52	21.73	199.64	41.72	20.90
6 - 14 - 6	271.27	64.16	--	95.28	21.73	181.17	90.10	49.73

Note: Columns 1-7 in new cruzeiros per metric ton.

aWhere the soluble component was not specifically given, the more expensive soluble equivalent price is given in this table. This probably results in overestimation of equivalent costs for some mixtures.

bThis should be considered as the margin for blending above and beyond the gross margins for straight material.

Source: Prices for mixed fertilizers supplied by sales managers of three mixing plants in Pôrto Alegre. The equivalent costs for nutrients in straight form were calculated on the average cash payment prices for the relevant fertilizers prevailing in Pôrto Alegre in December, 1968.

There is considerable variation in the margins between mixtures, even for the same company. It should be remembered that the mixing margin is in addition to the normal profit and overhead margin on straight products.

Another method of estimating mixing margins is via regression analysis.

$$P_i = a_o + a_1 N_i + a_2 PSOL_i + a_3 PISOL_i + a_4 K_i + u_i \qquad (8)$$

where

P_i = the cash price per ton of mixture i
N_i = kilograms of nitrogen per ton of mixture i
$PSOL_i$ = kilograms of water-soluble P_2O_5 per ton of mixture i
$PISOL_i$ = kilograms of nonwater-soluble P_2O_5 per ton of
         mixture i
K_i = kilograms of K_2O per ton of mixture i
u_i = disturbance term

A function of the form (above) was fitted to cash prices and nutrient contents shown on the price lists of a major fertilizer company. Two regressions were run, one for 1967 and one for 1968, and the summer price lists for each year were used. Values in parentheses are t ratios.

P = 54.39 + 936.6 N + 546.5 PSOL + 225.3 PISOL +
   (1.875) (4.147)   (5.558)   (2.318)
   297.9 K 1967
   (2.956)
   $\bar{R}^2$ = 0.859

P = 65.63 + 878.2 N + 541.0 PSOL + 214.7 PISOL +
   (1.764) (2.963)   (3.822)   (1.721)
   338.8 K 1968
   (2.646)
   $\bar{R}^2$ = 0.761

There were sixteen observations in 1967 and fourteen in 1968. The constant term may be considered as an estimate of bagging and distribution margins. Although the intercept terms were significant only at the 10 percent level, when converted into percentages of the average prices for mixed fertilizers, they fell in the same range as the estimated gross margins for overhead and profits shown in Table 47. The percentages were 29.8 and 34.3 percent, respectively, in 1967 and 1968.

The next step was to compare the cost for nutrients in NPK blends, as estimated by the regressions, with the prices of the same nutrients in the form of straight fertilizers. Straight fertilizers chosen for this purpose were ammonium sulphate for nitrogen, triple superphosphate for soluble phosphorous, ground phosphate rock (hiperfosfato) for nonsoluble phosphorous, and potassium chloride for potassium. For each of these fertilizers, the inverse of the nutrient to total weight ratio was multiplied by the constant term of the regression, and the resulting product was subtracted from the price per ton of nutrients in straight form in order to eliminate the bagging and distribution margin from both items being compared. The estimated mixing margins calculated in this fashion are given below, expressed as percentages over the cost of straight materials.

Nutrient	1967	1968
Nitrogen	9	33
P_2O_5, soluble	1	11
P_2O_5, nonsoluble	32	28
K_2O	16	61

Mixing margins appear to have increased for all nutrients except nonsoluble P_2O_5 between 1967 and 1968, which is rather surprising. The explanation for the extremely low margins shown for soluble phosphorous may well be that diammonium phosphate is used as the source of soluble phosphate rather than triple superphosphate. According to the import statistics, diammonium phosphate is the cheapest source of both nitrogen and phosphorous for all imported fertilizers. The problem is to allocate the total cost between the nitrogen and the phosphorous components if price comparisons are to be made. In 1968, the import price per unit of nutrient (including nitrogen in the ratio 18/64, and soluble phosphorous in the ratio 46/64), was the same for diammonium phosphate as for triple superphosphate (also entirely water-soluble 46 percent P_2O_5), in spite of the fact that nitrogen is generally at least 50 percent more expensive per unit than phosphorous.

No data on the cost of blending were available for Rio Grande do Sul. In the late 1940's, blending operations in the United States added approximately 14 percent to the value of equivalent straight materials.[17] It is doubtful that all of this was cost. At any rate, even if blending costs were as much as 14 percent of the raw material costs, it is extremely likely, on most mixtures being sold in Rio Grande do Sul, that considerable profits were being made, over and above those made on straight products. In addition, it is not beyond question whether the analysis of blended products is always up to specifications. The existence of at least six blending companies, all operating out of Pôrto Alegre and Rio Grande, and some of them quite small, suggests that duplication of sales effort and unnecessary product differentiation may be increasing the cost of nutrients to the farmer.

To summarize the findings of this section, the principal opportunities for reduction in fertilizer prices to farmers in Rio Grande do Sul other than direct subsidies appear to lie in improving the efficiency of the ports, increased (preferably exclusive) use of high-analysis fertilizers, and a reduction in mixing margins. Local production of nitrogenous and phosphatic fertilizers is more likely to result in price increases rather than decreases.

POTENTIAL DEMAND

If we assume that farmers in Rio Grande do Sul applied fertilizers at optimum rates, what would the potential demand for major nutrients be in the early 1970's? Supplementing the data on response functions with some rough-and-ready approximations, crude estimates can be obtained for nitrogen and P_2O_5. No such estimate is made for K_2O, in view of the apparent lack of response to this nutrient, as was observed in the experiments reported earlier in this chapter.

Two alternative, nutrient-to-product-price ratios were chosen, those actually prevailing in 1967 and a set 25 percent below those for 1968. The value of $s + v$ (share of production delivered to landlords plus the ratio of variable costs associated with fertilizer use to the value of output) was set at 0.3. A number of other assumptions upon which the potential-demand estimates are based are set forth below. Many of them are necessary because of the lack of response functions for soybeans and artificial pastures as well as even a moderately reliable phosphorous function for corn. The area assumed planted to each crop (in hectares), in Rio Grande do Sol, was as follows: irrigated rice, 400,000; wheat, 800,000; soybeans, 600,000; corn, 2 million; and artificial pastures, 1 million. Fertilization levels are optimum as estimated from response functions, except for those indicated by *:

Crop	1967 Price Ratios		25-Percent-Less-Than-1968 Price Ratios	
	N	P	N	P
Rice	26.2	60.3	32.7	68.5
Wheat	0.0	72.0	29.7	125.0
Corn	19.9	50.0*	62.3	80.0*
Soybeans	6.0*	87.0*	10.0*	100.0*
Artificial pastures	0.0*	20.0*	0.0*	30.0*

Finally, two more alternative, potential-demand measures are provided by assuming that if varieties of rice and wheat can be developed which are more efficient utilizers of nitrogen than those currently available, the optimum nitrogen-fertilization rates for each of these crops (under the assumptions set out), would be 100 kilograms per hectare for the 1967 price ratios and 120 kilograms per hectare for the 25-percent-less-than-1968 price ratios.

The optimal demand for nitrogen and phosphorous under the area assumptions and four combinations of the price and varietal assumptions are set forth in Table 50. It should be emphasized here that these demands would not simply materialize, given the price conditions postulated, even if all other assumptions were correct. Rather they would have to be developed through an intensive campaign of soil analysis and extension work similar to that of Operação Tatú and, in the case of the high-yielding varieties of wheat and rice, an accelerated research effort to breed nitrogen responsiveness into Brazilian varieties.

From Table 50, it may be seen that the prospects for achieving anything like the required demand for the minimum-scale, centrifugal-process ammonia plant are very poor unless there is a pronounced fall in the nutrient-to-product price ratios and/or success in developing nitrogen-responsive rice and wheat varieties. The conduct of an extremely successful extension and sales campaign is a precondition in either case. Another alternative would be to greatly expand the area under the five crops; however, the values chosen were already higher than those prevailing in 1967. Another possibility would be development of markets in neighboring states, including Uruguay, Argentina and Paraguay.

On the other hand, the possibilities for a large-scale, concentrated-phosphates plant, perhaps producing diammonium phosphate with imported ammonia, which could also be marketed directly in the form of liquids, are considerably more favorable, at least as far as demand is concerned. However, the production of high-analysis phosphates is a weight-gaining process. If both phosphoric acid and ammonia had to be imported (assuming that it would be more economic to convert phosphate rock to the acid form near the mines), it is doubtful whether the operation would be particularly attractive compared with importing diammonium phosphate, urea, and possibly liquified ammonia directly as finished fertilizers.

TABLE 50

Potential Demand for Nitrogen and Phosphorus
in Rio Grande do Sul
(metric tons of N and P_2O_5)

Nutrients and Assumptions	Rice	Wheat	Corn	Soybeans	Artificial Pastures	Total
1967 price ratios, existing varieties						
Nitrogen	10,496	7,032	39,802	3,600	--	60,930
Phosphorus	24,120	57,607	100,000	52,200	20,000	253,920
25 percent decrease from 1968 price ratios, existing varieties						
Nitrogen	13,076	23,760	124,525	6,000	--	167,361
Phosphorus	27,388	88,296	160,000	60,000	30,000	365,684
1967 price ratios, new rice and wheat varieties						
Nitrogen	40,000	80,000	39,802	3,600	--	163,402
Phosphorus	24,120	57,600	100,000	52,200	20,000	253,920
25 percent decrease from 1968 price ratios, new rice and wheat varieties						
Nitrogen	48,000	96,000	124,525	6,000	--	274,525
Phosphorus	27,388	88,296	160,000	60,000	30,000	365,684

Source: See text.

NOTES

1. For a discussion of the employment and social implications of overly-rapid mechanization, see Bruce Johnston and
John Cownie, "The Seed-Fertilizer Revolution and Labor
Force Absorption," American Economic Review (September,
1969), 569-82.

2. For a detailed study of the process of agricultural
colonization, decline, and outmigration, see M. R. Pebayle,
"Geographie rurale des nouvelles colonies du Haut Uruguay,"
Bulletin de l'Association de Geographes Français (January-
February, 1967), 15-34.

3. See B. S. Minhas and T. N. Srinivassan, "New Agricultural Strategy Analysed," Yojana (January 26, 1966). A
collection of Indian papers on fertilizer response, with emphasis on the differences between the best local varieties and
high-yielding varieties of grains such as the Mexican wheats
and rices developed at the International Rice Research Institute
is contained in Indian Journal of Agricultural Economics
(Conference Number; October-December, 1968). See especially
T. N. Srinivassan, "Raporteur's Report on Economic Aspects
of High-Yielding Varieties Programme," 48-60, for methodo-
logical comments and a review of the papers presented. One
paper by A. S. Kahlon and J. L. Kaul found significant interaction between phosphorous and nitrogen, but the rest analyzed
nitrogen response alone. I am indebted to Ralph W. Cummings,
Jr., of USAID/New Delhi, for sending me much of this material
as well as his paper with Robert W. Herdt and S. K. Ray,
"New Agricultural Strategy Revisited," Economic and Political
Weekly (October 26, 1968), that presents some evidence on
nitrogen response of Mexican wheats which shows profit
maximizing doses of nitrogen as high as 176 kilograms per
hectare.

4. Minhas and Srinivassan, loc. cit.

5. Cummings, Herdt, and Ray, op. cit., explain the
differences between the two curves, which are both for irrigated wheat, by the fact that the experiment stations were not
yet accustomed to working with the high-yielding varieties in
the 1965-66 season.

6. International Rice Research Institute, Annual Report, 1967, pp. 244-46.

7. Universidade Federal do Rio Grande do Sul, et al., Plano Estadual da Melhoramento da Fertilidade do Solo (Pôrto Alegre, 1969).

8. Ibid.

9. The basic Pôrto Alegre prices were obtained from IRGA, Lavoura Arrozeira (November-December, 1968).

10. For rice, those reported in IRGA, Anuário Estatístico do Arroz; for wheat, the official producers' price for bulk wheat in the interior of Rio Grande do Sul as given in the portarias; and for corn, the average value of output as calculated from SEP data on value and production.

11. Yield and cost data are calculated from Universidade Federal, op. cit. Prices received by producers were calculated from IBGE, Anuário Estatístico do Brasil, 1969 for soybeans and corn. The wheat price is that paid by the Bank of Brazil.

12. Roger G. Johnson and Jorge G. de Oliveira, "Uma Avaliação Econômica de Pastagens Cultivadas Para Terras Orizicolas," Lavoura Arrozeira (November-December, 1966).

13. Calculated from data supplied by SEEF, Ministério da Fazenda, Rio de Janeiro. Disaggregated f.o.b. data were not available for the entire period, 1955-67.

14. Some useful references are Donald Erlenkotter and Alan S. Manne, "Capacity Expansion for India's Nitrogenous Fertilizer Industry," Management Science (June, 1968), 553-72; OECD, Supply and Demand Prospects for Fertilizer in Developing Countries (Paris, 1968); United Nations Industrial Development Organization (UNIDO), Fertilizer Manual (New York: United Nations, 1967); and USAID/India, "Trombay Fertilizer Expansion," Capital Assistance Paper, no date, apparently 1968 or 1969.

15. Program of Joint Studies on Latin American Economic Integration (ECIEL), Martin Carnoy, ed., Industrialization in a Latin American Common Market (Washington, D.C.: The Brookings Institution, 1969, multilithed).

16. Banco Nacional de Desenvolvimento Econômico, Mercado Brasileiro de Fertilizantes, 1950-1970 (second edition; Rio de Janeiro, August, 1965), pp. 20-21.

17. Gian S. Sahota, Fertilizer in Economic Development: An Econometric Analysis (New York: Frederick A. Praeger, 1968), p. 114.

7

SUMMARY
AND
CONCLUSIONS

In Chapter 1, evidence was presented to support the hypothesis that Brazil's economic growth in the early 1960's was constrained by a shortage of foreign exchange. The rapid rate of economic advance that was experienced in the 1950's was led by an import-substituting industrialization which had succeeded in substantially reducing the import coefficient, but only at the cost of neglecting, and at times outrightly exploiting, the agricultural sector. This industrialization process depended on substantial inflows of foreign capital which, by the early 1960's, were seen by many Brazilians as larger than desirable for political reasons.

Productivity grew rapidly in the transformation industries but stagnated or retrogressed in the agricultural and service sectors. The result, in spite of the increasing importance of the industrial sector in terms of output, was that its share of the labor force actually declined during the decade of the 1950's. Brazil increasingly could be characterized as a paradigm of the dual economy, with a sophisticated and capital-intensive modern sector on one hand and large masses of illiterate peasants and urban slum dwellers who remained largely outside the modern, monetary economy, on the other. Regional and sectoral income inequalities were severe and placed in jeopardy Brazil's future as a unified society and a potential world power.

The process of extensive agricultural growth which permitted the industrialization effort without more than cursory attention to the agricultural sector on the part of policymakers threatened to grind to a halt, its momentum exhausted by the increasing burden of transport costs as foodstuffs were

delivered to consumption centers from an ever-receding
frontier. The failure to introduce many features of modern
agricultural technology in the regions relatively close to the
major urban centers was particularly notable, the principal
exception being parts of São Paulo State.

All projections of import demand suggested that hoped-
for high rates of economic growth would require an increasing
flow of foreign exchange in the 1970's. If this were to be
supplied without so heavy a reliance on foreign capital as to
be politically unacceptable, policymakers would have to give
a high priority to export expansion. This would require a
very rapid growth in agricultural exports (other than the
traditional mainstay of coffee), as well as in minerals, forest
products, and manufactured goods.

The needs to increase agricultural exports, widen the
domestic market for manufactured goods, provide higher levels
of nutrition for the large proportion of Brazilian citizens who
live in hunger, and achieve greater equality in income distribution all converged in such a manner as to make agricultural
modernization a high priority for Brazilian development in
the 1970's.

To shed some empirical and analytical light on the past
performance of the agricultural sector and its potential for
rapid growth, attention was focused on a group of agricultural
products, characterized by relatively favorable demand conditions, coupled with productivity stagnation over the postwar
period. All these products--beef, rice, wheat, soybeans,
and corn--are produced in the state of Rio Grande do Sul,
which is also the dominant exporter of beef, rice, and soybeans, and the state was selected for a detailed analysis of
the factors influencing production of the five products.

In Chapters 2 and 3, it was shown, in spite of a long
history as an exporting state, that Rio Grande do Sul's beef
and rice exports were in a precarious position throughout the
period studied, while corn was never exported in significant
quantities. Faced by increasing costs for domestically produced inputs in the case of rice, as well as growing competition
from other producing regions in Brazilian markets and an
exchange system which implicitly taxed the agricultural sector,
the economic environment facing the producer and potential
exporter was hardly favorable. The existence of direct export
controls was documented in Chapter 3 and, together with a
variable expressing the relative attractiveness of exporting
as opposed to selling in the domestic market, this information
was used to achieve a reasonable degree of statistical

explanation of Brazilian exports of beef, rice, and corn. It was also found, when the ratio of the export to the domestic price for beef, rice, and corn declined to a certain critical level, that exports were severely restricted if not entirely cut off. Only in the case of soybeans and soybean-meal exports, which the domestic market could not absorb, was there an almost unbroken expansion which was dominated by a trend in domestic production.

In Chapter 3, it was also found that significant, inverse, seasonal-price movements between Brazil and northern-hemisphere suppliers of rice, soybeans, and corn existed which could make careful timing of exports of these products advantageous for Brazil.

Chapter 4 examined the production of a high-cost import substitute, wheat, in Rio Grande do Sul. The operation of a multiple-price system, whereby both consumption and production of this commodity were subsidized, was examined and the extent of the subsidies estimated. It was shown that to save a dollar of foreign exchange by producing and transporting wheat cost Brazil $2.20 in domestic resources in 1967. Of the five products studied, wheat was shown to require the largest amount of domestic resources to earn or save a dollar's worth of foreign exchange. The reasons for the high cost of wheat production in Rio Grande do Sul were also examined. Marginal wheat production (a) took place on land of low, natural fertility and high acidity, (b) required relatively expensive manufactured inputs, (c) came from varieties which were inefficient users of nitrogen, (d) suffered from difficult climatic conditions, and (e) had obtained insufficient technical support. Finally, arguments in favor of domestic wheat production were reviewed, and most of them were judged to be of doubtful validity. It was concluded that while there would be some social costs in cutting back wheat production, a rapid expansion without substantial advances in wheat breeding and a reduction in the cost of inputs would be an expensive way to increase economic and political autarky.

In Chapter 5, it was shown that the entire postwar period had witnessed no significant trend in per hectare of herd productivity and that technological change had not proceeded fast enough to more than offset increasing soil exhaustion and the extension of agricultural production to more marginal lands. The possibilities for further agricultural growth in Rio Grande do Sul in the 1970's were found to be virtually nil unless productivity were increased, as there was no longer an extensive agricultural frontier within the state. In the final

section of Chapter 5, evidence was presented to show that
when advances in technology were intelligible and accessible
to agricultural producers, such advances were rapidly adopted
and resulted in substantial gains in productivity.

Fertilizers have played a key role in raising agricultural
productivity in many countries, and in Chapter 6 the use of
fertilizers in Rio Grande do Sul was examined in considerable
detail.   Improved fertilizer use was shown to offer a number
of significant advantages as the leading edge of a process of
agricultural modernization compared with, for example,
mechanization.   The profitability of fertilizer use was
examined, by making use of fertilizer-response functions
fitted to experimental data for rice, wheat, and corn.   The
nitrogen response of existing varieties of wheat and rice was
shown to be markedly less than that of the new, stiff-strawed
varieties developed at the International Maize and Wheat
Improvement Center in Mexico and the International Rice Research Institute in the Philippines.   Response to phosphorous
was generally strong, as Rio Grande do Sul soils were poor
in this nutrient.   No significant response to potassium was
observable, which might be expected, as statewide tests
found a high percentage of the soils to have adequate levels
of available potassium.

Formulas for calculating optimum fertilization levels
from response functions under varying conditions of land
tenure, variable costs associated with fertilizer use, and
assumptions concerning farmers' price-expectations formation were derived and applied for rice, wheat, and corn.
Evidence that the degree of suboptimality of apparent fertilization levels for rice and wheat may have fallen in the late
1960's was presented, but accurate tests were not possible
due to a lack of fertilizer-consumption data by crop.   Very
little fertilizer was used in the production of corn, despite
the favorable response observed for this product.   This was
probably due to the fact that most corn producers were small
farmers and had limited access to credit.   Soil-acidity correction by the use of lime was shown to be highly profitable,
but generally to require several years in order to pay back
the investment, which had a life of at least four years.   It
was noted that a shortage of medium-term credit may have
been responsible for underutilization of this input in Rio
Grande do Sul.

On the demand side, some efforts were made to obtain an
explanation of apparent per hectare fertilizer consumption, on

the assumption that all fertilizer entering the state in the period
1955-67 was used on rice and wheat. No significant response
to ratios of nutrient-to-expected-product-prices was observed.
Several hypotheses concerning the formulation of the latter
by farmers were tested. The best explanation of total consumption of nutrients was obtained by using area planted to
wheat and rice and, for nitrogen and potash, a time trend,
as independent variables.

There was some evidence of a significant increase in per
hectare consumption in 1967 and 1968 for all three major
plant nutrients, again assuming that all fertilizer was used
on rice and wheat land.

Turning to an examination of the various components of
delivered fertilizer prices, it was found that the principal
opportunities for reducing the cost of fertilizer to the farmer
in Rio Grande do Sul, other than direct subsidies, lay in improving the efficiency of the ports, increased use of high-
analysis fertilizers, and a reduction in mixing margins.
Local production of nitrogenous and phosphatic fertilizers
was more likely to result in increases than decreases in
prices to farmers, especially if the production of ammonia
were attempted.

The response functions and some rough-and-ready
assumptions were used to estimate the potential demand for
nitrogenous and phosphatic fertilizers in Rio Grande do Sul
under several assumptions concerning both the development
of nitrogen-responsive grain varieties and nutrient-to-
product price ratios.

If any general conclusion may be drawn from this study,
it is that, while there is substantial scope for rapid gains in
agricultural productivity in and increased exports from Rio
Grande do Sul, to achieve these will require more than the
manipulation of the pricing system for agricultural commodities and inputs, although favorable price incentives are
certainly of great importance. Policymakers will have to de-
vote considerable attention and financial resources to achieving the objective of productivity growth without increasing
existing inequalities in income and employment opportunities.
Research, extension, adult rural education, and, in some
cases, land reform--all endeavors requiring a strong organizational base and continuing political as well as financial
support--will have to be considerably strengthened.

Economics as a discipline can offer useful insights concerning how resources should be allocated and incentives
arranged to achieve specified objectives in agricultural

modernization. Yet, without a political commitment to the attaining of such objectives and a significant reordering of development priorities, it seems unlikely that Rio Grande do Sul (and, by extension, Brazil), will be able to improve its rather unimpressive record in agricultural productivity and exports, much less attain broader objectives of national policy such as a reduction in sectoral and regional inequalities.

APPENDIX

APPENDIX

FACTORS INFLUENCING THE SLAUGHTER
OF BEEF CATTLE IN RIO GRANDE DO SUL

This appendix presents the results of statistical experiments attempted with the objective of determining the influence of current-year cattle prices on slaughter rates in Rio Grande do Sul.

Separate time series are available on the slaughter of steers and cows, both for all charqueadas and frigorificos in the state--that is, all meat produced for out-of-state consumption--and for a single, large, packing plant, that of Swift, located at Rosário do Sul, in the southwestern part of the state. Three price series were available: the average steer price for Rio Grande do Sul as given by INSTICARNE and the average net prices paid to producers for both steers and cows by the Swift packing plant. The model chosen was adapted from one used with some success by Guilherme Leite da Silva Dias.[1] It contains two separable equations.

$$S_t = a_o + a_1 PS_t + a_2 C_{t-5} + u_t$$

$$C_t = b_o + b_2 PC_t + b_2 C_{t-t} + v_t$$

Where

S_t = number of steers slaughtered in year t

C_t = number of cows slaughtered in year t

PS_t = the producer price for steers in year t

PC_t = the producer price for cows in year t

u, v = disturbance terms

The number of steers slaughtered in year t is a function of the current steer price; the number of cows slaughtered is for five years previously. The lagged cow-slaughter term is included as the average age of steers at slaughter appears to be close to five years in Rio Grande do Sul. In São Paulo, a four-year lag was used with success by Silva Dias. Three- and four-year lags were tried for Rio Grande do Sul, but both resulted in statistically insignificant coefficients, lending support to the estimate of a four-to-five-year average slaughter age. This is because cows slaughtered will not produce offspring, and those not slaughtered generally calve the following spring, if at all. Slaughter for export both to the rest of Brazil and foreign countries normally takes place in the fall.

The cow-slaughter equation is perfectly analgous to that for steers. The models were run in both linear and logarithmic forms for the state as a whole as well as for the slaughter of the Swift plant. Because there was a strong downtrend in the statewide steer-slaughter series, probably explained by growing requirements (enforced by direct controls) for the supplying of fresh meat to the local market, an explicit time variable was introduced. (The population of Rio Grande do Sul increased at an annual average rate of 2.72 percent between 1950 and 1960 and was estimated to be increasing at 2.56 percent in the 1960's.[2]) The results, with only significant variables included, are given for both cows and steers, the equations being in double-logarithmic form.

Statewide:

$$S_t = 7.328 - 0.2646 C_{t-5} - 0.2093\ t \qquad \overline{R}^2 = 0.552 \qquad DW = 1.995$$
$$\qquad\quad (2.396) \qquad\qquad (5.045)$$

$$C_t = 6.238 - 0.2710 C_{t-5} \qquad\qquad\qquad \overline{R}^2 = 0.042 \qquad DW = 1.233$$
$$\qquad\quad (1.371)$$

Swift - Rosário do Sul

$$S_t = 7.828 - 0.4128 C_{t-5} \qquad\qquad\qquad \overline{R}^2 = 0.183 \qquad DW = 1.691$$
$$\qquad\quad (2.191)$$

$$C_t = 7.785 - 0.4817 C_{t-5}$$
$$\qquad\quad (1.806)$$

Neither the Swift nor the INSTICARNE prices were significant in any equation, either at the statewide level or for the Swift plant. The lagged cow-slaughter variable had the

expected negative sign in all equations, and was significant
at the 5 percent level at both the statewide level and for the
Swift plant. The significance was less for the cow-slaughter
equations, at the 10 percent level for the Swift plant and only
the 20 percent level at the statewide level. The elasticity
of both cow and steer slaughter with respect to lagged cow
slaughter was very similar for both cows and steers at the
state level and at the Swift plant. However, between the two
levels of aggregation, there was a great difference, the
elasticities being close to twice as high at the plant level as
at the state level. There is no ready explanation of this fact,
although the aggregation process itself may be the reason.
The Rosário plant is located in the heart of one of the most
important cattle zones where commercial slaughter for export
is a higher proportion of the total than for the state as a
whole. A conclusion which can be drawn from the regressions
is that cycles in cow slaughter have a tendency to perpetuate
themselves, although in damped form.

The lack of a significant price response in these equations
could, in part, be due to a simultaneity problem, since one
might expect that if more cattle are slaughtered, the supply
of meat will increase, causing the price to fall. However,
Rio Grande do Sul's beef market is tied to the national, and,
to a varying extent (depending on the severity of export and
import controls), also to the international market, and the
quantity of Rio Grande do Sul beef offered is unlikely to have
a substantial impact on the price. Rio Grande do Sul beef
production averaged 13 percent of total Brazilian output in
the years 1965-67. Brazil is a marginal supplier in the
international market.

It is also possible that producers respond perversely to
current-year prices. Suppose the price is unusually low,
and expectations regarding future prices are highly elastic.
Rather than holding cattle for fattening under adverse circumstances (low prices), young steers may be slaughtered earlier
than would otherwise be the case. The result would be a
statistically confused price coefficient. The same would be
the case if fazendeiros, seeking to maintain some customary
level of income, are "forced" to slaughter more cattle in
years of low prices. Again, if a capital constraint is
operative, high prices may provide a flow of funds which
releases the constraint and permits fazendeiros to fatten
cattle longer. In any of the cases cited here, an insignificant
price coefficient might be expected in a model of the type

used. What actually happens cannot be determined without more complete data and probably would include extensive interviews with cattlemen.

NOTES

1. Guilherme Leite da Silva Dias, Alguns Aspectos da Pecuária de Corte na Região Centro-Sul, Estudos ANPES, No. 7 (São Paulo, date unknown).

2. Data from IBGE, Anuário Estatístico do Brasil (Rio de Janeiro, 1967).

BIBLIOGRAPHY

BIBLIOGRAPHY

Books and Articles

Baer, Werner. Industrialization and Economic Development in Brazil. Homewood, Illinois: Richard D. Irwin, 1965.

Balassa, Bela. "The Purchasing Power Parity Doctrine: A Reapparisal," Journal of Political Economy (December, 1964), 584-96.

_____, and Schydlowsky, Daniel. "Effective Tariffs, Domestic Cost of Foreign Exchange, and the Equilibrium Exchange Rate," Journal of Political Economy (May-June, 1968), 348-60.

Bayma, Cunha. Trigo. Two volumes. Rio de Janeiro: Serviço de Informação Agricola, Ministério da Agricultura, 1960.

Beck, Mario de Lima. "Pronunciamento do Dr. Mario de Lima Beck, Presidente do IRGA," Lavoura Arroziera (January, 1965), 5-9.

Bergsman, Joel. Brazil's Industrialization and Trade Policies. New York: Oxford University Press, 1970.

_____, and Candal, Arthur. "Industrialization: Past Successes and Future Problems." The Economy of Brazil. Edited by Howard S. Ellis. Pp. 29-73. Berkeley and Los Angeles: University of California Press, 1969.

_____, and Morley, Samuel. "Import Constraints and Development: Causes of the Recent Decline of Brazilian Economic Growth: A Comment," Review of Economics and Statistics (February, 1969), 101-2.

Brown, Lester R. The Seeds of Change: The Green Revolution and Economic Development in the 1970's. New York:
Praeger Publishers, 1970.

Bruno, Michael. Interdependence, Resource Use and Structural Change in Trade. Jerusalem: Bank of Israel, 1963.

Chenery, Hollis, and Strout, Alan. "Foreign Assistance and
Economic Development," American Economic Review
(September, 1966), 679-733.

Cohen, Benjamin. "Foreign Exchange Constraints in Economic Development and Efficient Aid Allocation: Comment," Economic Journal (March, 1966), pp. 168-70.

Congresso Estadual da Orizicultura, Anais. Pôrto Alegre,
Etica Impressora, 1966.

Conjuntura Econômica. Monthly publication of the Fundação
Getúlio Vargas, Rio de Janeiro.

Cummings, Ralph W., Jr., Herdt, Robert W., and Ray, S.
K. "New Agricultural Strategy Revisited," Economic
and Political Weekly (India), October 26, 1968.

Dias, Guilherme Leite da Silva. Alguns Aspectos da Pecuária
de Corte na Região Centro-Sul. Estudos Associação
Nacional de Programeçao Econômica e Social No. 7.
São Paulo, date unknown.

Ellis, Howard S., ed. The Economy of Brazil. Berkeley
and Los Angeles: The University of California Press,
1969.

Erlenkotter, Donald, and Manne, Alan S. "Capacity Expansion for India's Nitrogenous Fertilizer Industry," Management Science (June, 1963), 553-72.

Federação das Cooperativas Triticolas do Sul, Ltda. (Fecotrigo). Trigo: Estudo do Custo de Produção No Rio
Grande do Sul. Pôrto Alegre: 1965, 1966, 1967, and
1968 (annual).

Fetter, Adolfo Antônio. "Pecuária Bovian de Corte no Rio
Grande do Sul," Lavoura Arrozeira (September-October,
1968), 45-52.

Freitas, Luiz Medonça de, and Netto, Antonio Delfim.
    O Trigo No. Brasil. São Paulo: Associação Comercial
    de São Paulo, 1960.

Fundação Getúlio Vargas. Projeções de Oferta e Demanda
    de Produtos Agrícolas para o Brasil. Rio de Janeiro,
    1966.

Furtado, Celso. Dialético do Desenvolvimento. Rio de
    Janeiro: Editôra de Cultura, 1964.

Haberler, Gottfried. A Survey of International Trade Theory.
    Princeton University Special Papers in International
    Finance, No. 1. Princeton, July, 1961.

Harberger, Arnold C. "Some Evidence on the International
    Price Mechanism," Journal of Political Economy (De-
    cember, 1957), 506-21.

Hayami, Yujiro. "Innovations in the Fertilizer Industry and
    Agricultural Development: The Japanese Experience,"
    Journal of Farm Economics (May, 1967), 403-12.

Herdt, R. W., and Mellor, J. W. "The Contrasting Response
    of Rice to Nitrogen: India and the United States," Journal
    of Farm Economics (February, 1964), 150-60.

Holmes, James. "The Purchasing Power Parity Theory: In
    Defense of Gustav Cassel as a Modern Theorist," Journal
    of Political Economy (October, 1967), 686-95.

Huddle, Donald L. "Balanço de Pagamentos e Contrôle de
    Câmbio no Brasil: Diretrizes, Políticas e História,
    1946-54," Revista Brasileira de Economia (March, 1964),
    5-40.

_____. "Balanço de Pagamentos e Contrôle de Câmbio
    no Brasil: Eficácia, Bem-Estar e Desenvolvimento Eco-
    nômico," Revista Brasileira de Economia (June, 1964),
    pp. 4-45.

_____. "Postwar Brazilian Industrialization: Growth
    Patterns, Inflation, and Sources of Stagnation." The
    Shaping of Modern Brazil. Edited by Eric Baklanoff.
    Baton Rouge: Louisiana State University Press, 1969.

Johnson, Roger G., and de Oliveira, Jorge G. "Uma Avaliação Econômica de Pastagens Cultivadas Para Terras Orizícolas," Lavoura Arrozeira (November-December, 1966).

Johnston, Bruce, and Southworth, Herman, eds. Agricultural Development and Economic Growth. Ithaca, New York: Cornell University Press, 1967.

Johnston, Bruce F., and Cownie, John. "The Seed-Fertilizer Revolution and Labor Force Absorption," American Economic Review (September, 1969), 569-82.

Kafka, Alexandre. "The Brazilian Exchange Auction System," Review of Economics and Statistics (August, 1956), 308-22.

Khrishna, Raj. "Agricultural Price Policy and Economic Development." Agricultural Development and Economic Growth. Edited by Bruce Johnston and Herman Southworth. Pp. 497-540. Ithaca, New York: Cornell University Press, 1967.

Klackmann, Raul Edgard, et al. Regiões do Trigo no Brasil. Estudos Técnicos, No. 28. Rio de Janeiro: Serviço de Informação Agrícola, Ministério da Agricultura, 1965.

Krueger, Anne. "Some Economic Costs of Exchange Control: The Turkish Case," Journal of Political Economy. (October, 1966), 466-80.

Leff, Nathaniel H. The Brazilian Capital Goods Industry, 1929-1964. Cambridge, Massachusetts: Harvard University Press, 1968.

_____. Economic Policy-Making and Development in Brazil, 1947-1964. New York: John Wiley and Sons, 1968.

_____. "Export Stagnation and Autarkic Development in Brazil, 1947-1962," Quarterly Journal of Economics (May, 1967), 286-301.

_____. "The 'Exportable Surplus' Approach to Foreign Trade in Underdeveloped Countries," Economic Development and Cultural Change (April, 1969), 346-55.

_____. "Import Constraints and Development: Causes of the Recent Decline of Brazilian Economic Growth, " Review of Economics and Statistics (November, 1967), 494-501.

_____. _____. "Reply to 'A Comment' by Joel Bergsman and Samuel Morley, " Review of Economics and Statistics (February, 1969), 102-4.

de Lemos, Raimundo Costa, et al. O Solo na Cultura de Trigo no Brasil. Estudos Técnicos, No. 37. Rio de Janeiro: Serviço de Informação Agrícola, Ministério da Agricultura, 1967.

Manneh, Alan S. , ed. Investments for Capacity Expansion: Size, Location and Time-Phasing. Cambridge, Massachusetts: The Massachusetts Institute of Technology Press, 1967.

McKinnon, Ronald. "Foreign Exchange Constraints in Economic Development and Efficient Aid Allocation, " Economic Journal (June, 1964), 388-409.

_____. _____. "Rejoinder to 'A Comment' by B. Cohen, " Economic Journal (March, 1966), 170-71.

Mellor, John W. "Toward a Theory of Agricultural Development. " Agricultural Development and Economic Growth. Edited by Bruce Johnston and Herman Southworth. Pp. 21-60. Ithaca, New York: Cornell University Press, 1967.

Minhas, B. S. , and Srinivassan, T. N. "New Agricultural Strategy Analysed, " Yojana (India), February 26, 1966.

Morley, Samuel A. "Import Demand and Import Substitution in Brazil. " The Economy of Brazil. Edited by Howard S. Ellis. Pp. 283-313. Berkeley and Los Angeles: University of California Press, 1969.

Paiva, Ruy Miller. "Apreciação Geral Sôbre o Comportamento da Agricultura Brasileira, " Revista de Administração Pública (January-June, 1969), 55-117.

_____. "Bases de uma Política para a Melhoria Técnica da Agricultura Brasileira, " Revista Brasileira de Economia (June, 1967), 5-38.

Pebayle, M. R. "Geographie rurale des nouvelles colonies du Haut Uruguay, " Bulletin de l'Association de Geographes Français (January-February, 1967), 15-34.

Sahota, Gian S. Fertilizer in Economic Development: An Econometric Analysis. New York: Frederick A. Praeger, Publishers, 1968.

Schultz, Theodore W. Transforming Traditional Agriculture. New Haven: Yale University Press, 1964.

_____. Economic Growth and Agriculture. New York: McGraw Hill Book Co., 1968.

da Silva, Ady Raul. Melhoramento das Variedades de Trigo Destinadas às Diferentes Regiões do Brasil. Estudos Técnicos, No. 33. Rio de Janeiro: Serviço de Informação Agrícola, Ministério da Agricultura, 1966.

Skidmore, Thomas. Politics in Brazil, 1930-1964: An Experiment in Democracy. New York: Oxford University Press, 1967.

Smith, Gordon W. "Brazilian Agricultural Policy, 1950-1967." The Economy of Brazil. Edited by Howard S. Ellis. Pp. 211-65. Berkeley and Los Angeles: University of California Press, 1969.

de Souza, Alvaro Ornellas. "Um Estudo Sôbre Exportação, " Lavoura Arrozeira (January, 1965), 5-9.

Srinivassan, T. N., et al. "Economic Aspects of High Yielding Varieties Programme, " Indian Journal of Agricultural Economics, Conference Number XXIII, No. 4 (October-December, 1968), 48-151.

Stakman, E. C., Bradfield, Richard, and Mangelsdoff, Paul G. Campaigns Against Hunger. Cambridge, Massachusetts: The Belknap Press of Harvard University Press, 1967.

Yamada, Saburo. "Changes in Output and in Conventional and Non-Conventional Inputs in Japanese Agriculture Since 1880," Food Research Institute Studies, II, 3 (1967), 371-413.

Public Documents

Agency for International Development. Brazil: Ultrafertil S.A.: Proposal and Recommendations for the Review of the Development Loan Committee. Washington, D.C., August 18, 1966.

_____. India: Trombay Fertilizer Expansion: Recommendations for the Review of the Development Loan Committee. Washington, D.C., no date, apparently 1968 or 1969.

_____, Brazil Agriculture and Rural Development Office. "Problems and Needs of Brazilian Agriculture." Rio de Janeiro, October 15, 1960. Mimeographed.

Banco do Brasil, CACEX. Comércio Exterior do Brasil, 1954-1963. Rio de Janeiro, no date.

Banco Nacional de Desenvolvimento Economico (BNDE). Economia da Carne no Rio Grande do Sul e Aspectos dos Mercados Nacional e Internacional do Produto. Rio de Janeiro, March 25, 1963.

_____. Mercado Brasileiro de Fertilizantes, 1950-1970. Second edition. Rio de Janeiro, August, 1965.

Comissão Central de Levantamento e Fiscalização das Safras Tritícolas (CCLEF). Anuário Estatístico do Trigo (1966-67 and 1967-68 crops); for 1963-64 through 1965-66 crops, Levantamento das Lavouras Tritícolas; 1962-63 crop statistics are contained in Trigo Nacional, two volumes.

Economic Commission for Latin America (ECLA). "Agricultural Development in Latin America." E/CN.12/829. February 12, 1969. Mimeographed.

_____ . "Fifteen Years of Economic Policy in Brazil," Economic Bulletin for Latin America (November, 1964), 153-214.

_____ . "The Growth and Decline of Import Substitution in Brazil." Economic Bulletin for Latin America (March, 1964), 1-59.

Escritório de Pesquisa Econômica Aplicada (EPEA), Ministério do Planejamento e Coordenação Geral. Diagnóstico Preliminar, Setor de Comércio Internacional. Rio de Janeiro, March, 1967.

Food and Agriculture Organization of the United Nations (FAO). Agricultural Commodities: Projections for 1975 and 1985. Two volumes. Rome, 1967.

_____ . Fertilizers: An Annual Review of World Production, Consumption and Trade, 1966. Rome, 1967.

_____ . Production Yearbook, 1967. Rome, 1968.

_____ . Trade Yearbook. Rome. Various issues.

_____ and ECLA. Livestock in Latin America: Status, Problems, and Prospects. Volume II. Brazil. New York: United Nations, 1964.

Governo do Estado do Rio Grande do Sul. Balanço Geral do Estado do Rio Grande do Sul, 1967. Pôrto Alegre, 1967.

_____ . Os Problemas do Trigo. Pôrto Alegre, 1961.

Instituto Brasileiro de Geografia e Estatística (IBGE). Anuário Estatístico do Brasil. Rio de Janeiro. Various issues.

_____ , Serviço Nacional de Recensamento. Censo Agrícola. Rio de Janeiro, 1950 and 1960 censuses.

Instituto de Pesquisa Econômico-Social Aplicada (IPEA), Ministério do Planejamento e Coordenação Geral. A Industrialização Brasileira: Diagnóstico e Perspectivas. Documentos IPEA No. 4. Rio de Janeiro, January, 1968.

Instituto de Pesquisa e Experimentação Agropecuárias do Sul
(IPEAS) and Centro de Treinamento e Informação do Sul
(CENTRISUL). Pastagens na Zona Fronteira do Rio
Grande do Sul. Circular No. 32. Pelotas, February,
1967.

Instituto Rio Grandense do Arroz (IRGA). Anuário Estatístico do Arroz. Pôrto Alegre. Various Issues.

_____, Departamento de Obras e Assistência Técnica.
"Estimativa do Custo de uma Quadra Quadrada de Arroz."
Pôrto Alegre, January, 1968. Mimeographed.

_____. Subsídios para Reestructuração: Relatório
Preliminar do Grupo de Trabalho Criado pela Portaria
538/66 de 3 de Novembro de 1966. Pôrto Alegre, 1967.

International Monetary Fund. International Financial Statistics. Washington, D.C. Various issues.

International Rice Research Institute. Annual Report, 1967.

Ministério da Agricultura, Departamento Econômico, Servico
da Estatística da Produção (SEP). Carnes, Derivados e
Subprodutos, 1966. Rio de Janeiro, September, 1967.

_____. "Contribuição ao Planejamento da Política
Brasileira do Trigo." Rio de Janeiro, May 26, 1965.

Ministério do Planejamento e Coordenação Geral. Programa
Estratégico de Desenvolvimento, 1968-1970. Versão
Preliminar. Two volumes. Rio de Janeiro, June, 1968.

_____. Programa Estratégico de Desenvolvimento:
Áreas Estrategicas I e II, Agricultura, Abastecimento.
Rio de Janeiro, January, 1968.

Organization for Economic Cooperation and Development
(OECD). Supply and Demand Prospects for Fertilizers
in Developing Countries. Paris, 1968.

Secretaria de Agricultura do Estado de Rio Grande do Sul.
Área de Pastagens Cultivadas no Rio Grande do Sul.
Pôrto Alegre, 1966.

United Nations Industrial Development Organization (UNIDO).
    Fertilizer Manual. New York: United Nations, 1967.

Universidade Federal do Rio Grande do Sul, Faculdade de
    Agronomia e Veterinária, Ministério da Agricultura,
    Instituto de Pesquisa e Experimentação Agropecuárias
    do Sul, Superentendência da Região Sul, Secretaria dos
    Negócios da Agricultura, Instituto Rio Grandense do
    Arroz, Associação Sulina de Crédito e Assistência Rural.
    Plano Estadual de Melhoramento da Fertilidade do Solo.
    Pôrto Alegre, 1969.

Unpublished Papers, Studies, and Dissertations

"Ata da IIª Reunião Anual da Cultura do Trigo." Pelotas,
    1968. Mimeographed.

Bethlen, Francis R. "Effects of Brazilian Economic De-
    velopment and Price Policy on Brazilian Wheat Imports."
    Ph.D. dissertation, Purdue University, January, 1962.
    Mimeographed.

Clark, Paul G. "Brazilian Import Liberalization." Williams-
    town, Massachusetts: Williams College, September,
    1967. Mimeographed.

_____, and Weisskoff, Richard. "Import Demand and
    Import Policies in Brazil." Paper prepared for AID,
    February, 1967. Mimeographed.

Knight, Peter T. Agricultura, Tecnologia e Comércio Inter-
    nacional: Estudos da Realidade Brasileira. Rio de
    Janeiro: Editôra APEC, 1971.

_____. "Agricultural Modernization in Rio Grande do
    Sul, Brazil." Paper prepared for USAID/Brazil, May
    28, 1969.

Lakos, Ivan Andras. "The Effects of Brazil's Foreign Ex-
    change Policy on the Value of Her Exports and on the
    Flow of Private Investment with Respect to Brazil's Eco-
    nomic Development: 1946-1960." Ph.D. dissertation,
    Harvard University, March, 1962.

Love, Joseph L. , Jr. "Rio Grande do Sul as a Source of
    Political Instability in Brazil's Old Republic, 1909-1932."
    Ph.D. dissertation, Columbia University, 1967.

McDonald, John C. "Brazil's National Wheat Campaign Be-
    gins." Rio De Janeiro: U.S. Department of Agriculture,
    Foreign Agricultural Service, November 6, 1969.
    Mimeographed.

Pardi, Miguel Cione. "Elementos Para a Formulação de
    Uma Política de Carnes." Rio de Janeiro: Ministério
    da Agricultura, 1966. Mimeographed.

_____, and Caldas, Ruy Brandão. "Plano Nacional de
    Combate á Febre Aftosa." Ministério de Agricultura,
    unpublished typescript, no date, probably 1966 or 1967.

Peterson, Willis L. "The Returns to Investment in Agricul-
    tural Research in the United States." Paper presented at
    the Symposium on Resource Allocation in Agricultural
    Research, University of Minnesota, Minneapolis, Febru-
    ary 23-25, 1969.

PLANISUL. "Estudo Econômico Sôbre a Bovinocultura No
    Rio Grande do Sul." Pôrto Alegre, July 30, 1968.
    Mimeographed.

Program of Joint Studies on Latin American Economic Inte-
    gration (ECIEL). Industrialization in a Latin American
    Common Market. Edited by Martin Carnoy. Washington,
    D.C.: The Brookings Institution, 1969. Multilithed.

Smith, Gordon W. "Agricultural Marketing and Economic
    Development: A Brazilian Case Study." Ph.D. disserta-
    tion, Harvard University, October, 1965. Mimeographed.

_____, and de Alencar, Geraldo. "Relatório Sôbre
    Estudo de Perspectiva de Oferta e Demanda para Produtos
    da Agricultura Brasileira." Rio de Janeiro: Escritório
    de Pesquisa Econômica Aplicada, August, 1967. Mimeo-
    graphed.

INDEX

INDEX

ABOUT THE AUTHOR

Peter T. Knight is Research Associate, The Brookings Institution, Washington D.C. He has taught economics at the Center for Training and Research in Economic Development (CENDEC) in Rio de Janeiro and is currently serving as coordinator of the International Study of Industrial Efficiency, a project involving research institutes in eleven Latin American countries and part of the Program of Joint Studies on Latin American Economic Integration.

Dr. Knight has published articles on the economics of technological change and has prepared several papers on Brazilian agricultural policy for the Agency for International Development. He has traveled extensively in Brazil and elsewhere in Latin America, as well as in Europe and the Middle East.

Field research for the present book was done in Brazil in 1968 with the support of the Foreign Area Fellowship Program. Dr. Knight holds degrees from Dartmouth College, Oxford University (where he was a Fulbright Scholar), and he received his Ph.D. in Economics from Stanford University in 1970.